Meet the family...

Fifty true stories from diverse grassroots communities in Bolton

Edited By

Michael Carroll

Published by
Bolton Multicultural Arts
7 - 9 Bold St.
Bolton
BL1 1LS

Email: multiculturalarts@hotmail.com

ISBN-13: 978-0-9553610-0-5
ISBN-10: 0-9553610-0-1

Contents

Bolton Multicultural Arts

Formed in April 1999, Bolton Multicultural Arts was set up to bring diverse communities together in Bolton through the arts and develop integration whilst recognising, understanding, respecting and appreciating cultural traditions. A series of innovative projects have been accomplished to lessen the 'we – they' dichotomy between cultures and forge greater links between sections of the community. These projects have increased access to the arts and affiliated activities for members of the community who would not normally have such access. In the process, the arts has been utilised as tool for awareness raising, education and community development.

The first major project, a multicultural community production of A Midsummer Night's Dream in 2000, brought people together from diverse cultural origins in Bolton, with little or no experience of theatre[1]. Rehearsals explored the theme of culture and created a diverse cohesive team willing to trust and support each other. Aspects of culture were represented and expressed through gesture, costume and set design. In turn, this brought together a diverse audience to performances at the Festival Hall, Bolton and Bury MET. Again, The Pot of Gold in 2001 brought people of diverse cultural origins together to explore and perform Plautus' Roman comedy about greed using Commedia Del Arte masks and techniques, incorporating Bollywood dance[2]. In 2002, a traditional Indian tale The Peddler and His Hats was translated from Gujarati, adapted for performance, and toured to a number of community venues in Bolton[3].

Bolton Multicultural Arts was commissioned by Bolton Community Network in 2003 to devise a short play about Bolton's Compact. The play made a dry subject matter humorous and accessible, enabling community members to understand and explore the issues regarding the development of the funding code of good practice[4].

Dirty Laundry was a challenging and sensitive piece of forum theatre exploring changing communities and ignorance of cultures. Performed at the Connecting Communities Conference, Mere Hall,

1 Plate 1, back cover.
2 Plate 2, back cover.
3 Plate 3, back cover.
4 Plate 4, back cover.

Bolton in 2005, people from a variety of cultural backgrounds and faiths contributed their ideas and participated in the forum theatre[5].

The completion of Meet the family... is a major achievement and milestone in the development of Bolton Multicultural Arts. The book will be utilised as a resource for community groups and schools to explore issues regarding diversity and community cohesion.

5 Plate 5, back cover.

Acknowledgments

Firstly, I'd like to thank in particular The Baring Foundation and Trafford Hall, Manchester (Making Things Happen Grant) for the funding to initiate this project and their patience. It helps tremendously when funders understand the complexities of a project and can be flexible if a project encounters certain difficulties. Thanks also to the Community Chest fund, administered by Bolton CVS, a very important local source of funding to empower community groups.

I am very grateful to Jeannette Fowler, Shahla Holgeth and Helen McHugh of Bolton Community College for their support with funding for the project and the facilitation of the participatory appraisal training.

Apologies and thanks to the line manager of my 'proper job' at Bolton Community Network, Carol Latham, who often tried to kick me out of the office over the past four years when I was supposed to be on leave, but gave up before she tore her hair out. I would like to express my appreciation to all the staff at Bolton Community Network for their comments on the stories and use of the facilities.

I am very grateful to the Community Cohesion Sub Group, Stronger Communities Group and Bolton Vision (Bolton's Local Strategic Partnership) for supporting the printing of this book. It is refreshing to know that Bolton Vision is prepared to invest in smaller community organisations, therefore recognise and value their work in the community.

Many thanks to Ray Collett, Malcolm Ngoala and Sylvie N'guessan for enabling access to members of BRASS and for helping with translation during interviews. Thanks also to Kairen Smith and Helene Morris for giving up their time to proof read the stories.

Last, but by no means least, thanks to Nazeera Atcha, treasurer of Bolton Multicultural Arts, for always being available to sign the cheques!

Foreword

The concept of this book may seem simple enough, now you hold it in your hands, as a product, a material object. You are invited to let the weight of the human experiences in this book, seep into your hands, your senses and your imagination. For, the stories are true stories that have been lived, collated from people at grassroots level in the community who have never had the opportunity to express a true experience from their life to a wider audience. They are from people who are used to having self-appointed representatives speak on their behalf. Therefore, the book has provided members of the community with a voice.

This Bolton Multicultural Arts' project actually began in 2002 when twenty-four local people from diverse cultural origins and backgrounds in Bolton, were trained for a week in basic participatory appraisal[1] techniques. Twenty-two of them were interviewed to undertake six hours a week of work. This was a very significant part of the project as it provided the majority of the community interviewers with their first few steps on the employment ladder. Their job was to go out into the community to reach people who had true stories to tell about a defining moment in their life, an important memory. The group prepared lists of people and community groups they could contact then set about making appointments and collating stories using the tools they had learned. The group was supported by weekly drop-ins, designed to guide them on the structure and content of the stories and to assess their progress. The process has culminated in many achievements and opportunities for those who have participated in the project. Most of the group involved in collating the stories have since progressed on to further education and employment. Some have either started up their own community group or have become members of existing groups and therefore play an active role in their community.

One of the most positive aspects of the project has been the

---

1 Participatory Appraisal is a family of tools and approaches that facilitate a process of individual and community reflection, analysis, decision making and action planning. PA developed from Participatory Rural Appraisal, an approach that evolved from international development in the 1980s and 1990s.

group's bilingual skills, which enabled them to reach people in the community with language barriers. However, the varied levels of English in the group and those contributing the stories resulted in many difficulties regarding the written expression of the material and its integral details. This was overcome with an investment of more time and patience. In some instances, contact details of people were lost or people had moved, leaving a number of unfinished stories. All these obstacles hindered the progress of the project considerably, whilst trying to chase the set target of fifty stories. However, at least on my part, the project became a labour of love with a relentless determination to accomplish this goal, no matter how long it took. This meant that the project had to be extended, relying on countless hours of voluntary time over a period of four years.

Throughout the process of this book, the participants have been empowered to overcome confidence and language barriers. In many cases, a couple of hours of asking questions, rephrasing questions, checking the interpretation of answers, then exploring the material from different perspectives, has just provided the minor details of a small paragraph. On average approximately twenty-five hours have been spent on each story. To illustrate this point further, one story from a French speaking Congolese man, involved a series of interview sessions where questions and answers were translated from English to French, and vice versa through an interpreter. Also, bear in mind that in the process of translation there are no exact definitions for certain words, ideas and phrases. As you can imagine there was a lot of frustration from all parties involved, as well as laughter!

Some of the stories in this book raise questions about the definition of culture and whether anyone can truly say that they belong to a specific culture. If we are living in a multicultural society with many 'cultures' overlapping and merging, can we as individuals be multicultural? Are we a part of a conglomerate culture that has not been defined or are we each hybrids of different cultures with our own specific mix? Is there too much emphasis placed on cultural identity and the need for it to be defined, in an attempt to assign people to a particular group or category? What implications does this categorisation have? Aren't we all unique individuals, belonging to the experiences that have shaped us? If so, should the term diversity apply to every individual's uniqueness rather than cultural origin?

When first beginning the project it was envisaged that somehow an ideal representation of Bolton's cultural make up could be portrayed. However, it is impossible to 'represent' every cultural origin in Bolton and one story from an individual of a particular cultural origin cannot mean that they 'represent' that culture, as they are precisely an individual with their own particular personal experience, perspective and therefore, voice. Having collated the stories it became apparent that the book is about valuing everyone first and foremost as human beings with their own unique experiences and therefore perspectives on life. It is on this level of understanding that they are united. The stories are from many diverse backgrounds offering a rich, broad range of alternative experiences, obliterating Bolton's own stereotypical mask of mills and cloth caps as well as many other preconceived ideas about cultures. At the same time, many of the stories raise awareness about aspects of culture and provide a great insight into how people's lives are shaped. Because of the subject matter expressed in some of the stories and because some members of the community generally do not want to be identified, approximately half of the stories are marked as anonymous or contain just a first name.

I hope you enjoy your journey through this book, identifying, engaging and empathising with each human experience, whilst recognising that each story could be from the person next door, a friend, or, as we are all connected in some way, a relative. So come on in and meet the family...

Michael Carroll BA Hon's., MA, PGCE
Bolton Multicultural Arts

In the Face of Tradition

(Sahora)

My name is Sahora and I used to live in the Daubhill area of Bolton. I went to Deane School. My family lived in a terraced house, but it was a big house with quite large rooms. I was a tall, slim, bubbly and talkative fourteen-year-old Asian girl. I liked Bollywood movies and music, but also liked the band Aha and Tom Cruise! I particularly remember the design, technology and chemistry classes at school because we had to work in pairs. In chemistry, I had to work with a boy called Paul. He was a familiar face from other lessons, but I had never really worked with him before. When we worked together, I noticed that Paul listened to me. He wasn't like the other boys, who just acted like fools. We began to get on well together, then one day Paul asked me out. Being a Muslim girl I was a bit apprehensive at first because Paul was not Asian and his religion was Church of England. However, I agreed. As we were both still at school, there could be no serious relationship anyway.

I used to see Paul at lunchtimes. We sat in the school canteen to eat together. I ate salads, chips and peas, whereas Paul usually just ate chips, but we shared each other's drinks. Sometimes we used to meet after lessons in the park near Brandwood School. I often went there with my Asian girlfriends. For them it was quite a novelty that I was seeing a white English boy, but as they were my friends, they were sworn to secrecy. Paul used to meet me in the centre of the park later, where no prying eyes could see us. We sat on the grass, becoming engrossed in each other's company. I had to keep an eye on the time, but I could not help lose myself in the moments we shared together. This meant that sometimes I was late home. I had to lie to my parents, telling them I was in detention for talking in class. I tried not to make too much of a habit of this and limited it to once or twice a week.

Each Saturday I went to Bolton town centre with my Asian girlfriends so everything appeared all above board to my parents. Sometimes my friends came to my house to pick me up just to make sure my parents did not suspect anything at all. After arriving in town, I used to buy two pasties from Greggs the bakers, then went up to the top of Debenhams' multi storey car park to meet Paul. I secretly arranged to meet him there because it was very unlikely that I would bump into anyone else there I knew. It was in Debenhams' car park that had we had our first kiss. I remember it so well, a sweet kiss, not too intense, not too quick. I felt all tingly and could not stop smiling afterwards. After a few hours together, I met up with my friends again elsewhere in town, then went home. This carried on for two years until we both left school. Our relationship grew stronger and stronger. Paul and I had deep feelings for each other. However, it was always at the back of my mind that my family were very strict Muslims. I wasn't even allowed to go out with a Muslim boy never mind anyone else from outside our religion.

The local Bolton South College was close to my home so it was the most convenient college to attend once I had left school. For Paul it was a longer distance to travel and he had to catch a bus. He had told his parents that most of his friends were going to this college, which was true to a certain extent, but of course our relationship also had an influence over his decision. I suppose we didn't overtly plan to go to college together, but I don't think we were entirely objective about our choice either. At college we carried on in very much the same way as we had done at school. We met each other in the canteen and whenever we both had free periods we'd walk into town together. I established a routine of going to college at eight thirty in the morning and arriving home at four fifteen in the afternoon. We continued to enjoy each other's company and were very close to each other. Our relationship was not physical; we had a mutual understanding and respect for one another. I loved him for the sense of freedom he gave me.

One day, after Paul and I had met in Debenhams' car park, we decided it was time to go back to college, so we entered the lift to descend to the ground floor. We were so captivated by each other's presence; laughing together, our smiles mirroring each other, whilst we held hands. When the doors of the lift opened, all of a sudden the life drained out of me as if sucked out by a vampire. In front of us stood one of my father's friends. I immediately let go of Paul's hand, cowering my head. My heart seemed to have a life of its own as it pounded away. I cringed in terror; this man did not look too impressed. After we had passed by him, Paul and I tried to reassure each other that everything was going to be all right, but I feared the inevitable inquisition would be awaiting me back home. I caught the bus back to college, all the time, imagining the incident being reported back to my parents.

After college, I made my way home with my friends, telling them what had happened earlier. As I approached the house, my legs became more and more shaky. My heart was thumping in anticipation of my parents' reaction. As soon as I walked into the house the air was filled with gloom, a foreboding of what was to come in the temple of doom. It carried with it the weeping of my mother in the next room. Now I knew for definite they had found out, I was scared and was tempted to go back out again. However, their presence summoned me towards them as if I was destined for my execution. I slowly walked into the living room and there was my father sitting sternly in his chair. The atmosphere was crushing me. My dad just sat there very quietly. Then my mother looked at me and hysterically wailed 'Why...! Why...!' I did not answer. She moaned that I'd put them to shame. Then my dad looked at me with his piercing dark eyes and said 'From tomorrow Sahora is not going to college, she will stay at home'. I couldn't believe what I was hearing. I screamed back at them saying I would go to college and they could not stop me. Besides, I had exams coming up shortly. All he could say was that I should have thought about that before I started seeing the English boy behind their backs. He ranted on about how he couldn't believe I'd do such a thing, as if it was some kind of criminal act. He informed me that from now on he'd be looking for a suitable Asian boy for me to marry. I was furious and I told him I'd say no to every boy he introduced me to. Despite my fiery resistance, I knew they were determined to enforce their demands.

So that was that, no more college. The first week at home was hell, all I could think about was Paul. I missed his company madly, which made me determined not to speak to my parents. I was tempted to phone him, but it was too risky with my parents around, it would be like stoking up a volcano if they found out; besides, I wouldn't have put it past them to have bugged the phone. However, I did manage to get a friend to pass on a message to Paul about what had happened. There was no point in doing any college work anymore and I found myself becoming restless in my prison of reform. My friends dropped by to offer me support. They advised me to try to forget about Paul, as I knew deep down nothing could ever become of the relationship. They also gave Paul the same advice. He was sensible enough to know not to pursue the matter.

The time spent in the house seemed to drag on and on until after three weeks I couldn't stand the boredom anymore. I decided to tell my parents that I'd find some sort of job and get on with my life. I managed to find myself a job in the town centre as a sales assistant. My father issued a warning not to see Paul or any other boy. If I did he threatened to marry me off without my permission. I knew he meant what he said. Nevertheless, I became happy with my job as a sales assistant in a clothes shop. I enjoyed meeting people and having money of my own to spend. I heard from friends that Paul had finished studying at college and had gone on to university.

Fortunately, my dad didn't mention marriage for a few years.

When I was twenty years old he sat me down and told me it was now time to get engaged. He informed me that a boy was coming to visit me within the next week. I agreed to the meeting, but told my father if I did not like him I would say no to the marriage. My father accepted my answer.

The next week came and there was a tremendous air of anticipation in our house. My mum spent most of the day cooking nice food. I invited two friends over to give me moral support, as I was extremely nervous. Finally, the big moment arrived when Rahil came with his parents. They were led into the living room. I was then invited to sit with them. Everyone was fairly tense underneath all the pleasantries. His parents seemed quite nice and not too old fashioned, saying they would not impose their values upon me. After a quarter of an hour, I went upstairs to my bedroom, then Rahil followed a few minutes later. He sat at my desk where I used to do my work and put my make up on, whilst I sat on my bed. From the first glance of Rahil I thought he looked OK. We began to talk and he told me he was a primary school teacher. From then on the conversation began to flow, something clicked inside me and I felt at ease talking to him. He appeared less nervous than when we'd first met downstairs. Before we rejoined our parents, Rahil asked me if he could see me in a different environment away from them and without their knowledge, as he felt it was too soon to give an answer about marrying me. I was pleased as I felt the same. We decided to meet in a couple of day's time at Pizza Hut. We went downstairs and our parents said their goodbyes, whilst Rahil and I agreed to let each other know if we liked each other in due course.

Two days later, I met Rahil in Pizza Hut and we talked at length. I began to like him and agreed to meet him again the next day for lunch. After a week had passed by, my father asked me if I liked Rahil enough to marry him. I said yes. Then he revealed that Rahil had made the same decision. So both sets of parents were happy. After this it was easier to see Rahil with my parents' knowledge. We were married at a local mosque and held a big wedding reception at Bolton Deane School. It still took me a year to really get to know Rahil, but I grew to love him very much. I thought I had been in love with Paul, but looking back, at the time I was too young to know what real love is.

I now have two girls aged six and nine and live in London due to Rahil's job. I am very happy that I found the right partner, even though my marriage was through a formal introduction. Before, I did not believe in arranged marriages, but they do work out as long as the couples are not forced into it.

Collated by Selma Kadva

The Pool

(Afsaneh Karbla Zadeh)

Afsaneh was born in Tehran, the capital of Iran in 1976. At the age of six, she started school. She recalls a short story about one of her life's experiences that happened during her girlhood when she was nine years old. On one hot summer's day, she went to Saee Park off Vali Asr Avenue, near her home to play with her friend. The park is one of the capital's main thoroughfares; it is very big, much bigger than Queen's Park in Bolton. It is known as the 'Lovers Park', where couples sit at dusk beneath a canopy of fragrant chinar, cypress and pine trees, exchanging gossip and intimacies. People go there to study or read, but also to play games such as football.

Apart from benches and most other things that many people would expect to see in a park, there was also a deep pool in the centre. Afsaneh and her friend were playing by the pool, being very boisterous, messing around, giggling, laughing and having so much fun. They were playfully teasing each other and Afsaneh, in particular, was fully immersed in her playful mood. She was quite keen to extend the boundaries of this fun. Both were very warm and took their shoes off, to dip their feet in the pool. As they sat down on the edge of the pool, they experienced the cool relieving sensation of the water on their feet. A dip in the pool, however, was not enough to calm their lively spirits. Dipping soon turned to splashing each other with their feet. Afsaneh had a better idea, she spotted her friend's shoes on the pool's edge and threw them into the water, laughing so much she nearly cried. Now for the first time that afternoon the moods of the two friends contrasted each other. It was as though Afsaneh had cast her friend's happy face into the pool as well as her shoes. Her friend's immediate expression was one of shock and disbelief, but very soon, it grew with rage and suddenly with a surge of anger, she pushed Afsaneh into the pool.

The humour of the afternoon was now well and truly broken. Afsaneh didn't know what had hit her, her body was in a deep shock at being engulfed by the water, her arms and legs whirled frantically as she struggled for breaths of air above the surface of the water, as she could not swim. With every spare breath she cried for help, she panicked in her fight for air. Now it was dawning on her friend exactly what she'd done, but she could only stand there motionless not knowing what to do.

A middle-aged gentleman who was sitting on a bench not so far from the pool heard Afsaneh's cries for help and saw that she was clearly struggling in the water. Without a second thought, he ran and dived in. Afsaneh began to lose her fight for air as her body submerged with tiredness. Meanwhile other people in the park noticed all the commotion and started to gather around the pool's edge to see what was going on, one of the passers by called a medic. All eyes and hope were on the middle-aged gentleman as he attempted to save Afsaneh. He reached her, then was able to turn and swim to the pool's edge with her. Afsaneh's lungs spluttered, coughed and expelled spouts of water. An ambulance arrived promptly and immediately sped her off to hospital.

Fortunately, after a few days Afsaneh was discharged from hospital safe and sound. She knew that this incident would stay in her memory forever and that she would be eternally grateful to the man who had saved her from drowning. To this day, as she reflects upon this story from her home in Bolton, she still has not forgiven her childhood friend for pushing her into the pool and has never spoken to her since the incident.

Collated by Nasim Rezaei

The Hunter and the Hunted

(Anonymous)

I am a young man from Sulaimaniya, Kurdistan, in the north of Iraq. I was born in 1965 and lived in the western Sorani region, a very mountainous environment. When I was around the age of ten I'd climb the mountains with my friends. Once at the top we'd then embark on the next stage of our adventure, involving hunting and catching birds such as the cowbird which flies high and nests in the mountains. Sometimes we hunted pores in the forests surrounding the mountains. The pore is a heavy bird, a bit like a chicken, and cannot fly very much, so it lives in the forest for protection and does not go out into the open. Many years ago, this hunting was very popular, especially in the winter, when the snowflakes float down through the mountain air. As the pore bird cannot fly a long distance the hunters would follow it whilst it was briefly airborne, then catch it fairly easily when it landed. I have fond memories of this adventurous childhood.

After attending primary school, secondary school and college, I was conscripted to join the Iraqi army in 1987. Two years later I was married, but could not enjoy the marriage very much because I was away most of the time. Being a Kurd I hated serving for the Iraqi army. However, in 1991, two weeks into the Gulf War there was a big uprising in Kurdistan against the Iraqi regime. I was caught up in this and left the Iraqi army to join the PUK[1] party, fighting for them as a peshmager[2]. The PUK paid me for this service and I played a very active role in helping them to successfully overthrow the Iraqi regime. All the Kurds were extremely excited and happy about their liberation and celebrated it in every part of Kurdistan, and many Kurdish people were married in this joyous year. They had waited a long time to be free from the

1 Patriotic Union of Kurdistan.
2 A type of Kurdish soldier.

persecutions of the Iraqi government. Fittingly, my first child was born symbolising the beginning of a new life.

Unfortunately, over the next couple of years, the situation in Kurdistan became more complex as political groups developed. Disagreements between the two main political parties, the PUK and the KDP[3] led to a big civil war. The ordinary people of Kurdistan felt despondent because after fighting for freedom and independence they were now fighting amongst themselves. The civil war led to Kurdistan being divided into two parts, Badinani in the east and Sorani in the west. The freedom of Kurdistan had only lasted for two years. Now families and relatives were separated by a border between the two regions. They could not travel easily from Sorani to Badanani to visit friends and relatives because of the tight security checks on border crossings. There was still ongoing fighting between the two parties. Everyday the situation grew worse and worse with more killings and many began thinking of leaving their homeland as there was no food, no money, and no freedom. However, I still remained a peshmager for the PUK party.

On 30th July 1997, the KDP gathered a huge army together and attacked the PUK governed city of Arbil, the capital of Kurdistan. I was serving in the city of Arbil that day, when it was surrounded by the KDP army. Lots of people died during the fighting and many were arrested by the KDP including myself. I was put in prison where the conditions were very bad, the food was very basic, only two small meals a day. It was very cold in the cells, especially at night. We were treated badly by the soldiers of the KDP. During this empty void, all I could think about was my wife and son. I dreamed about them during the cold lonely nights. Many prisoners became ill and sick because of the conditions. I spent a year in there. When I was released in 1998 I was unrecognisable, very ill, thin and

3 Kurdistan Democratic Party.

frail because I had lost a lot of weight.

I arrived home in Sulaimaniya to be greeted by my wife. She could not believe how different I looked. We were both lost for words. After a prolonged pause, we hugged and cried, as we were so happy to see each other again. However, when I saw my son in shabby clothes I felt so guilty, even more so when the first thing he wanted to know was where his father had been. He told me he had missed me very much. The house was also in a very poor state, many things had changed, my family had been living in poverty. There was no heating because diesel oil was too expensive to buy. I said to my wife 'The PUK, did they not help you?' She said they had only given her a little money at the beginning of my prison sentence, but that was all. I was extremely angry about this as I had expected the PUK party to return my loyalty by supporting my family whilst I was in prison.

The PUK did not appear to be paying any attention to the public anymore. This turned me against the party. I believed, like others, that they were just looking after their own interests. I wanted nothing to do with them anymore. Although I had no money at all, I decided to ask a friend to lend me just enough to buy an arabana[4] and some fruit. It was the only thing I could think of to try and make a living.

I took the arabana to the city centre of Sulaimaniya every day to sell the fruit, but from time to time members of the PUK party approached me asking why I was no longer one of their soldiers. They tried to persuade me to rejoin the party, but I asked them why they were not there to help my family whilst I was in prison. I told them I no longer believed in what the party stood for. This did not deter them, but I stuck to my principles despite their harassment and the lure of a salary once again.

4 Fruit barrow.

Like others, I now believed that the party was more like a dictatorship. It was as though life had ground to a halt in Kurdistan, there was no future at all, there was no freedom. So, I had to make the hardest decision in my life, to leave my family before having to undergo more harassment from the PUK authorities. I knew five friends that felt the same way, so we got together and began to discuss plans to escape illegally over the border of Iran, then through Iran into Turkey. We soon discovered a further six men who also wanted to escape, so we all arranged a meeting together. Each man had to pay seven thousand dinas to a guide who was going to help us. Including the guide, there were twelve of us in the group. We soon became aware that many had lost their lives on the route we had chosen. Just ten days before, fifteen people had been killed, shot by Turkish soldiers once they had crossed the Iranian and Turkish border.

We did not have any other choice but to travel by foot at night. Crossing from Iraq into Iran was fairly easy, but we knew that Turkish soldiers were stationed high up on top of the mountains keeping watch along the border between Turkey and Iran. So when we arrived at this border, in groups of twos and threes we attempted to creep through these positions very slowly, being extremely careful not to make the slightest sound. It was a nervous ordeal and a great amount of patience was required to negotiate the crossing, dodging the spotlights and torches. There was always a tense, conscious feeling of being watched and hunted. The Turkish soldiers were very vigilant. We had all nearly made the crossing when gunfire interrupted the silent night. Everybody began to run in panic. A member of the last group had been shot. He had to be left, and the other two ran for their lives through the darkness in and out of trees as fast as they could, not stopping at anything that was in their path. They ended up separated from the main group. The rest of us managed to meet up together. After hearing the gunfire we thought the three crossing in the last group were dead. Later that night the guide went out looking for them and to everyone's surprise and relief, he was able to locate two of the group that had survived. Having assembled together, we all travelled further on and hid in a cave where we rested during the daylight.

Once darkness had fallen we set off again. After three days of travelling we arrived at the town of Wan. We were very tired, hungry and still lamenting the loss of our friend. For four days we stayed at a secret hiding place in a house. Then, group by group, we moved from Wan to Istanbul by bus, all the time fearing that the authorities would board the bus and detain us. Fortunately, we arrived at the bus station in Istanbul, extremely happy and very relieved to have reached that stage of the journey. We had realised the first part of our dreams. We had a brief look around for an hour before my cousin's friend turned up to meet us. He took us to his house where we stayed for three weeks. It was the first time that we had stayed in another country, the views were wonderful and the weather was warm. It felt so nice to be able to bask in the pleasant sun as we visited all the attractions in Istanbul. However, my cousin's friend warned us that we were not here to enjoy it, we had not come for a holiday. He told us to focus on the second part of the journey and feel very worried because many people had died on this section. During these three weeks we consulted a number of people with experience and knowledge about the different ways of crossing the border of Turkey into Greece. One night my cousin's friend took us to see a group of eight people who provided advice on the crossing. After a while another man turned up. He was a navigator who had taken many people across the heavily mined military border separating Turkey and Greece. He asked us if we were ready for the next stage of the journey. We were ready. He informed us that the next stage would involve four days' walking, then we would be able to board a bus to Athens.

The next day we made sure that we gathered enough food together for the journey ahead, and set off that night in a minibus to the borders of Turkey and Greece. There was an air of journeying into the unknown again after our comfortable stay in Turkey. As we approached the border, our driver and navigator noticed that we were being followed by a police car. They probably suspected an attempted border crossing. He told us he was going to speed up then stop, at which point everyone had to run from the van as fast as they could. Everybody did as he said, we just jumped out of the minibus, some wanted to take the backpacks we had prepared with food and clothes, but there was no time, we had to leave everything. We ran and ran as fast as we could. We became conscious that the police had not followed us, so eventually we could afford to slow down and walk. We realised that we were actually in fields of crops full of watermelons and cucumbers. We searched around in the dark, eating some and saving some of the crops for our journey. We must have trudged through these fields for about three hours, then trees began to enshroud us as we journeyed for another three hours into dense forests. The route took us to a big wide river with strong fast-flowing currents, the river Evros. Many people had lost their lives crossing here. Its rushing sound haunted the night. We couldn't believe we were expected to cross such a dangerous river and were very scared. We knew we had no choice. Near where we were standing was a little wooden platform at the river's edge. Our navigator knelt down and took up a couple of wooden planks. He brought out a deflated dinghy and oars that had been hidden underneath them. He proceeded to blow up the dinghy, then asked one of us to hold the end of a rope. We watched in amazement as he began to make his way across the roaring river, skilfully resisting the pull of the water. More rope was released as he progressed further. Eventually, after a tremendous battle against the current, he made it to the bank on the other side and tied the other end of the rope to a tree. The same was done on our side. He made his way back with the dinghy and in groups of five, we were able to haul ourselves across the river. I was the last to cross the river. It scared me so much as I could not swim. I could not even look at the water.

After about two hours we had all made the crossing. The energy had been sapped from all of us, but we had to continue our journey. We walked for a further four hours into a big forest. The cold dark air was biting into us. I was so tired and cold; I told our navigator that I couldn't go on anymore. He told us to carry on for another half hour then we could rest. We trudged on in the crumpling snow until we arrived at an old dirty wooden shed. It was bare inside. Our navigator told us to sleep there until the next night's travel. There were no windows or doors to prevent the extreme cold air coming in. The hut also stank of dampness. Our navigator disappeared for twenty minutes, then came back with five sleeping bags. He went to get some more for the rest of us. Now we had stopped travelling the freezing cold gnawed into our still bodies, preventing us from sleeping for some time.

After we had slept during the daylight and eaten, as soon as the night's darkness began to fall again, we travelled on. At least the cold was less severe now we were moving again. Following this pattern, over the next five days, the biting cold, the tiredness and the hunger began to seep deeper and deeper into our morale. We ran out of food and our navigator lost his way, though he did not tell us at the time. On the fifth night of travelling after the river crossing, we were like the walking dead. We ground to a halt as the sound of wolves echoed in the mountains. The howling meant that the wolves could sense us. Most of the party didn't want to carry on, wanting to rest for the night. Our navigator assured us that we could carry on and told us not to worry. During the next few hours, the howling sifted nearer and nearer, until we were sure that we were surrounded. Our navigator asked us to take out our knives in preparation for a fight, otherwise we could die. There was an air of hunger amidst the barren white terrain, we felt isolated. The wolves were accustomed to the harsh environment. Our party merely represented a meal for them.

We could sense them slowly edging in on us. We waited tensely for them. Suddenly they struck from every angle, their snarling breath melting the frozen silent night. They charged with gnashing teeth, ravaging, ripping, shearing and tearing through skin and bones as we thrust, slashed and stabbed with our knives. Screams and cries emitted from the men in the frenzy, struggling to escape their predators. The wolves knew all about hunger and were not about to let their meal pass by. The fortunate ran blindly, screaming into the night, wherever their legs could take them. Four were eaten alive, others counted themselves lucky to escape with torn clothes, and badly bitten legs, bleeding from the chomping jaws. We managed to kill about five wolves.

We sought refuge in a cave, which was difficult to get into, but once in there we felt safer. Many of our group had received bad injuries from the wolves, so the next day our navigator left us to get some dressings for their wounds and some food. He also returned with some clothes. Four of the party in particular were badly wounded. He led them down into the village to get help. To try and avoid too much attention, in groups of three or four we descended from the mountains into the small village below, every three or four hours. From here there was great relief as we all eventually managed to secure bus rides through Greece to Athens.

From Athens I eventually travelled to Britain, where I now reside in safety. I would like to dedicate this story to the memory of Alana Sour, the navigator who led us across the Evros river. After many crossings later, he eventually lost his life in that river around 2002. We shall always be grateful to him.

Collated by Faruk Amen

Death toll in Evros River illegal immigrants incident reaches 23

11th September 2003

The number of bodies believed to be of illegal immigrants who drowned while attempting to sneak into Greece from Turkey across the Evros River continues to rise and has reached 23, local authorities said Wednesday early evening.

On Tuesday, authorities discovered 12 bodies along the banks of the river, marking the border between Greece and Turkey, while an ongoing search operation has turned up another 11 bodies.

In a related development, authorities believe that the body of a young woman discovered four days ago downstream, also belongs to the group of those discovered over the past two days.

According to initial estimates by medical examiner Pavlos Pavlidis, the 23 victims - 21 men and two women between the ages of 25 and 35 - had been dead for approximately four days, and the cause of death was drowning. They were all of Asian descent. Authorities believe that either the boat they were using to cross the river overturned, or a rope that had been tied on the two sides of the shore across the river broke off as they were attempting to cross the water.

The bodies were taken to the Alexandroupolis University Hospital for post mortems.

Source: ANA (Athens News Agency) daily news bulletin

No Bhajis on the Beach

(Anonymous)

My family and relatives lived close by each other in Daubhill, Bolton. I used to be a very cheeky girl and was a bit of a tomboy when I was younger. I wore jeans, tops and trainers and had a short haircut. I was always playing with boys and would come back home with dirt all over my face and hands, much to the disgust of my mother. My mum longed for me to wear dresses, but I refused as they were too soppy. Daubhill is a very built up urban area, but as a young Asian girl growing up there I didn't know anything different until I was about seven years old. I heard my family talking of this magical place they were planning to visit called Blackpool. I remember trying to imagine what this place could be like ...a kind of never-ending wonderland of fun and adventure maybe.

When you're young the days are years long with waiting and anticipation. Finally, the day of the trip arrived. I grasped it with both hands very early in the morning for it had not come soon enough. What was wrong with everyone? I was ready to set off straight away! Well, at least after deciding I'd better have a bath first. There appeared to be some action in the kitchen with the smell of samosas creeping up the stairs from my mum's frying pan. I got out of the bath, hurriedly got changed and dashed downstairs to have breakfast. Mum had also fried some chicken. The food smelled delicious and I could not help but have a piece of samosa. As my mum was very focused and busy, she told me to sit down, have my breakfast, and not to bother her so she could finish the cooking in peace.

My mum, dad and brother had been to Blackpool before and were tired of me pestering them for more details. I'd never been to the seaside before, but I had seen luxurious pictures of it. The weather seemed perfect for the trip. My parents had organised a minibus to take the family and loads of relatives.

There was a tremendous buzz as my aunts talked amongst themselves and us kids were hyperactive with crisps and sweets once inside the minibus. We set off from Bolton on our great adventure wondering what the fair and the rides would be like and which ones we'd like to go on first.

As soon as we arrived in Blackpool, me and the rest of the kids squeezed out of the minibus and started running about all over the place such was our excitement, but this was soon curtailed by the sharp voice of my mum. She got us all together and told us to stick with each other at all times. Of course, the parents had no choice, but to take us to the pleasure beach. The air was different here, it was fresh sea air, certified by the sound of the seagulls. The fresh air also bred pangs of hunger in us, so we found a bench on the way where we could tuck into mum's delicious food. Soon our energy levels were up again and we continued to drag the parents to the pleasure beach. It was exciting, but noisy and scary at the same time, with loads of people, some going up, some coming down, some spinning all around. There were rolling oily squeaky wheels on metal tracks, announcers, flavours of music mingling in the air with thrilling screams here and there. The shapes and colours of each attraction pulled me this way and that enticing me to their mini adventures and I whirled in the heavenly cloud of doughnuts, fish and chips and candy floss. Finally, my first ride arrived. I clambered onto a colourful horse on a merry-go-round and off we went together gliding up and down racing through fields and over hedges, but every now and again passing the smiling face of my mum. I enjoyed this so much. I went on the log flume with my dad crashing though the water, then went on a big slide and a few other rides. Now I wasn't scared at all, I wanted to go on everything! I succumbed to that tempting smell of candyfloss which I persuaded my aunt to buy, together with a fizzy drink. I could not believe how quickly candy floss disappears as soon as you put it on your tongue; I so wanted it to retain its cotton wool texture so that I could chew it indefinitely.

The adults had now decided to take us off to the beach. We were soon heading out from the hustle and bustle of the fairground to the open sea shimmering in the distance beneath the blazing sun. There were loads of people here too, lying on deck chairs, eating ice cream, but all I wanted to do was drag my dad through the icing sugar sand towards the seagull sea. I was struck by the enormity of the sea, a vast, breathing carpet of water reaching as far as the eye could see, right up to the sky. Yet thin layers of it seeped in over the sand and I paddled, kicked and splashed in it with my dad. Then, out of the corner of my eye, I saw my brother playing with the sand. He was building a sandcastle, I wandered up to him to investigate, but he told me to go away and build my own. However, as I turned around I spotted a bigger sandcastle being built by some other children. They were more accommodating. A little girl told me she would be back in a minute and gave me her bucket and spade. The other girls showed me what to do and I became extremely involved in the construction of the wonderful architecture. We all worked very hard and once it was finished the rest of the girls went to bring their mums and dads to show off the glistening piece of work. I turned around to tell my mum …but I could not see her …I could not see my dad …my brother …or any of the relatives. My stomach sank to the bottom of my insides; it became clear my family had vanished. A delirious feeling came over me, as though a fever was spreading through my body. My stomach turned and tightened as I began to wander the beach and it became more and more apparent I was isolated in this sandy people world. All my happiness had suddenly turned to despair. Surely, someone would recognise me, but they all appeared like aliens, some looked at me curiously as I wandered about, some didn't look very nice… Perhaps I would never see my mum again! Tears began to well up in my eyes, I began to cry. Then a lady appeared before me, slim with kind eyes. She knelt down, stroked my hand and spoke to me very softly. She asked me what was the matter. Through my tears I told her I'd lost my mum. She told me not to worry and to hold her hand, but I was very uncertain as my mum had told me not to talk to strangers. However, I felt I had no choice but to trust this one. She led me up the steps off the beach to where the trams ran along the road. She spotted a policeman and took me up to him, explaining I was lost. The policeman thanked her and actually told her that my family were looking for me! He got on his radio and told a colleague that he'd found the little girl, asking me my name to make sure.

I waited and waited with the policeman who assured me that everything would be fine. It seemed like ages, but then I saw my family in the distance and I ran as fast as I could towards my mum. She was crying with relief, engulfing me in a big motherly hug, she made me cry also. In the background I could hear one of my aunties' scolding tongues, lashing me for wandering off on the beach by myself. Meanwhile the policeman had wandered up behind me. He told me I was very lucky and in future to make sure I stayed with my family at all times. When he had gone, my uncle warned me sternly never to let go of my mum's hand ever again, as I could easily get lost in a crowd. I was just happy to be in the sea of my family. We went for a final treat of fish and chips and I did not let go of my mum's hand once. My dad kept checking on all the kids to make sure we were all present.

On the way back home everyone was content. All the kids dozed off to sleep through exhaustion and sea air. After that day I learned my lesson and always stuck to my mum like glue wherever we went. Even now that I am twenty-three years old, my mum still worries about me wherever I go. I will always be her baby.

Collated by Summaiya Kadva

Shanta Bai

(Anonymous)

Shanta Bai was born in Uganda, in 1940, and had four sisters. She finished her education at the age of twenty-one and shortly became married to her husband, Rakesh, who owned a chemist. They lived in a big farm house on land where there were mango trees, plum trees and even a grapevine next to the side of the house. There were four servants in their home, one for cooking, one for cleaning and two for washing and ironing. Shanta lived the life of a princess in her house as she didn't have to do any work at all. She gave birth to three children, two boys and one girl. The servants always had dinner ready for the children when they returned home from school. When Shanta's husband Rakesh came home from work they would often go for a long drive in the car. They lived a luxurious life and were a very happy family.

In Uganda, a politician called Idi Amin had worked his way up to President. Amin was a massive, fat, round-faced, ugly, black man. People used to respect him and called him 'Dada' because he wanted to be known as a father figure. When people saw him in the streets they bowed and greeted him. Every month, he used to throw grand parties at his home, inviting businessmen and rich people from different fields of work. He used to show off his indoor swimming pool to all his guests, but he also used to show off the heads of decapitated bodies to them, which he stored in his chilled freezer room. Whoever praised him and took his side, Amin showered with treasures. Whoever rebelled against him, he threw in his pool, beheaded them and showcased them in his chilled freezer room. It was during one of Amin's parties that he cast his evil eye on Shallu, a Hindu Gujarati girl. Amin liked her very much and lusted after her. He had plans to marry her. However, Shallu did not like Amin at all, she knew that he behaved like a gangster and found him very imposing.

Amin grew impatient at Shallu's reluctance to accept him and so he tried to force her to marry him. Shallu was scared of Amin because he was such a powerful man. How could she reject him? He threatened to make trouble for her if she did not accept his proposal. Shallu could only confide in her family about the threats. If she complained to anybody in authority, Amin would hear of it and only make her family's life intolerable. The only option left was for the family to leave Uganda forever and go to India[1].

When Amin heard the news that Shallu had left the country, he was very angry and upset. He was so angry that he inflicted revenge on all Indians in Uganda, he decreed that all the Indians would have to leave the country. On 4th August 1972, Amin gave Uganda's fifty thousand Asians (mainly of Indian origin) ninety days to leave the country or face imprisonment in military camps. However, the most well known and common reason for this course of action is that Amin was losing control over his country and decided that the best way for it to recover was to expel the Asians, as they owned a lot of businesses. 'I am going to ask Britain to take responsibility for all Asians in Uganda who are holding British passports, because they are sabotaging the economy of the country', Amin declared at the beginning of August 1972. 'If they do not leave they will find themselves sitting on the fire' Amin warned.

Amin's gangs began to rob the Indian houses and their businesses. There was a big conflict between black African and Indian people. Many Asians owned big businesses in Uganda and many Indians were born in the country. Their ancestors had come from India to Uganda when the country was still a British colony. Those who remained were deported from the cities to the countryside, although most Asians were granted asylum in Great Britain.

1 There is little historical evidence of this. The following may or may not refer to Shallu: 'We know that when Ugandan Chief Idi Amin wanted to marry a rich Gujarati girl, her family had to abandon all properties and run back to India' (http://dravidaperavai.50megs.com).

Amin enforced a curfew; no one could leave their houses to go anywhere once the sun had set. Shanta Bai hadn't enough money to buy a ticket to leave Uganda. Her husband Rakesh wanted to sell the chemist to raise the money, but no one wanted to buy it as they were all leaving the country. They asked friends, family and anyone they could think of to lend them the money, but everyone was too concerned with their own plight. There were only four days left until the deadline to leave Uganda. Fortunately, they were able to sell their chemist to someone at a very cheap price just in time. Rakesh went to pick the money up, he was very scared because of the curfew, but he managed not to be detected. Shanta was waiting for her husband at home, she was very worried because it was getting late. She didn't want to leave the house and risk breaking the curfew and also had her children to consider, who were fast asleep. At four o'clock in the morning there was a bang on the door. Shanta hurriedly opened it, only to see her husband there crying in excruciating pain. On his journey back home a dog had attacked him and bitten him on his hand, which was covered in blood.

Shanta was very scared now; she couldn't take her husband to the doctors because of the curfew. She panicked and ran into the street, knocking on everyone's door seeking help, but no one would open their door to her. A man from a Punjabi family who lived at the end of the street was kind enough to accompany Shanta to her house, bringing with him a bottle of chillies. He looked at Rakesh's badly bitten hand, then poured the chillies on the wound. Rakesh screamed so loud that everyone in the street could hear him. His wound was painful enough without having the burning chillies cast on to it. They managed to wash and dress the wound as best they could.

Early in the morning workers from the airport arrived to pick up the remaining Indians. Shanta Bai's family were forced to leave for the airport immediately without the children having washed or eaten. It was very upsetting, all the family had tears in their eyes because this was their country, they were leaving forever, their homeland. The family flew to London, arriving as refugees. The government put them in a detention centre where Rakesh managed to get some proper medical treatment for his hand. Eventually the family moved to Bolton, where Rakesh began work in a factory. However, in 1996 he had a heart attack and passed away. Even now, Shanta thinks back to that night before they left Uganda and still hears her husband's scream ringing in her ears.

Collated by Samim Vali

A Mother's Possession

(Anonymous)

In a city called Ahmedabad, India, lived a little girl called Gita with her family. Gita was very spoilt as she was the only child to her parents. Her parents always fulfilled Gita's demands and wishes. When she was twenty years of age, she got married to her husband, Sanjay, from a middle-class family. Gita was very happily married to Sanjay, who also fulfilled her wishes and demands. They had three children, two girls and one boy. The two girls were called Pinky and Pooja and the boy was called Raj. Raj was the eldest by a year and there was a one-year gap between his younger sisters.

Raj was sixteen years old when his father Sanjay died from cancer. As his father had been the head of the family, earning money to keep them all, it was now very hard for them to live properly and pay the bills. There was no longer any money coming into the house. Because of this, Raj had to take responsibility and do small jobs like washing cars, waiting on tables in restaurants, and various other jobs so that the family could make ends meet.

Although Raj was studying, he eventually took it upon himself to get a full time job and support his family. He found employment in an office where he worked alongside a girl called Rani. They became good friends and worked together everyday helping each other in their work. Because of the pressure Raj was under, he found in Rani a good shoulder to lean on. She was someone whom he could tell his troubles to and was very supportive. Rani admired how Raj had handled the situation resulting from his father's death. They both enjoyed each other's company. After months and months of working together, Raj and Rani fell in love and began to spend more time together. They were both so in love that if Rani did not come to work, Raj would feel lonely and miss her very much.

Raj was now twenty years old. His mother, Gita was very over protective of her children and didn't let them do anything without her consent. She still saw them as children and wouldn't even let them go out of the house if she did not think it was necessary. However, in Raj's case it was a necessity. Raj's sisters, Pinky and Pooja, were very quiet, they hardly got out of the house at all. Gita would occasionally tease Raj about getting married, whilst secretly dreading this day because she and her daughters had become so dependent on him. So she sought reassurance that he would always be there to look after them.

One day Raj came home late from work and sat with his mother. Because of his lateness, Raj jokingly said to his mum 'Don't worry I haven't been out to get married or anything'. Though his mother laughed along with his joke, she read deeply into this and became suspicious. She dwelled upon his words and light heartedly said to Raj 'Tell me, who do you want to marry, my son?' Raj then began to tell his mother about Rani. His mother was eager to meet her, so the next day they went to Rani's house. As far as Gita was concerned, it was just a visit, but before she knew it, a wedding was proposed, all the relatives agreed and she was swept along by the tide of enthusiasm. Everyone approved, including Gita, but secretly she was not happy with the wedding and found herself reluctantly putting on a brave face for the sake of her son. She did not want him to marry Rani. Gita feared for the future, she feared the loss of control over her household.

The wedding went ahead as planned and Rani moved into Gita's home, as is the custom. The house was full of happiness apart from Gita who was very jealous. She lay awake in her bed at night thinking how her agreement to the wedding had changed the family. She couldn't sleep. She could only think 'Why did I agree to the marriage?'

After a year Raj and Rani had a son, this meant that Gita

became even more peripheral to the family unit. Her jealousy caused an endless vendetta against Rani, she didn't like her and tried to cause as much trouble for her as possible. Gita made stories up to tell Raj so that he became angry with Rani. She would tell Rani to put specific ingredients into a meal, then complain to Raj when he arrived home from work that she'd mixed the wrong ingredients into the food. Gita created fights for the sake of it and always complained to her son that Rani was the cause of the trouble. Rani, however, was too honest, caring and loving to cause any trouble. Gita exaggerated any fabricated evidence to convince her son that Rani was no good for him. Raj was beginning to get sick of the atmosphere in the house. The tension between Gita and Rani grew, but Rani just kept quiet because she did not want to inflame the situation. She wanted her marriage to last and didn't want to upset her husband. She was such a patient girl who never complained.

Rani's father was very old and had all kinds of illnesses, but his health began to deteriorate with each passing day until one day he lay on his deathbed. Rani was extremely worried about him and asked her mother-in-law, Gita, if she could go home to visit him. Seizing the opportunity to demonstrate her authority in the household and express her grudge against Rani, Gita refused. This really upset Rani. That night her father passed away. When learning of this Rani became distraught, it infuriated her that Gita had denied her the opportunity of saying goodbye to her father. Rani never disobeyed Gita no matter how badly she treated her; she did not want to bring any shame to the family. However, she could no longer remain silent and withhold her pent up emotions.

Rani confronted Gita about the issue concerning her father. For the first time she began to raise her voice venting her anger at Gita. She shouted and raged for the lack of respect Gita had shown her. Gita was stunned and could not reply, but as Rani ranted at her, Raj entered the house and saw everything. In desperation, Gita ran to her son saying 'This is what happens all the time when you're not home'. Raj was already in a bad mood and now he'd walked home straight into this, when all he wanted to do was relax after his hard day at work. He had grown sick of the complaints and immediately grabbed Rani, attempting to push her into the room where their son was asleep. A tremendous struggle ensued. Rani cried and screamed at her husband, but Raj's rage had taken control, he could not stand the tension in the house anymore. Gita revelled in the torrid climate and shouted to her son 'Burn her! Burn her!' Raj grabbed a petrol can. One of the timid sisters dashed out trying to grab it from his hands and pull him away. She was no match for Raj's strength and could not prevent him from throwing the petrol over Rani. The sisters cried and shouted at their brother to stop, but Raj was possessed with fury. He lit a match and threw it towards Rani, engulfing her in flames. Raj heard his son crying in the background and quickly strode towards him, but Rani grabbed hold of Raj tightly, clinging to him as though he was her last breath of air. She gently whispered with fading words 'We both lived together, we both die together'.

Raj, Rani and the baby were taken to hospital. The police came and took a statement from Rani just before she died. Raj died three days later. The evidence from the statement was enough to put Gita into jail, but it was the impact of losing her son that truly hit her. She realised she was wrong and regretted everything she had done, but was jailed for fourteen years. Pinky and Pooja were sent to an orphanage[1]. Gita could not handle the guilt and lost control. Slowly, over the course of time, memories of that terrible night tortured her so much, they drove her to madness. After ten years in jail she died.

Collated by Zahida Abbas

---

1 Even at this age, young people are sent to an orphanage or hostel if no relatives are willing to look after them, as there are no social services in India. In an Indian orphanage, young people learn life skills and vocational skills that will enable them to obtain work. There are also ceremonies where they can choose marriage partners. Everything is geared towards integrating them back into society.

The Phoney War

(Anonymous)

I used to live on Leonard Street, near Higher Swan Lane in Bolton. There used to be a lot of mills in this area. Around 1938 I was looking after my two sisters, as my mother had died when I was sixteen years old. Fortunately, I did manage to get some time to myself at the local social club belonging to a mill on Settle Street. It had a tennis court and a function room where they played records. It was here that I met my first husband, Burt, an employee at the mill. After dating Burt for a while I soon began to realise that he was a good man, he liked a laugh and we enjoyed each other's company very much. Then of course we fell in love. However, there was an air of uncertainty about the future. Although the papers were full of war talk, the general attitude was that the war clouds would soon drift away. I became engaged to Burt and we talked about getting married in the coming year around Easter time in 1940. Burt made me promise that if the country went to war we would get married straight away.

One night I remember coming home from work through the train station in Bolton and I was surprised to see Burt waiting for me there at the top of the steps. I asked him what he was doing there. The first words he uttered were 'The Germans have marched into Poland, are we getting married?' I was so overwhelmed by these words as it meant we could be going to war, but I was also getting married. Burt reminded me of the promise I had made to him. That afternoon, we went to the TSB to withdraw some savings and then on to Prestons of Bolton to buy my wedding ring. The next day we went to the local church to put the banns up. This is the religious law requiring the announcement of the couple contemplating marriage in order to discover any objections. The announcement is read at church each Sunday for three weeks before the marriage. You were expected to attend church on these days whether you were a regular churchgoer or not. On the Sunday of that weekend, September 3rd 1939, war was declared. I was at Burt's house with all of his family and listened to the moment it happened on radio. We were all shocked and hoped it would soon be over with.

During the months following the declaration of war, nothing seemed to happen; we weren't engaged in any military action, so people began to call it a 'Phoney War'. Burt and I soon made the wedding arrangements and were married on 30th September 1939. Both my sisters were bridesmaids and wore pink. However, one of them didn't feel well on the day. She was so looking forward to being a bridesmaid, but she fainted as the car arrived. She was so upset at missing everything and did eventually make it to part of the reception, all wrapped up. I was fortunate to get married in white satin as later on in the war people could not afford to spend their clothing vouchers on wedding dresses, so they would get married in suits or clothes that could be worn on other days. Sometimes people would pool their clothing vouchers together to buy wedding outfits.

The 'Phoney War' soon changed after I became pregnant in December 1939. In January 1940 food rationing began. Each person was given a ration book. Only a few foods were rationed at first, but more foods were included as the war developed. Butter, sugar and some meats were the first products available to buy in shops with ration cards only. The ration cards also kept a record of how much people were buying according to the size of their family. Later that year, food became scarcer and everyone had to make sacrifices. The local chip shop only opened on a Friday night because of the rations on fat and even though the opening time was eight o'clock, children would begin queuing at six.

The German army overran the Low Countries. Belgium, Holland, Norway and finally France, all fell to the German war machine. By June 1940, the German army was virtually at our doorstep. I was getting very worried about my pregnancy. I heard stories from France about people fleeing the cities as their houses were being bombed, that mothers were having babies in fields and at the roadsides. I could not help thinking that this might happen to me. It started to appear more of a reality when the authorities began taking all the road signs down to make it difficult for the Germans to find their way around, should they arrive in Bolton. I prayed and prayed that I would have the baby before the invasion. After the fall of France in 1940, Hitler turned his attention to us. His plans to invade Britain depended on crippling our Royal Air Force. In July 1940 the Luftwaffe, the German air force, began its attempt to bomb Britain into submission. The resulting conflict became known as the Battle of Britain.

It became law that we had to carry gas masks with us everywhere we went. They were very frightening things to look at and had an awful rubbery smell. The German air force was bombing all the major cities. Sometimes it lasted all night. I remember when the sirens went off the first night, Burt and I jumped out of bed. My sisters were staying in the back bedroom; one of them jumped up out of bed too, to switch on the light, but smashed her nose on the bedroom door. Her nose was a right bloody mess.

During the pitch black nights, we watched the sky light up with flames. From this you could tell where the bombing was taking place. Burt used to say 'Oh Liverpool's getting it tonight' or 'Manchester'.

Finally, the day arrived when I was due to go into hospital. Burt was very concerned about me. From the hospital I could hear the sirens and the bombs every night, such death and destruction whilst I was waiting to give birth. One night there was a very close explosion on Punch Street. The nurses laughed because Burt, bless him, visited me in hospital at seven thirty in the evening, then cycled home, wrote me a letter, cycled back to the hospital and slid it under the door the same night. The nurses joked saying 'You've got another love letter here!' Our husbands helped us to go down the cellar steps and seat us on deck chairs down one side of the cellar, but then they had to leave. Newborn babies were wrapped up in blankets on the other side of the room. The sirens used to begin at eight in the evening. We stayed in the cellars until we were given the all clear, but this would not be until around six in the morning.

I heard Mr Churchill's speech in hospital when referring to the efforts of our fighter pilots. 'Never in the field of human conflict was so much owed by so many to so few'. This was a very rousing speech and made everyone in the hospital feel safer and confident.

I remember the night my baby, Paul, was born on 5th September 1940, the same night the Germans bombed Bolton, they dropped a bomb somewhere near Wigan Road. Paul was a few hours old then. Burt anxiously rang the hospital fearing the bomb had landed on us.

Soon after Paul was born we were provided with a special cot for him. It had a see through lid, in case of gas. It was a horrible looking contraption and I couldn't imagine having to place my baby in that capsule. Yet somehow, the war became a normal way of life. It is surprising how you can be in the middle of something like that and just get on with it; it's a coping mechanism I suppose. We were anxious about getting enough food for Paul because of the rations. Burt's mother laid her hands on anything she could get hold of for him. I had more Farley's rusks lined up in my kitchen than in any of the local shops!

Collated by Rehana Makkan

My First Fast

(Anonymous)

I was eight years old living in the village of Sherpura, India. India is a very hot country, and at this particular time, it was the Islamic Blessed Month of Ramadan. Ramadan involves having to fast from sunrise until sunset each day for a month. This means not eating or drinking anything during this time. Being just a child I had never been allowed to fast before. It is not healthy for a child to fast in a hot country. They aren't expected to fast at all until they have reached puberty.

However, this time I felt left out, so I asked my mum if I could keep a fast, just for one day. Mum tried to put me off by saying I would not have the desire to keep the fast all day and that I would soon break it. She didn't even think I would be able to get out of my bed before sunrise. I pleaded with her to let me try and pestered her so much that in the end she relented. I went to bed that night determined to wake up before sunrise the next morning and slowly drifted off to sleep with this thought harboured in my mind.

Under the dark blanket of the morning, still half asleep, the sound of the household waking began to filter through my senses, calling me to consciousness. Then with the alertness of a soldier, I rose out of bed, washed my face, brushed my teeth and went down to join the rest of my family for Sehri, an early morning meal eaten just before sunrise, followed by the first prayer of the day, called Fajr. Sehri is a Sunnah act, meaning a deed carried out in the custom of the prophet Mohammed.

Mum was surprised to see me up so early with the rest of the family. She thought I would forget and would not be able to resist the temptation of staying in bed. My dad appeared pleased that I had made the effort to join them and told me that if I could keep the day's fast without cheating, he would give me ten rupees. Ten rupees was a lot to a small child in India. Now I was even more determined than ever to keep a fast.

Before we knew it, the morning's sun was beginning to raise its glowing head. After Sehri, because it was still very early in the morning, I went back to bed. I didn't wake up until later that morning. Fortunately, it was a school holiday, but the weather was extremely hot. The sun felt as if it was constantly hanging over my head. So I kept washing my face with cold water to cool myself down. I wanted to drink the water so much to quench my thirst, but managed to persevere for the sake of the fast. For a short while, I wished I had never vowed to keep the fast, as the heat was becoming unbearable, but the reward my dad had promised acted as an extra incentive.

I decided to go to my friend's house a few plots away, along the dusty paths created by the villagers walking back and forth. The heat was worse outside where the earth baked in the sun. I was eager to tell my friend I was fasting and that my dad was going to give me ten rupees if I succeeded.

My mouth and throat felt dry. My thirst was growing so much that my one wish was to stand under a refreshing waterfall with my mouth wide open. However, I had to be resolute and stick to the fast. My friend and I played outside for a few hours in the sun, running around on the dusty land. I began to feel dizzy and disorientated, I couldn't stand straight. My friend became scared and rushed towards her house to get some water for me, but I shouted after her. She was going to tell her mum that I was fasting, but I forced her not to, fearing her mother would shout at me and force me to drink the water.

I went home immediately and told my parents what had happened. My dad said that if I broke the fast he would still give me ten rupees. I thought this was generous of him, he was obviously concerned about me, but as there was only a couple of hours remaining before the fast for that day could be broken, I refused. Instead, I decided to go to bed. My mum agreed to wake me up just before sunset in time to break the fast with the rest of the family.

When I awoke, I couldn't believe it, everything was set for the meal. There was fruit, dates, and many fried savouries. My mum had made it all, even though she was fasting and I realised that throughout the day she had just carried on with her daily chores as normal. This made me appreciate her even more. I broke my fast with a date and a glass of lassi[1]. We all ate fruit together. Then my mum went to perform her namaz[2] in another room. When my dad came back from the mosque, we ate properly. He was very impressed that I had kept my fast and gave me ten rupees as promised, then amazingly, my mum gave me ten more. I was also very pleased with myself, I told my friends about it the following morning. They were very envious that I had received twenty rupees as a reward.

I was very glad I did not have to keep the fast for the whole month, but my first fast gave me an insight into how difficult the experience can be. It wasn't until a few years later, when I was eleven years old that I fasted for a whole month.

Fasting makes you realise there are people in the world who are starving, with no food or water. This is one of the reasons why Allah wanted his people to fast for thirty days, to make us appreciate what we have and to think of the less fortunate. I will never forget my first fast.

Collated by Rehana Makkan

1 Like a milkshake made with yoghurt, with a savoury or sweet flavour such as mango.
2 Prayers.

My Secret

(Anonymous)

Life had started off quite normally. I lived with my mum, dad and my sister. Mum and Dad were quite strict, but looking back, the routine of daily life, interspersed with family days out and holidays, made me feel safe and secure. Shortly after my thirteenth birthday, something happened that turned my life upside down. I was walking through a park, when suddenly I was grabbed from behind and dragged into some bushes. I was raped. I ran all the way home and made my way to the bathroom, where I scrubbed myself in a bath full of cold water until my skin was red raw. Because I felt so dirty and ashamed I could not bring myself to tell anyone. How could a girl my age bring up such a taboo subject anyway? The attack had lasted just a few minutes, but those few minutes changed my life. I felt I had been transformed from an innocent child into a dirty, shameful slut. The strain of hiding such an awful secret made me snappy and rebellious.

As the years passed by, I married a man several years older than me. He promised he'd look after me. For a few months I believed him. After a while, I started to tire of having to have sex whenever he wanted. It wasn't unusual to be woken up during the night. If I ever dared to say no he just slapped or punched me into submission. A couple of years later I fell pregnant; I was delighted, and so was he at the beginning. As my bump grew, he began to call me fat and ugly, so he started having sex with other women; lots of them. He often came home with love bites on his neck, sometimes he didn't come home at all. He even tried talking my best friend into having sex with him! At the time, I just felt grateful for the fact that he stayed with me and continued to provide for me. After all, no one else would have wanted me. At least that was what I believed. When the time came for me to give birth to my daughter, for just a few hours, he gave me all his attention, holding my hand as I pushed my baby out into the world. I gave birth to a beautiful baby girl. We stayed in hospital for two weeks, as there were a few problems. He only visited us twice, but I didn't care. I was enjoying being cared for by two wonderful motherly nurses. They washed, dressed and helped me hold my daughter to my breast. For the first time in eight years I didn't flinch at the touch of another person. All too soon it was time to go home. My husband came to collect us, looking just like any other happy doting new father. However, his mask slipped a few hours later when my hungry little girl demanded to be fed. 'Shut the little brat up!' he shouted, attempting to be heard above her crying. From this moment I was on tenterhooks. Each time my baby stirred or made the slightest little noise, I whipped her out of the cot and cuddled her close, to keep her as quiet as possible. I found this new routine, coupled with postnatal depression, to be an exhausting and punishing way of life. Yet it was nothing compared to the excruciating pain I woke up to one night, as he tore my stitches in the process of satisfying himself. I don't know if it was guilt, fear or the fact that he simply couldn't care less, but afterwards he would not take me to hospital. Twenty four hours later I was in so much pain, I couldn't even walk. I phoned my neighbour to come round and look after my baby daughter then called for an ambulance. I was admitted to hospital where they operated to repair the damage and kept me in overnight for observation. The following day I returned home, to be met by my neighbour. She still had my little girl, as my husband hadn't come home. This was not unusual for him as he often spent the odd night away. I never knew where he was or who he was with. I stopped asking him ages ago as he always retorted that it was nothing to do with me!

Days passed and there was still no sign of him. By now I had run out of both food and money. As we were living out in the country, I had no alternative but to walk the five miles to the nearest town where I could cash my family allowance. I ambled around town whilst doing my shopping and treated myself to a cup of tea and cream cake in a café overlooking a lake, before making my way to the bus stop. Once on the bus I sat back and gazed out of the window as we sped past field after field of yellow blossom.

I was abruptly brought back to the present when I recognised his car parked outside the house of another woman who had a reputation in the village for sleeping with other women's husbands. A couple of hours later, I was fetching the washing off the line. As I walked in through the back door carrying the basket piled high with laundry I didn't notice the fist; his fist, waiting for me. Some time later I was aware of a banging noise; I couldn't move and could barely make a noise. The front door opened. With some relief I realised it was my neighbour. She phoned for an ambulance and again I was taken back to hospital. Mum and Dad came to visit me after my neighbour had called them. I felt so ashamed when I saw the expression of disgust on their faces as they looked at the state of me. However, I was so grateful when they offered to take my baby daughter and me home with them. They told to me to inform the neighbours that we were just visiting for a while. Mum and Dad said they couldn't face them if word got out that there was to be a divorce in the family.

Weeks turned into months and I found the strain of living a lie in the claustrophobic confines of my parents' home too much. So my daughter and I moved into a flat by the seaside; a very draughty flat with carpets blowing three or four inches up from the floorboards on a windy night. And yet, for the first time in ages, I felt at peace. I decided that I wanted a better life, both for my daughter as well as for myself. I enrolled on a full time secretarial course whilst my little girl went to a very kindly childminder. My confidence was at an all time high as I completed the course and was awarded the college's 'Student of the Year' title. I was even in the local paper!

I ended up with a really good job and even started dating

again. However, as soon as a man started to get too close, I'd behave badly so that he would be forced to dump me. Life followed this self-destructive pattern for several years until I let my guard down at university. In my second year at university I met a man who was intelligent and sensitive. Within a few weeks we fell head over heels in love. We became inseparable and only parted from each other to go to lectures and tutorials. It was so sweet to walk out of the lecture hall to find him waiting for me. However, he tired of studying and gave up after his first year, then proceeded to make life very difficult for me to continue with my own studies, but continue I did!

I became pregnant and so he put even more pressure on me to leave university on the grounds that it would be more responsible for me to undertake paid work. Every now and again he lost it and slapped me round the face, pulled my hair or locked me out, but he was always so sorry afterwards. I put up with it because I actually felt sorry for him at times. He had been married before he met me, but hadn't seen his children for more than two years. Apparently he had gone home from work one day to find his wife and children had left him, completely out of the blue. Of course, he didn't tell me that they had actually moved into a women's refuge. Three months into my pregnancy, he attacked me kicking and punching like someone possessed, brandishing a pair of scissors in front of my face. He then cut the clothing off me and imprisoned me in the bedroom for more than a week, telling everyone I had gone away to stay with relatives. Eventually, I returned to university shrouded in a mask of make-up, which he had very kindly gone out and bought for me, to cover the bruises. And believe me I did have to thank him for it! I also had to wear big baggy jumpers with roll necks.

The physical attacks continued and intensified over the next few months, to the extent that I gave birth to my second child with a leg in plaster and a bald patch on my head, where he'd pulled out a clump of hair. He often kept me awake all night, knowing that with two children to look after, I wouldn't be able to catch up on my sleep during the day. He insisted on moving us further and further away from any friends and family until eventually we were living in an isolated area with no neighbours, no shops, no telephone, no buses, and he also ensured that I had no money.

Several years passed and my health had started to suffer as a result of all the beatings. I realised I couldn't carry on living under his regime any longer. I was watching daytime television one day and a survivor of domestic violence was being interviewed. In that moment I realised that I too was a victim of domestic violence. The programme highlighted the help that was available for women like me.

It took several weeks to put any kind of plan into action. I managed to save a little amount of money and started packing a bag I kept hidden in the garage. I was so scared of being found out that I struggled to look him in the eye, fearing that he may even be able to read my mind! Yet, despite this, I also felt excited, so much so that I was sure I'd give the game away, but I didn't! Then the unthinkable happened. He went out and left me, the children and the car at home. As soon as he had gone I quickly bundled the children and the packed bag into the car and we were off. At last, after years of hell, I was free.

At this stage I didn't know exactly where we were going, but I just kept on driving. I wanted to put as many miles as possible between us and him. I knew some relatives that I could ask for help. Sure enough, one of them agreed we could stay with them until we found alternative accommodation. That alternative accommodation became the refuge in Bolton and it turned out to be the best thing to happen to me for many years. Not only did my children and I have somewhere safe to stay, but I was able to talk to the other residents and also a counsellor who helped kick start the long healing process.

Years on I'm happier than ever before. I've been able to lay many old ghosts to rest, some going back to when I was thirteen years old. I also have a good career now, working with homeless people. Most importantly, I am able to make my own choices and I will never take my freedom for granted. And yes, I do go out on dates now and again, but I'm not putting my life on hold in the hope that my Mr Right comes along. For the time being, I'm happy just the way I am!

Halima and the Tree

(Halima Mayat)

I was born in the village of Warathi in the state of Gujarat. I grew up there and attended school, studying up to the fifth level in the same village. This is the equivalent to finishing primary school in the United Kingdom. Girls weren't allowed to study any further in those days, though I would have liked to, if there had been the opportunity.

I remember a beautiful sunny afternoon, when I was twelve years old. I had been itching for a sense of adventure all morning, so I was very excited when three of my friends arrived to see if I was going out to play. With the permission of my mother, we went off into the fields. We loved playing in the fields and frequently spent hours there, climbing trees, laughing and having a wonderful time. First of all, we sat by a tangy tamarind tree. The leaves of this tree are used to spice up Indian cooking. We chatted about school, home and clothes, the usual things girls talked about at that age. The birds chirped away and the chatter of female workers could be heard from the fields, interspersed with laughing and giggling. We decided to play a chasing game. As I was the chaser, my friends ran as far away from me as possible. One of them scrambled up a tamarind tree to escape from me. She shouted down 'You can't get me now!' She thought I wouldn't dare climb up the tree, as I was afraid of heights. I was determined to prove her wrong. I made a tremendous effort to grip the dry tree and begin my ascent, whilst focusing on her, in order to try and eliminate any fear from my mind. I panted in time with my heart whilst my will and fear battled against each other inside me. I stretched, trying to reach a branch for security and so I could pull myself further up the tree. My friend looked down at me, knowing I was petrified, so she reached out her hand to help me up.

I couldn't help looking down even though my friend advised me not to. I began trembling. I couldn't help thinking that I would fall. This feeling engulfed the whole of me, until I became disorientated and dizzy. As I tried to reach out to my friend, I lost my balance and yelled as I plummeted to the ground. There was a thud at the end of a long fall down. It wasn't a straight fall as my foot had got caught on a barbed wire fence nearby. I shrieked as I lay on the ground with a piece of wire piercing the heel of my shoe and my foot. I cried out with pain at the sight of blood dripping from the wire. My friend jumped down to help. We both attempted to extract the piece of wire. This only caused more agony. The wire wasn't shifting at all, as it had penetrated a good two inches into my foot. All we could do now was try and make our way back home. I cried most of the time as I leaned on my friend for support. The five minute journey home took twice as long as usual. Apart from the pain I endured, we both feared we'd get into trouble from our parents. However, apart from the initial shock, my parents were just relieved that nothing serious had happened to me. My uncle now had to take me to the hospital in the village nearby, about three miles away. I could not walk at all. I could feel a great stabbing pain shooting from my foot right up my leg as the tears kept on rolling off my face.

As it was the monsoon season, the footpaths were very muddy which made the journey even more difficult for my uncle. He had to carry me in his arms. The squishy mud squirmed beneath his feet as he negotiated the terrain. He breathed heavily, with sweat dribbling down his face. My weight had begun to take its toll on him. After a while he had to stop to put me down and relax his arms and shoulders. However, I was anxious about getting my foot treated and couldn't understand why he had stopped. My uncle explained that the conditions had slowed us down and the journey would take longer than anticipated. Having rested for a while we carried on, but had to stop and start for the remainder of the journey.

Finally, much to the relief of my uncle, we arrived at the hospital after three and a half hours. The waiting room was full of people, with the air conditioning whizzing away. We both sat down and quenched our thirst with cold chilled water from the water cooler. My uncle poured a little over his sweating head. He fully appreciated the refreshing cold water trickling down his face and neck. It was as though he had been walking forever judging by the sighs of relief emitted as he rested.

A nurse took me into a separate room, then held my foot as I screamed the place down. Without giving me any anaesthetic to numb my foot, a doctor took a pair of tweezers and yanked the wire out. It was all over in a few seconds. My foot was then dressed and bandaged and I came out of the hospital crying with pain. Once again, my uncle carried me along the perpetual tiresome trek back home. He reassured me that everything was going to be all right. However, the arduous journey and my constant crying wore my uncle's calmness into submission. He finally snapped, yelling at me that I was stupid for climbing the tree, considering I was scared of heights! After his outburst, we both suffered the long tiring journey home in silence.

Collated by Rehana Makkan and Summaiya Kadva

Give and Receive

(Anonymous)

I was born in Istanbul, the capital city of Turkey, but my parents had a traditional village upbringing in Balchik. This village is situated in the town of Susehri, which is in the city of Sivas. Men were traditionally looked upon as the heads of each household and families were not really respected until they had produced a male child. With this cultural tradition engrained within them, my parents desperately wanted a baby boy. There were no women's rights, women were nothing compared to males. The men always took control of the money that came into the house. Women were never expected to get a job, just to look after the family and follow their husband's orders. They cooked, cleaned, looked after animals and even worked in the fields growing and harvesting crops. The word 'love' was never mentioned, it was kept secret. Most girls were not allowed to go to school, however if they were lucky, some did manage to go to primary school. There was not even a calendar, nothing in the village to keep accurate records of when people were born. As a result, quite a lot of people actually celebrate their birthday on 1st January. This is the usual date that is entered by the authorities when people register with them, if they do not know their exact date of birth. I was born on 1st June, but even my birth was registered on 1st January!

Growing up in this village, my mother was no different from the other women there, but she had lots of pride. She so yearned to give birth to a baby boy. However, fate seemed to taunt her. Her first child was indeed a baby boy, but he was born dead. It wasn't long before she gave birth again to another baby boy, but he only lived for eight months due to a problem with his internal organs. Despite being devastated by these experiences, in the true tradition and culture of this Turkish village, she was not allowed to express her feelings, though her tears could be caught glistening in the sun by the other women as they harvested the crops.

In the face of this trauma, my mother was resolute in her quest for a baby son. It wasn't too long before she became pregnant again. This time she gave birth to a baby girl. Fortunately, the baby girl survived. In a period of about four years, my mother gave birth to three more girls, but still no sign of any sons. Eventually, once more she fell pregnant, this time with a son, but again he was born dead. Even following this she gave birth to another son, but of course, he too suffered the same fate. So she came to the conclusion that she was never destined to have the son she craved for. To add insult to injury, an uncle of mine who had often treated my mum badly through out her life, told her that in order to have a son she must first kiss his feet. This is an indication of just how badly women are treated in our culture.

From the other women in the village, my mother came to hear about a shrine in the village of Gölova İlçes, dedicated to Karayakup Evliyasi, a Muslim martyr who was buried there. He was one of seven brothers who died during an ancient war. She heard how prayers had been granted from people who had visited this shrine. There was no way she was going to miss out on this opportunity. Immediately she arranged to travel there with my dad, my auntie and my uncle. They travelled fifteen miles from the village to the shrine in the back of a trailer, pulled by a tractor which was driven by my uncle.

After arriving at Gölova İlçes, she climbed the rugged hill to where the small enclosed shrine was located. She washed to cleanse herself in the small stream there before praying as Muslims do[1] and prepared to stay in the shrine overnight. There she knelt, praying and praying so hard reading namaz[2], reciting specific verses from the Quran to be granted a baby

1 A ritual called Wudhu.
2 Prayers.

boy. She even made a pledge that if her prayers were granted, she would sacrifice seven sheep; one sheep when the child was born; one when the child attended primary school; one when he was circumcised; one when he joined the army; one when he finished military service; one when he married and one when he too had a child. Following this, she prepared herself for sleep hoping for some kind of sign. Gradually she sunk into a deep, deep sleep and amazingly in her unconscious state she actually saw the image of Yakup Evliyasi. Dressed in white clothes and a white beard, he spoke with a very loving gentle voice, telling her she was already pregnant with a male child and his name would be Yacup. She suddenly woke up feeling as though a small stone had entered her womb. She reflected upon her dream and could not believe she had seen the martyr. She was both shocked and ecstatic, but as always she had to keep her feelings inside as the women had to be seen to be mature and not emotional.

Nine months later, after my family had moved from the village of Balchik to Istanbul, my dad had started a business, driving his own bus, transporting people from Istanbul to the surrounding towns and villages. One day he had just driven a bus load of people back to the village of Balchik, where in this village of his upbringing, he received the joyous news that my mum had given birth to a baby boy. Despite all the previous misfortune, celebrations in the village began immediately and just as my mother had pledged in the shrine, they sacrificed a sheep. My parents were so happy to finally have a baby boy and of course called him Yacup. In Istanbul my mum made a sweet dish, helva, usually made on very special days. She invited the neighbours and extended family. They gave a big feast with recitals from the Quran in praise of her newborn son.

My parents now thought that there was potential to have another son, so they tried again. Three years later my mother became pregnant. News of the birth came from the hospital.

Two of my sisters who were aged ten and eleven at the time went to the post office and bought tokens for the phone to ring the hospital. They asked a nurse there if my mother had given birth to a boy or a girl. When they found out it was a girl, my sisters cried and threw the rest of the tokens on the floor. My mother had given birth to me!

After I was only eight weeks old my uncle died and my mum had to go back to the village of Balchik for his funeral, leaving me for twenty days. She was so upset at the death of her brother. At the same time, my cousin was considering divorcing his wife because she had not conceived a child. Because of these events, my mother became very close to offering me up for adoption to my cousin.

I was born three years after my brother and became extremely jealous of him. Of course, because of cultural tradition and the adversity my mother had conquered in conceiving her one and only son, Yacup was my parents' most prized possession. He had all the attention and my parents bought better gifts for him. My earliest memories of my brother are from when I was about five or six years old. He would often hit me, even in front of my parents, but they never stopped him or even told him off. All I could do was try to hit him back. When I was seven or eight years old at primary school, I remember him taking my pocket money on more than a few occasions and keeping it for himself. Whatever he wanted in life he got it. My sister knitted a red jumper for me and a blue one for my brother. My jumper was very plain and simple whereas his was very intricately knitted with rich wool, containing sophisticated patterns. Right from the time he was born, my parents constantly told him that he would be the boss of the family as he was the boy. So this spoilt child began to demand things such as his pocket money, crying and crying until he got it. Believing that everything was his, even when he was ten years old, the day came when he demanded my father's driver's licence, insurance papers and vehicle registration documents, just as we were about to leave the house for a trip to town. He cried and cried to have them and keep them with him. In Turkey the driver of the vehicle always has to carry the vehicle's documents. My father relented as usual and passed them over to him to look after. So, acting the big boss with the papers and the keys, my ten-year-old brother led the way to the car parked in the back street. He was so caught up in his moment of authority that he failed to notice an open man hole and disappeared straight down it. Then of course he cried for a different reason, this time he needed their help. He was not badly hurt at all, but the keys and papers to the car could not be found so our day out was ruined. They were never recovered and my father had to go through the process of obtaining new keys and documents.

After Dad finished with his bus driving business, he then went into selling cars, which led to my brother, who was about fifteen, becoming even more obsessed with them. This influenced him about ten years later, when he was twenty-five years old, to borrow a lot of money from my sister's husband to start a business buying and selling his own second-hand cars. The money he earned from this totally changed his lifestyle. He stayed out late at night and always ate at the best restaurants. He went to clubs, spent his money on holidays and gambling. He even paid the rent and the bills for his girlfriend's apartment, though he did not move in with her.

For a short while my mother and father moved away to a village house they had built. This meant I was living with just my brother at the family home. In Turkey, it was felt unsafe for a girl to be left home alone even though I was twenty-three years old. Therefore Dad told my brother never to leave me alone in the house. Yacup ignored this advice. Sometimes he came home from his nights out, sometimes he did not. I started to complain. One morning I was cleaning the house and had just mopped the tiles, when he arrived home from a late night out. The floor was wet, so I told him not to come in with his shoes on, but he just walked right in. I kept telling him to take his shoes off. He quickly turned around and slapped me across the face. I fell and banged my head on the tiles. I was unconscious for a few minutes. He rang my sister telling her to talk to me, as according to him, I was causing problems. I rang my friend crying, she told me to go straight to her house at once. All this happened on the day of my exams for Open University.

In February 2001, the Turkish economy took a turn for the worse affecting everyone, especially businesses and my brother became bankrupt. He did not work for a while after this and suffered a nervous breakdown. On 15th August 2001, I was due to fly to the UK. As I was doing some last minute packing, my father and Yacup were arguing about the business my brother had lost through his gambling, extravagant lifestyle and not reinvesting in the business. Yacup could not accept this. My father is very patient, but Yacup is so spoilt he could not listen to the truth and threatened to hit him. My father said 'If you hit me, then I'll hit you!' I tried to split them up, shouting 'Please, please stop!' They were not listening. It made me extremely upset; I fell to the floor crying. My mother could only say to me 'Are you stupid? What are you crying for?' She did not even question her spoilt son's behaviour. My friend who was present, was also upset, but told me not to worry. Then Dad said he was leaving as he was deeply hurt. I pleaded with him not to go. My mother did not even support him. He went to the car and I rang him shortly afterwards on his mobile. Dad went to the corner shop and waited for me as he was supposed to take me to the airport.

About a year after my brother was recovering from his nervous breakdown, he began to work for my dad's taxi business, eventually taking over the business around February 2002. I already had shares in the business from about 1999 and my Dad had eventually paid me some money earned from my shares, once the business was in profit. However, since my brother took over the business, although my investment has grown, I have never seen a penny.

As I sit down, here, now in the UK, I realise through telling this story, I have actually found the true reason why I am here. First of all, I have never felt my parents' love. My parents never cared about any of their daughters. All their daughters have been made to pay for their brother all through his life and we have never received the respect we deserved. I am just too heartbroken about my family because they never cared. They did not look after me, they just let me be and never considered my thoughts and feelings. The one time I asked for the income from my shares that the taxi business had generated, because I was not working, my brother refused, just saying in his usual spoilt way that the money was his. I will never see the money from those shares. I haven't kept in touch with my brother now for two years. I am here because I escaped them and the way women are treated in that culture. Here I am more independent. If I had ever married someone from Turkey, I probably would have been suppressed forever, like my sisters.

In Turkey, if women cover themselves with a headscarf, they are not allowed to work in government places and most big companies. My family expected me to become more European and modern when I came to the UK, but instead I have gone the other way. I am religious and wear a headscarf, so I am a disappointment to them. I was even disappointed in myself, just like my mother, when I thought I was going to have a baby boy and had a girl instead. It is all part of the psychology stemming from the culture I was brought up in.

Collated by Michael Carroll

Taxi Driver

(Faizal Makkan)

You can imagine the kind of tales taxi drivers have to tell from the variety of characters they meet. Faizal has been a taxi driver for United Taxis in Bolton for about seven years. He drives a combination of day and nightshifts. There is one story in particular that sticks in his mind.

It was very early one morning, around two thirty, during the Christmas season about five years ago. For taxi drivers, Christmas is the best and busiest time of year, and this particular day had proved to be very hectic. Faizal was just coming to the end of a gruelling night shift, there were no passengers in his car and he was relieved that all his hard work was now behind him. He could afford to relax a little and drifted up towards the traffic lights, on red, alongside Bolton train station, heading up Derby Strcet in his Toyota Corolla 2-litre GTI. As he was feeling tired, he didn't mind resting at the lights for a while. The roads were now very empty and quiet; a peace had descended upon Bolton town centre after all the hustle and bustle of the nightlife. His radio played very low, underscoring the sights through the wide screen television of his car.

As he waited for the lights to turn green, he watched other taxis transporting people home and the odd couple of people walking home from their night out. Gradually he became aware of a peculiar booming noise creeping upon him, becoming louder and louder. He looked towards the lane on his right and saw a boy racer Ford Escort pull up alongside of him. Inside the car there were three boisterous young lads partying, as if in a mobile nightclub. They appeared very drunk, swinging cans of beer in their hands and jumping up and down to the music blasting from the speakers. As soon as they saw him looking at them, they began hurling abuse, calling him an old man, pulling strange faces and making all kinds of obscene gestures at him. For Faizal, they typified the type of yob culture that was infesting the town. They focused all their attention on Faizal, trying to wind him up. This made him angry, but he still managed to keep a straight face as he shook his head with contempt.

As the youths were so full of themselves, Faizal decided to enter their little game and revved up his 2-litre GTI engine. Sure enough their driver responded, but revving his engine even louder. Aware of what was going on around him, Faizal noticed another car in his mirror, approaching from behind in the distance. As it drew nearer, he realised that it was a police car. A moment of inspiration entered his wise old head. He looked back at the boys, as he revved his engine harder and nodded to their driver. Of course, this was the signal that the youths had been waiting for. The race was on. Both cars revved their engines as if on the starting grid of a formula one grand prix circuit. Hands raised aloft, all the youths encouraged their driver and cheered him on in between their swigs of beer. Adrenalin rushed through Faizal's veins, his heart beating like the pistons of his engine.

The lights turned green, the engines roared and the tyres screeched. As soon as Faizal's car sped a couple of yards, he slammed on the brakes, letting the other car zoom off into the distance. The youths were fully immersed in their drag racing scene. However, the police existed in the real world. Faizal's moment of inspiration worked and he laughed as he watched the police car with blaring siren and flashing lights, chase the youths up the road. His laugh was fuelled by the knowledge that he had got one over on the youths. He felt so pleased with himself. Faizal drove to the side of the road and stopped for a short while to calm himself down and get some fresh air. He then got in his car and began driving up towards the base of United Taxis on Adelaide Street. Further on up the road he was delighted to see that the Ford Escort had been pulled over by the police and the driver of the vehicle was being booked for speeding, drinking and probably a whole range of other offences. Faizal continued to drive with an air of pride and satisfaction in the knowledge he had brought a sense of justice to the world. He'd helped to 'clean up the streets'[1].

Faizal radioed a colleague to tell him about the incident. His friend also laughed with great satisfaction and congratulated him. As soon as Faizal arrived back at base, he told the story to the rest of the drivers in the taxi rank. They were all in stitches and wished they had been there to see it. This is Faizal's favourite story from his work as a taxi driver. He still chuckles to himself every time he thinks about it.

Collated by Rehana Makkan

1 Relating to the character Travis Bickle in Martin Scorsese's film Taxi Driver, starring Robert De Niro.

The Story of Mohammed

(Anonymous)

Mohammed was born in Pakistan. He came to England when he was seven years old. He used to live in Manchester, but soon moved to Bolton. When he first arrived in England he really missed his homeland; he didn't like the different lifestyle, the cold environment and the weather. Mohammed became confused and disorientated in his new world. He missed picking sweet corn on cobs, sugar canes, and catching fish from the small pond near his house with his friends in Pakistan. He struggled at the beginning of his life in England because he could not speak English. Gradually he began to settle down and make new friends in Bolton. He went to Bolton Parish Church School then to Breightmet High School, which is now known as Withins School. Mohammed has a story about his childhood life, which he will always remember.

Most of my friends and I used to travel home from school on the number one six two bus, which went all the way to Bolton town centre, Great Moor Lane bus station. I used to get off early at the stop, which was just near my house on Bury Road, but my friends would carry on to the bus station. Sometimes when they got off the bus they were beaten up and bullied by skinheads from another school. One day the skinheads broke one of my friend's arms so the next day my friends asked me if I would go with them to the bus station just in case the skinheads attacked them again, so I agreed.

That day was a nice sunny summer's day. After school had finished, we all got together and arranged to go down to the bus station. Each one of us had found some kind of weapon to take; most of us were carrying sticks and stones. I had my nanchuks, which are two sticks held together with a chain in the middle. There was about forty of us from the first year to the fifth year. The gang was full of vibrant youth and there was a collective excitement as we travelled on the bus towards our destination. We got off at the bus stop in town outside the YMCA and headed towards the police station and the magistrates' courts, just before the bus station, because we wanted to catch the gang of skinheads by surprise.

As we walked towards the bus station, all of a sudden about two hundred skinheads came charging towards us. There were a few seconds of hesitation at the sight of them, but I pulled my nanchuks out and stood my ground. I looked behind me only to see all my friends running away, now I was surrounded. I fought and I hit the first three or four of them with my nanchuks. Then I became drastically out-numbered and quickly turned around, running after my friends. They all piled into the YMCA and ran to the top of about thirty stairs. There all my friends huddled together. I followed them up the stairs, shouting at them for leaving me on my own. I grabbed a big stick from one of them. Crash! The doors at the bottom of the YMCA flew open and the skinheads began running up the stairs. I charged downstairs at them with the big stick and to my surprise, they all ran back outside as I chased them. I caught one of the lads and I was just about to hit him when I was grabbed from behind. A voice said 'That's enough!' It was a police officer. I threw the stick in a bin, but the policeman told me to pick it up, so I did as he asked. He said that he was arresting me for carrying an offensive weapon. I was taken to the police station just around the corner. I felt that I had been mugged because they had taken me and left the skinheads behind. I was also very angry with myself. I was put in a cell for about two hours which was long enough for me to calm down and realise how stupid I had been. I thought to myself that it had not even been my own fight yet I was the one who had been arrested. I knew I would now have to go to court. My mother came to the police station and took me home.

The next day at school I was a hero, I was the talk of the school, I had stood my ground, fought and got arrested. The whole school was proud of me. Everyone said that if I was fined at court they would all chip in to pay it off. A few months later, I attended court. The police officer who arrested me gave evidence saying that on such and such a date and time, he saw me chasing about one hundred white youths outside the YMCA with a big stick, which he produced in court. The magistrate smiled and asked me why I was chasing one hundred white youths. I explained to the judge about the trouble my friends had been having and the reason that I was chasing them was that if the fighting had started in the YMCA, there would have been a lot of damage. The judge smiled at my response and said that he would let me off as long as I did not get into any more trouble.

The following day at school, I told everyone that I had been fined three hundred pounds. Everyone chipped in; some put in a few pounds, some fifty pence. Together, they raised the full three hundred pounds. With the money, I threw the biggest school leaving party at the YMCA in the school's history. I had party tickets printed, which I sold for sixty pence, raising even more money. I splashed out on food and drinks and I bought the teachers' leaving presents from all the fifth year pupils.

Collated by Mussarrat Shafiq

Liar's Day

(Halil Zeqiri)

The day that will never leave my memory is 1ˢᵗ April 1999. In my country, this day is traditionally called Liar's Day where people tell lies and play jokes on friends and family, much like April Fool's day in the UK. I wish that what happened on that day was a lie, but unfortunately, it was the bitter truth that I had to accept. It took place in the city of Pristhina, the capital of Kosovo, which was now being run by the Serbian army and police under the regime of Slobodan Milosevic, who was attempting to ethnically cleanse the country of Kosovan Albanians. A year before this date, I was working as a lawyer and a chief administrator at the Central Prison of Pristhina and had Serbian work colleagues, but since the policy of ethnic cleansing began, like every other Kosovan Albanian I found myself out of work. They just wanted to get rid of us all.

I lived in a block of apartments five floors high, with three flats on each floor. In our flat, there was my wife, my sixteen-year-old daughter, eighteen-year-old son and my frail mother who was ninety years old. I woke up after very few hours sleep, with my clothes on, which was quite natural because we did not know what was going to happen from one day to the next. We had got into the practice of sleeping with our clothes on in case we had to leave everything at a moment's notice. However, the night before was the longest night in my life because I was constantly thinking about what had happened earlier that day. Upstairs, I had a very close Serbian neighbour whom I had known for twenty years. I had nipped out to do some shopping and happened to bump into him on my return. He was with the rest of his family holding suitcases and explained sheepishly that they were going to his son's for a short visit. However, I became suspicious that he was leaving for good, as he knew something was going to happen to us. Maybe he had informed the authorities about the Kosovan

Albanian people living here. I could not sleep for thinking about it. He was the only Serb living in our building.

We had our minimal breakfast of soup. It was just a meal to keep us alive. There was no appetite for its taste, just a vague appreciation of its value. Everyone seemed preoccupied with themselves, there was no conversation. Our phone was an important source of information to learn what was happening in the other towns and villages. We constantly wondered when it was going to be our turn. Every minute, each day, we received reports from friends and relatives about events elsewhere. Therefore, our minds were filled with anxiety and fear of what was going to happen to us. The days felt very long, one hour would feel like a whole day. We were just waiting and waiting. We could not stand the waiting. I could never think about what would happen to me, my mind was always occupied with thoughts about what would happen to my son, my daughter and my mother. We were all very nervous; we did not know what to do, or what to say to each other. We could see and hear the bombs from NATO dropping on Serbian targets in the city. This only made us more fearful that the Serbs would take revenge on us.

After eating, I walked across to the window where there was a good view of the surrounding area from the first floor. Just at this moment, two tanks and four armoured vehicles pulled up at the bottom of the flats. Armed police officers and militants approached our apartments. It was impossible to tell who was who for they purposely wore different combat jackets and uniforms, so we could not identify them from the police, the army or the paramilitary. I knew this was the moment. They got out of their cars and entered the building, their boots echoed through the hallways, the harsh knocks, the opening, slamming and kicking of doors, bounced along the walls of the corridors, eventually reaching our apartment. There was a knock on the door, there were four men, two in balaclavas and two with their faces painted. 'Five minutes to leave if you want to stay alive!' they stated brutally, no questions asked. We immediately grabbed the remaining bits of food, a small tin of sardines and useful bits of clothing such as jackets. A sense of panic gripped us, our hearts were beating rapidly. The corridors of the building reverberated with panic, as people rushed aimlessly to escape in fear of their lives.

A neighbour pleaded with me to help his disabled mother. How could I? I had my own mother to look after, but I felt so guilty, as I had known him for years. Everyone was preoccupied with saving only themselves and members of their family. The corridor was now sweeping with a frenzied, rushing tide of people, cries of women and small children who had not a clue what was happening and where they were going, their basic possessions flowing with them. 'What are you doing?' the soldiers asked one woman. 'I'm waiting for my son' she replied. The masked men grew angry at her disrespect for their orders. 'If you want to save your life give us your jewellery, your money! Now get going!' Some tried their best to hide their anxiety and panic so as not to disclose it to the militants. Some did not know if they would ever see family members or friends again who had gone into the town shopping. We all spilled out of our block of one hundred and fifty five flats, drifting like timid lost animals into a herd of five thousand others, streaming from seven neighbouring concrete blocks. A man went to get his car from his garage, below the flats, but the soldiers noticed his diversion. They walked up to him putting a Kalashnikov to his head, 'Why are you late? Get back and walk!' They took his car. I managed not to cause too much of a distraction as I helped my mother and the rest of my family climb into my small Yugo car parked at the bottom of the apartments. No sooner had I started the car and turned it around, we were just part of the herd, a mixture of cars and people all trundling along at a snail's pace. Everyone was 'just going' as they had been ordered with no clear direction, except heading south towards Macedonia and Albania, as the north was where the Serbs were based.

It was a mass exodus. We were sat in the midst of the herd, the windows wound down. 'Can you help my baby?'; 'Can you squeeze me in?' fellow Kosovans begged in desperation. Again, 'No' I replied 'I have my mother, there is no room in the car'. We felt helpless, as we could not offer any help. We had to ignore desperate pleas for assistance, even from individuals with their own family, willing to risk being split up from them and maybe not see them again. I had previously made sure the petrol tank was full in preparation for the inevitability of this day. This had involved taking my ID and relevant documents to the police administration in order to get some vouchers for fuel. As the car meandered along, I could not help wonder if the petrol would last because we were moving so slowly.

We crept past another car with its bonnet up at the side of the road. The driver pleaded for help, but the mass exodus of cars and people could not disengage themselves from their rolling momentum. No one could afford to stop and help for fear of reprisals by soldiers and the fear of losing touch with family, friends and relatives. The other side of the road leading back to Pristhina was completely empty. After an hour, we had only just reached the outskirts of the town. This would have normally taken ten minutes. At least we had now left the town and there was some relief to have got this far with all of the family intact.

Now there was an eerie atmosphere. As I glanced in my mirror, I could see the long trail behind us in the distance, those on foot now looking as small as birds, flagging behind. Elsewhere we could see the occasional flashing light followed by the thunder of the bombs in the distance. Ironically, this was comforting because during the bombings the Serb soldiers in their armoured vehicles scurried and hid for safety like crabs in the sand when the tide comes in. Later, of course, they reappeared when the bombs had died away. It was during one of these quiet periods, that a big armoured vehicle drove up alongside us, overtook the car in front and cut across them, forcing all of us, including my cousin's car behind, to stop in a lay-by. Three soldiers got out of the vehicle, all with blacked faces. They walked past our car to the one behind us. I could see them questioning my cousin through the mirror. After a few minutes, they walked back up to us. One of them was built like a gorilla. We were afraid just to look at him as his presence intimidated us so much. His solid heavy Kalashnikov rifle pointed at us. The presence of this weapon took my breath away. We all felt the immediate threat and power it contained. He occasionally adjusted his position, moving from side to side. He purposely let us see his trigger finger moving backwards and forwards, making us know that with just a little more applied pressure, we would be shot at point blank range. However, we dared not flinch, as one sudden movement would cause him to pull the trigger. We wilted in the domination of his overbearing power, crushing the fear out of our skins like a hydraulic clamp. 'Give me your documents' he said. 'Where are you going...? You are going to Albania?' He answered his own questions for us, he did not expect us to speak. He noticed my eighteen-year-old son. 'So you saved him for the KLA?[1]. Why did he not join the Serbian Military Service?' I tried to explain that I had an ID card from the Serbian prison I worked in and that my son was actually born in Serbia whilst we were on holiday there. This was thwarted by his overriding 'Stop! Don't say anything!' He threw the ID cards in the car. He asked me to get out and open the boot of the car. They saw that we only had bare necessities and no weapons. 'Close it and get back in the car!' he commanded. They went to inspect the car at the front and went through the same routine, whilst we wondered what was going to happen to us all. After they had finished, the gorilla grunted 'If we see you here when we come back, we will kill you!' All three then climbed into their armoured vehicle. They turned around going back past us, then turned right, behind us into a neighbouring village.

1 Kosovan Liberation Army.

I got out of the car exhausted with fear and discussed what had just happened with the other drivers. All of us needed the time to collect our thoughts together after the traumatic experience we had just encountered. As we climbed back into our cars, I saw the armoured vehicle again in my mirror. They obviously saw that we had not yet moved. It had only been a matter of minutes since they had left. They began to turn in our direction, but then changed their minds and went the other way. Maybe they could see we had just started our vehicles and were about to set off. By now the long line of vehicles that were behind us, had passed us by. My family were so frozen with shock, they could not speak, but time did not allow us to reflect upon our emotions. It was as though we had just set foot on a land mine, but this time it had not exploded. I was concerned whether or not it was a good idea to carry on. Though my frail mother could not tell what the soldiers had said, she certainly understood what had happened; there was a great fear in her eyes. I wondered if she could endure what lay ahead. Somehow we knew that this was only the first point of danger, that there would be many more to come. Nevertheless, we decided to continue our journey.

Our three cars were now the only ones on the road. As the road curved bending to the right, after half a mile, I could see the blue uniform of officialdom, awaiting us ahead. There was a big group of police. They signalled for our small group of cars to stop. We knew that if we showed them any lack of respect, or did any tiny thing wrong, we would be killed. 'Your documents!' one of them demanded arrogantly. 'Where are you going? Why?' I told him we were going to Macedonia. As if we were only venturing out for some kind of holiday, he said 'You cannot go with these documents. They are invalid'. I was afraid he was going to tell us we would have to go back. I even thought it better for them to kill us now, as going back would reawaken the ghosts from our graveyard of experience so far. He walked across to a colleague with our documents, pretending to discuss what he should do. It was just a psychological trick for them to instil more fear into us. After ten minutes, someone else came and handed our documents back to us. The car in front began to move. We assumed we could go too and followed.

It was ten miles until the next checkpoint, followed by another, five miles later, and another, ten miles after that. At each checkpoint, we had to go through the same harrowing procedure. Every time we passed one checkpoint, we wondered what was going to happen at the next. Each one held our lives in the balance, testing our nerves to their limits.

Now we assumed we were close to approaching the border. Surely this would be our final hurdle. We had heard of people coming here a while ago and queuing for one week, but only to be sent back to Kosovo. We knew that if we could only pass this border there would be a great sense of freedom. There were many mixed emotions going through our minds and our bodies. It reminded me of the temperature gauge in the car. We were like the car's engine all heated up, inflamed and bothered, our needle rising into the red. We needed the automatic fan to switch on, to cool us down and relieve us all of our plight.

Another three miles passed, then in our sights lay a small brick building with barriers to the side. This was it, this was the border! As we drew closer there was no one else there waiting to go through, so we just stopped about ten yards away from the barrier and waited. No one came out to us for twenty minutes. Then surprisingly a border officer stepped outside the building and just waved his hand signalling for us to go. The barrier rose and we drove through. Further off in the distance we could see another barrier, but we were stopped about half a mile before this, in neutral ground by two Macedonian police officers. They told us we could not drive through the Macedonian checkpoint with our cars. Even though the driver in the first car attempted to bribe them with money, they would not let us through. They told us to drive back to the barrier where we had just come from. So the rest of our families got out of the cars, whilst we drove back to the previous barrier. At the office, we were told to put our cars in the car park. Hundreds of cars had been left there. The border control officer sarcastically remarked 'Leave your documents and keys here on the table, we will give them to you when you come back'. The man that had been driving in front of us knew he had just lost his new Volkswagen Golf.

We walked back to our families further down the road where the Macedonian police were, then all of us walked towards the Macedonian checkpoint. I had to hold my mother up with the help of my son. My cousin had the same difficulties with his mother. The sky had darkened and it began to rain heavily. It was now as if someone had switched on the rain with a remote control just to make the situation worse. Our clothes, possessions and my mother began to weigh heavier and heavier with the rain. We could not stop as it was the final push to the Macedonian border.

We struggled for half a mile, drained of energy, drained of emotion, but finally we reached the Macedonian border checkpoint. We were exhausted. Despite the obvious state we were in, the police there could not afford us any politeness. They asked for our personal documents. My passport had expired a couple of years ago. My mother and daughter did not have a passport. My son was the only one with a valid passport. One of them arrogantly asked me 'How can your mother and daughter pass the border without a passport?' Again, they acted as if we were just going for a holiday. They gave us all forms to fill in to find out where we were going. We all just wrote Macedonia. Just then a UNHCR[2] bus drove up to the barrier. After filling in the forms, they told us to go. The fifteen of us climbed onto the bus.

2 United Nations High Commissioner for Refugees.

Now the fans switched on inside us. We realised we were free, we didn't care about where we were going. Everyone's faces relaxed into a smile. We were all so relieved, a tremendous pressure had been lifted from us. We had escaped with our lives. The bus drove about five miles. In the distance there appeared to be vast fields of mushrooms ahead. As we drew closer, it became apparent that they were thousands and thousands of tents full of refugees from Kosovo. We were given a tent to share with my cousin's family on a spare patch of ground. The conditions were very poor, the fields were soaking wet through with the rain. We could not change our clothes. Despite this, there was a sense of belonging, as the damp air whispered of everyone's story. This was the first step of a long journey to freedom in the UK. It was a day when everything was wiped away from my life. It was impossible to absorb, but it was the truth on Liar's Day, a truth I suddenly had to accept.

Collated by Michael Carroll

The Tea that wasn't Drank

(Zulekha)

Hi. I am Zulekha and I am seventy-five years old. I live with my son, his wife and four grandchildren in Bolton. I was born in India and have lived in England for around ten years. I was just remembering, the other day, when I was around thirteen years old, making tea in the kitchen back in India. It was four o'clock in the afternoon just after the siesta, when most people have had a snooze, due to the very hot weather, as it is too exhausting to do any kind of physical activity. I had not long been awake and was still feeling dozy. As I got up the sun shone directly onto my face through the glass window. I could feel the heat rays of the sun hit my face causing my skin to sweat. I decided to try and clear my head with a cup of tea. I didn't make the tea on an ordinary cooker, but a primus, a kind a mini gas stove, the kind used for camping. Into the pan went the water with the loose tea, to draw out the flavour, then the sugar and massala, then lastly the milk, which makes up most of the drink.

The tea bubbled as it came to the top of the saucepan, then I poured it through the strainer into the cup releasing the sweet, spicy fragrance into the air. I turned off the gas, but noticing that the flame wasn't fully extinguished, I leaned over and sprinkled water over the hot primus. In a flash a hot flame of fire shot up and blew in my face. I screamed, automatically closing my eyes and shielding my face with my hands. Everything was blank, but the skin on my face was stinging. I could tell that the front of my hair was all burnt because of the awful smell of singed hair. I could not stop coughing as the smoke entered my nose and mouth. I blindly gasped to gain intakes of breath, choking as tears rolled down my face.

I panicked, as I was alone in the house and out of desperation began to pour more water onto the primus attempting to douse the flames. This only caused the flames to roar in stature, threatening to engulf the place. I didn't realise this and just as I was about to pour another pan of water onto the primus a hand grabbed my arm. Luckily, it was the hand of a neighbour, dragging me away from the primus and out of the kitchen. I was in agony. I was scared, my face was a tight stinging mask. My neighbour then applied some cream to it. I was worried, I would end up in trouble for what had happened. Shaking with shock, tears streamed across my burning cheeks. My neighbour took me to the dining room and consoled me saying everything would be all right. She told me that if she hadn't arrived when she did, the fire would have been very severe and the consequences beyond imagination.

Meanwhile my brother had returned from the fields. He observed what had happened and quickly took the primus into the courtyard and sprinkled sand over it to cool it down.

My face felt red raw. I didn't have my face dressed with any bandages, but kept applying the cream as it had a cooling effect on the skin. It took about two to three weeks for the final scars on my face to heal and I will never forget that horrifying afternoon for the rest of my life.

Collated by Rehana Makkan and Summaiya Kadva

The Collective Farm

(Jerzy Chlebek)

My name is Jerzy, though some people call me George as that's how my name roughly translates into English from Polish. I am originally from the town of Drobobycz in Poland. This is where I spent my childhood. I have one brother and a younger sister. My story begins in 1939 at the beginning of the Second World War. The Germans and Russians had invaded Poland from different sides and in September 1939, under the German-Soviet pact, Poland became divided. The Soviets took, and absorbed, the eastern half of Poland including Byelorussia[1] and the West Ukraine. The Germans incorporated Pomerania, Posnania and Silesia into the Reich, whilst the rest of Poland was designated as the General-Government, a colony ruled from Krakow by Hitler's friend, Hans Frank. In the Soviet zone, one and a half million Poles, including women and children, were transported to labour camps in Siberia and other areas.

In 1940 many thousands of captured Polish officers were shot at several secret forest sites. I witnessed many of these horrific incidents. I even had to help dig their graves and bury their bodies, whilst they were still shaking and not quite dead. It was not until 1943 that evidence of the massacre by the Soviets in Khatyn, near Smolensk in the Ukraine, began to emerge, where four thousand, four hundred Polish army officers were murdered. However, it wasn't until about fifty years after the war that the total number of mass murders in Khatyn was revealed, which approximately totals twenty one thousand eight hundred and fifty seven[2].

1 Now known as Belarus.
2 In October 1992, Russian President Boris Yeltsin presented a copy of an original 1940 execution order signed by Stalin and five other Politburo members, from Gorbachev's private archive along with forty-one other documents to the new Polish president, former Solidarity leader Lech Walesa. During a 1993 visit to Warsaw's military cemetery, Yeltsin knelt before a Polish priest and kissed the ribbon of a wreath he had placed at the foot of the Khatyn cross. In a joint statement with Walesa, he pledged to punish those still alive who had taken part in the massacre and make reparations, a promise that has not been kept.

In April of 1940, when I was eighteen years old, I remember the morning when the Soviet officers came shouting and knocking on our door at four o'clock in the morning. My father had already been imprisoned by them about three weeks before. They said they were taking him for an interview, but we never saw him again. 'We're giving you one hour to pack your things' they said. They stayed there whilst we panicked, trying to get our most basic things together such as clothes. They did not say where we were going, but we knew that other people had recently been sent to Siberia. The rumbling engines of lorries waited for us outside. With our basic belongings, my brother, sister, mother and I were ordered to climb into the back of one of the lorries, along with two other families.

The lorries transported everyone to the train station. There, a cattle train awaited us. About sixty of us were ordered to climb into a metal boxcar. There were no windows, no toilets, just a small hole in the floor, no beds, just some wooden platforms with room for a few people to sleep on. When they shut the doors, we were in complete darkness. Everyone was terrified and confused because we hadn't done anything wrong. This was the beginning of a four week journey. The cattle train had no air. It was very stuffy, cramped with the putrid smell of animals. We were experiencing just how animals felt when transported from one place to another. During the journey, when the cattle train did stop and the doors opened, everyone ran, desperate for water. Sometimes they gave us hot water to drink. Men, women and children also went underneath the train to relieve themselves. People who died during the trip were simply unloaded at the first opportunity.

When the cattle train had passed over the Russian border, then they opened the doors, they knew that now there was no place for us to go. At the end of the four week journey, more lorries were waiting for us at the train station. They took people to different locations. After four hours of driving, we ended up in a small village in Kazakhstan, Central Asia in the very north, which is technically southern Siberia. We arrived at a collective farm[3] and were expected to find our own accommodation. Later, my mother was to die there.

There weren't any soldiers around, so we were as free as we could be, but were told by brigadiers[4] that if we didn't work we would not eat. They actually classed us as voluntary workers. The first day we arrived there, we were ordered to start work on the farm and we were given various work assignments. For months, our main task was to dig for stone, which was to be used for building a school. We had to dig one and a half metres underneath the hard ground before reaching the stone, then unearth it, from sunrise until sunset every day. This job was very hard and made my hands bleed. We also had to carry out tasks such as wheat cutting and making bread. Our reward was a small portion of food such as potato soup. This way of living depressed us and dented our morale, but we didn't have a choice.

One day, after dinner, I had to go out with my brother into the forest to collect the wood for the cooking and to keep ourselves warm. This wasn't a task we had to do every day, just when our stock of wood was running low. The sun was shining, but the temperature was so cold. It was approximately minus thirty degrees Celsius. We had to travel by foot about one mile through the white landscape of snow, into the forest. Even though the weather was so cold, I was only wrapped in fairly ordinary clothes, a shirt, trousers, shoes, an overcoat and some gloves. This certainly wasn't enough to keep out the bitter biting air. Whilst working my way towards the forest, I tried to move as quickly as I could in order to try and bring some sense of warmth to my body. Finally, we arrived at the white forest, very reminiscent of a Christmas card landscape, but with the severity of potentially freezing to death. We did our best to look for wood on the ground, to save having to cut

3 A farm or a group of farms organised as a unit, managed and worked cooperatively by a group of labourers under state supervision, especially in a communist country.
4 High ranking military officers.

it from the trees, as all we had with us was a scythe. You learn to appreciate the small things, as they matter so much and not having any choice, the more wood we collected, the happier it made us feel. Each piece represented preparation for later warmth. We tried to find dry wood, as it burns better. My fingers were gnawed into the bone with cold, which made tying up the bundles of wood very difficult. When we had finished, my nose was so blue with the cold and my ears were pained by the bitter breeze. We had been collecting wood for two hours. The sun had now gone down, which meant the temperature had dropped to about minus forty degrees Celsius. My brother and I carried a bundle of wood each on our backs as we set off towards our lodgings. I knew the weather had grown even colder because instead of pain, there was now numbness, I didn't know if my feet were part of me or not. I was also tired and weak and my legs had stiffened up. The journey to our lodgings seemed so far away, I felt as if I'd never get there. I trudged on through the snow with my dead feet.

As soon as we arrived, I attempted to take off my shoes, but I couldn't because they were frozen solid, fused onto my feet. I had to ask my brother for help. The only thing he could do was to cut the shoes off with a knife. After we managed to get them off, I looked down at my feet; they were so white, right up to my ankles. I knew it was frostbite because other people had previously experienced it on their noses and ears. My brother went outside and brought back some snow in a bucket. He began to rub it on my feet for a good half hour to restore the circulation. I remembered when we were younger, we used to put snow in each other's shoes, but this time I couldn't feel it. A friend rubbed snow on my other foot. Very slowly, feeling began to return to my feet, I felt some pain, but at least I could feel something. I couldn't forget about this story as later I realised that I could have lost my feet.

Towards the end of 1941 the Russians were losing the war

against the Germans. The Germans had reached Stalingrad and Moscow. After the German army invaded the USSR, the Soviets turned to the Polish as allies. The 1941 Sikorski-Maiskii Pact called for the formation of a Polish army in the USSR to fight the Nazis and it promised an amnesty to all Polish citizens inside the country. In 1942, around one hundred and fifteen thousand people were permitted to leave Soviet territory. I ended up joining the Polish army in Russia to fight the Germans until the end of the war.

Collated by Tahira Patel and Nyla Anwar

The Story of Miriam

(Zahida Abbas)

This is a story about my childhood friend Miriam. She lived very happily with her parents in a house rented from my friend in Jhelum, Pakistan, next door to her aunt. Miriam was fourteen years old; she was a nice, calm, beautiful girl and spent most of her time helping her mother with the housework. She was from a Christian family, but I never asked her about her religion because it did not matter to our friendship. We used to go to school on a tanga which is a carriage that seats four people and is pulled by one or two horses. As we travelled to school on the tanga every morning it was lovely to hear the birds singing from the trees, only, Miriam cringed when the driver of the tanga whipped the horse and pleaded with him not to be so cruel. She believed that animals shouldn't be treated in this way.

I remember in particular, one nice summer's day with a beautiful bright blue sky. There were some guava trees near the entrance to Miriam's house and to the side some pens where hens were kept. The hens strutted about and clucked in excitement as Miriam's aunt fed them, then collected the eggs they had laid. Following this, we went to school, playing with a skipping rope along the way.

After the morning lessons we went home for dinner, but no sooner had Miriam arrived at her house, she was given two big piles of clothes to wash by her mother. Her house had no water to wash clothes because there was no pressure in the water pump, so she took the pile of clothes across to her auntie's house where the water pump was in good working order. Her auntie's house had five rooms and a veranda. In front of the veranda, there was a big garden with beautiful flowers. Miriam was in a cheerful mood, as she began washing the clothes, she remarked to her auntie how pleasant the guava trees looked, which grew near the water tap. Because Miriam was so busy with her chores, I did not see her when I returned to school later that afternoon, after my dinner.

After a gruelling afternoon of washing, Miriam began to hang the clothes on the washing line to dry, but complained of tiredness to her auntie who stood beside her. Miriam was determined to finish her work and battled on until about six o'clock in the evening, when she finally completed her task. Miriam started to feel cold, but her auntie told her not to worry because she would soon warm up with a cup of tea inside her. So off went her auntie to make her a nice massala tea. As Miriam sipped her tea, she recognised the fragrance of curry drifting across from her mother's cooking. This was the signal for her to return home, so she picked some fruit from a guava tree and began to make her way. The birds had begun to quieten down because it was getting dark. A parrot perched on a branch of a guava tree caught Miriam's eye. It loved to peck and eat the fruit. She picked up a stick from the ground and tapped the branch, attempting to prevent the parrot from spoiling all the fruit. Some of the leaves fluttered down from the tree, but the parrot did not move at all. Miriam realised that her attention had been diverted and looked back at the clock in her auntie's house, thinking she must return home as it was getting late even though she lived just a minute away, around the corner.

As Miriam arrived home she explained to her mother that she was still not feeling very well. She had aches in her shoulders and felt very tired. Her mother wasn't surprised as she'd been playing early in the morning, studied at school, washed clothes and hung them out to dry for the remainder of the day. Again, tea seemed like an appropriate remedy and with cup in hand, Miriam went to her room to rest.

Miriam's aunt surveyed the calm of the evening as its deepening hush descended, but the tranquillity was soon broken by the sound of someone shrieking and crying. She ventured outside to find out who it was. The crying appeared to be coming from Miriam's house, so she wandered over to investigate. To her amazement, there was Miriam lying unconscious on the floor. Miriam's family was extremely worried and scared as there was a trickle of fluid coming from her mouth. Her mother had called the priest, as he was the first person she could think of.

The priest arrived and everyone's eyes gazed intensely as he examined Miriam. In a dark and eerie manner, he proclaimed that she had a devil inside her. Miriam's family tried desperately to wake her, but there was no response. The priest began to read. He uttered some holy words whilst flicking water on Miriam's body. There was an acceptance of the priest's words and actions, because he represented God in the eyes of Miriam's family. The priest explained that he would have to beat the devil out of Miriam. He picked up a stick made from the branch of a tree and swung it. The stick whooshed through the air, whacking Miriam on the shoulders. He then proceeded to beat her from the shoulders down to her stomach and then her legs. More fluid bubbled from Miriam's mouth. Every strike carried a driving intent to oust the devil from Miriam's body. Eventually the priest stopped the beating and announced that the devil had gone.

There was no sign of life in Miriam at all, for she had been beaten to death. The priest declared that the devil had been too strong, despite the fact that before he had arrived, at least Miriam had a pulse and was breathing. Miriam's mother screamed and cried as it dawned upon her that she would never see her daughter alive again. Miriam lay there with bruises all over her body. Despite this, there was a general resignation to the belief that Miriam's fate must have been the will of God.

The next day, when we realised that Miriam wasn't on the

tanga with us, we all thought she was not well. When we came home from school, we found out what had happened to her. We could not believe that no one had stopped the priest from beating her, from murdering her. We were very upset and angry as the police did not investigate her death, it was hidden from everyone.

The hens ran around as usual, the guava trees still grew in the sunshine and the parrot pecked at the fruit along the branches, but there was no Miriam. She was not here any more; she was sleeping, like sleeping beauty. She didn't like the horses on the tanga being whipped because it was cruel, but she ended up being beaten worse than an animal. Even though Miriam isn't here, she will always be in my heart, my memory, and will remain there for the rest of my life.

In memory of Miriam aged fourteen.

Friends

(Anonymous)

I used to live with my beautiful wife, Irina, and my lovely daughter, Svetlana, in Moldova, but moved to the city of St. Petersburg in 1988 and lived there until 1991. The city of St. Petersburg is, in my opinion, the most beautiful city in the whole of Russia. In contrast, Moscow is a grand city, but sometimes the people there are cold, unfriendly and unwelcoming. My first experience of St. Petersburg was on a holiday with my family when I was fourteen years old. The people there were the friendliest people I had ever met. They were more than happy to stop what they were doing to give us directions, advise us on the best sights to see and how to get there. One gentleman even missed his bus to work, whilst giving us detailed instructions on how to get to the Hermitage Museum. No one was too busy to talk to us; nobody ignored us as they would often do in Moscow. In my eyes, the beauty of St. Petersburg has never been exceeded by anything else I've seen. It is full of historical monuments crafted by the best artists of every era imaginable, including ancient statues, golden treasures of exquisite design, priceless art and the most wonderful architecture. The ancient streets, beautiful gardens, hallways of grand palaces, magnificent cathedrals, tombs of past Tsars, glorious temples with spiralling steeples, all mesmerised me so much I was speechless. There are no words to describe the thoroughly pleasant experiences of that time. The people seemed so happy to see us and the city was so beautiful, that when I went back home to Moldova, it became my lifelong ambition to go and live in St. Petersburg indefinitely.

In 1986 I was conscripted into the military service. As Moldova was part of the USSR, I could not believe how fortunate I was, when I learned that I was going to be assigned to the beautiful city of St. Petersburg. After I finished two years of service there, I decided to stay and live in the city of my dreams. Shortly after, my wife Irina who worked as a dentist and my daughter, Svetlana, joined me in St. Petersburg. However, in the USSR of 1990, the economy was tumbling fast. Prices were doubling in just a few days, wages were diminishing and it was difficult for everyone to make ends meet. We certainly couldn't afford to buy a house, so we had to rent a room.

We found a room within an apartment in the region of Kalinski Raion. The owner of the apartment was an elderly lady, a retired lawyer who lived in another room. She also let out a third room in the apartment to another family of four, the father, Vladimir, his wife, Ludmila, and their two children, Peter and Sasha. This family were our perfect housemates. They were so lovely and even kind enough to cook us a welcoming meal. Our children played together all the time. Their boys took care of Svetlana in the yard, making sure that she was never bullied or upset. Vladimir helped me to decorate the room and informed us that he had a friend who was selling some of his possessions cheaply because he was moving house. So we bought some furniture and picture frames off Vladimir. He helped me to frame some of my old family photos, then hang them on the wall. The room wasn't much, but now it felt like a real home, very cosy.

In the summer of 1990, whilst Ludmila was in the ninth month of her pregnancy, I decided to take Irina and Svetlana on a three week break back to Moldova. It was fantastic to see all our friends and relatives once again as we missed them very much. Whilst we were there we even bought a present for Ludmila's new baby.

When we arrived back home, I knocked on the main apartment door, but I heard no answer. We had not taken our apartment key with us on holiday, for fear of losing it. I couldn't see anybody through the chink in the doorway, but I became extremely concerned because the light in the corridor appeared to be shining from our room. This could only mean that our door had been unlocked and opened, which I could not believe as I had locked our door with a big heavy duty padlock before we had left for Moldova. There was no other option, but to take a penknife from my bag, break the lock of the main door and force it open. We immediately rushed to our room, but were halted by the sight that confronted us. I was so shocked; I dropped my knife onto the floor. My wife burst into tears, she was almost hysterical. Our once cosy room now looked like a bombsite, clothes were scattered everywhere. There was no television and all the furniture had vanished. Our child, Svetlana, was surprisingly calm. She couldn't appreciate what had happened. It gradually dawned on us that we had been burgled. Irina and I were totally devastated. It was a tragic situation because not only had our privacy been invaded, but our basic household belongings were now distant luxury items, which we could now only aspire to have. It would take as much as two years to replace them, such was the fragility of the USSR economy and unlike England, there was no house insurance.

Irina went to search for our neighbours to see if they knew anything about the burglary, whilst I stayed in the room to assess the damage. Our television, furniture, fridge, tape recorder, camera, rugs, sports clothes, books, lots of useful equipment and even the carpet were all missing. Everything else, that wasn't worth taking, was scattered around the floor in a big mess. All our old clothes, all of our underwear, all my little daughter's clothes were just lying around in a heap. A picture of my mother was lying on the floor, along with other family pictures. The burglars had just taken the frames and thrown the photographs on the floor. The shameless scoundrels had even stepped on them with their muddy boots on their way out!

Just as I bent down to pick the pictures up, I heard a piercing scream. My wife had caught someone in the kitchen red-handed with the most treasured of our family heirlooms under his arm, an old icon of the Virgin Mary, of great historical and sentimental value, passed on to me from my great grandmother. The burglar tried to barge past my wife in order to escape from the apartment. In the heat of the moment, she grabbed the knife I had dropped on the floor and threatened him with it, obstructing his exit, stopping the coward dead in his tracks. 'Thief!' my wife shouted as she stood in the corridor. I immediately dashed out. I could not believe it, the burglar was Vladimir! I immediately knocked Vladimir down and dragged him into our room. I was ready to kill him, but Irina stopped me. We held Vladimir and pinned him down on the floor until the police arrived.

Later, we found out that Vladimir's wife had run away with her two older children, deserting her newborn baby soon after we had gone on holiday. After the police had taken Vladimir away, my wife and I ended up taking care of the baby for three days. She didn't cry and it seemed that she had been well fed and clothed. At least it looked as if Vladimir had taken good care of her. However, as we couldn't afford to keep her, unfortunately we had to hand the baby over to a shelter.

Shortly after the incident, I found out how Vladimir had managed to get into our home. He had tricked one of the neighbours, who happened to be a locksmith, into believing our room was Vladimir's room. Vladimir had simply told the locksmith that he couldn't find his key. So our neighbour duly obliged and kindly picked the two locks for him, genuinely believing his story. Once Vladimir had access to our room, he began to sell all our belongings. He used the money to repay debts, but apparently spent most of it on drink. Even though debts were common in St. Petersburg at that time, I do not know why he had to stoop so low, as he did have a job. Maybe once we had left for Moldova and his wife left him, he had nothing to lose and took the opportunity to earn some easy money to help pay for his baby daughter.

News soon travelled all around the neighbourhood about what had happened. The locksmith came and apologised to us for believing Vladimir's story. Then we were very surprised when one of our neighbours from the next block of flats turned up with our fridge and offered to give it to us, absolutely free of charge! We were very thankful to him, he was very kind. He was very embarrassed and apologetic because he had believed another one of Vladimir's stories about a friend of his moving house and selling a fridge cheaply. It was beginning to sound all too familiar. We couldn't believe our good fortune when another neighbour turned up on our doorstep with our tape recorder and our camera. Then someone else brought our television. In fact most of our possessions were returned. That's how kind people in St. Petersburg can actually be, but then again, Vladimir was from St. Petersburg. Oh well, nothing's perfect, you can't expect the whole population of one big city to be decent. You get your good people, and your bad people, everywhere you go.

Collated by Elena Taban

Bus Stop

(George Powell)

George Powell was born in Jamaica on 26th April 1929. The weather in Jamaica can get very hot, up to one hundred degrees Fahrenheit. Jamaica is one hundred and forty four miles long from east to west with two international airports. George joined the army when he was still in school at a very young age. After leaving school, he trained as an electrician, and obtained work in this field at 'Citrus Company Jamaica Ltd'. His father had a farm where rice, green bananas, mangoes, oranges, pears, avocados, coffee, ginger and many spices were grown. George loved Bombay mangoes. He still cannot forget the smell and taste of them. George has always observed the religious concept of Shabbat[1] or Sabbath as part of the Seventh Day Adventist Church. The Seventh Day Adventist Sabbath is observed from sunset on Friday, until sunset on Saturday evening. During this period people stop work and carry out the rituals for the Shabbat, which makes them all feel part of one huge family. All the cooking has to be done before sunset on the Friday as this also constitutes work. In George's family, no one was allowed to watch television after sunset on the Friday.

George spent thirty years of his life in Jamaica. He married his wife in 1960 and in the same year they came to England, where George began working as a bus driver. George enjoyed his job and his married life in England. He soon had a family with three boys and one girl.

George recounts an incident from 1974 on a beautiful summer morning when the sky was a clear blue. George woke up, had a bath, then breakfast with his wife before setting off to work. He was in a good mood as he left his house at six thirty. He

1 Judaism's teachings about the Shabbat were
eventually adopted and instituted by other religions.

always said good morning to his passengers as they boarded his bus. This morning was no different and by seven thirty, he was driving on his second bus trip from Padbury Way in Breightmet, back to Moor Lane bus station in Bolton town centre. His number six bus was full of people, most of them on their way to work.

As the bus came to a halt at the station, all the passengers began to step off, each departing in their different directions. The last passenger to leave told George that there was still someone else upstairs, who had probably drifted off to sleep. George waited a few minutes to see if the remaining passenger was going to come down the stairs. There was no sign of him so George decided that he'd better go upstairs to see if anyone was actually there.

George climbed up the stairs of the bus, looked down the rows of seats and saw that there was a passenger still there, reading a newspaper held out in front of him. George made a polite remark, expecting the passenger to come to his senses and realise that the bus had now come to the end of its journey. However, there was no response, so George walked up to the passenger and tapped him on the shoulder to wake him up. To his amazement, the passenger just keeled over slightly to one side. George tried to be a bit sterner in his attempt to wake the passenger up, but there was still no response. George then became frightened as it dawned on him that something was obviously wrong, he took a few slow steps back, then turned and dashed down the stairs. He clambered off the bus to find the bus inspector.

The bus inspector rang for an ambulance and the police. As they arrived, everyone in the bus station was stopping and staring to see what was going on. The ambulance men entered the bus and went upstairs to investigate. They were up there for a long while, before bringing the man down on a stretcher, then, they carefully placed him in the ambulance and drove him off to hospital.

Later, George found out that the man was dead on arrival at the hospital. He had suffered a heart attack whilst on George's bus. After having a rest, as George was feeling a bit shook up, he decided to get back to work. Whilst driving, George could think of nothing else, but the man dying on his bus. Numerous thoughts and images revolved in his mind. He saw images of the man standing before him with his newspaper, paying his fare then going upstairs. Was he in any pain then? Why had no one noticed that there was a problem upstairs? George wondered what would happen if he too suddenly had a heart attack. What would then happen to his family? He realised that nothing is certain, there is no guarantee of life from one minute to the next. George could not get rid of these thoughts, they occupied and exhausted his mind throughout the rest of the day.

In the evening when a weary George came home from work, his wife was waiting for him; she had made him his special dinner. She noticed that something was wrong with him and asked if everything was all right. George then told her about his day. They sat down to eat, but George couldn't eat anything, he felt so tired that he went to bed early. As soon as he closed his eyes, he saw the face of the dead passenger. Where was he now? George thought, was he just in a deep sleep?[2] Despite George's tiredness, he could not sleep at all.

George could not stop thinking about that man for a couple of weeks. Every time he went on bus duty, he remembered him. Ever since that day George has learned not to take life for granted, he doesn't know how long he will be around, nor does anyone. George is now severely visually impaired. He has a stick to help him find his way around and relies upon a carer. He is still able to enjoy life and eats his traditional Jamaican food with his friends at the Afro Caribbean Day Centre and the Unity Centre. He also enjoys the odd flutter on the horses.

2 Adventists believe that death is an unconscious sleep, commonly known as 'soul sleep', and reject the idea of an immortal soul.

George will never forget the frightening experience of the passenger on his bus. At least George is very much alive and still able to appreciate life.

Collated by Samim Vali and Shamim Khan

The Story of Rabia Khan

(Anonymous)

Rabia Khan was born in 1958 in a very big rich landlord honoured family. Being in a big joint family system means people have to sacrifice their lives for traditions and customs. The whole family lived in a big mansion near Peshawar, in the northwestern frontier of Pakistan, next to Afghanistan's border. There were about thirty five people in the family living together, including the grandfather, grandmother, aunties, uncles, mothers, fathers, cousins, brothers and sisters. There were also servants who took care of the day to day duties around the house and cooked one lamb a day to feed everybody in the household. These people were very strict, they would not let any of their children marry outside of the family. For example, a son would marry an uncle's daughter.

Rabia had a basic Islamic primary school education. She could not further her education, as girls were only allowed to attend primary school. There was no education for girls at all, once they had reached puberty. It was thought they didn't need education once they had reached puberty because they were then expected to marry, stay at home and look after the family. Once they had reached this age, if the girls had to go outside the house they would have to wear a hijaab[1] or burqa to cover their bodies and faces.

When Rabia reached the age of thirteen, she became engaged to her cousin. At this time her brother Sarfraz, aged eight years old, was also engaged to the sister of this cousin. Rabia was married at the age of sixteen and had two children. She

---

1 In some Arabic-speaking countries and Western countries, the word hijaab primarily refers to a headscarf worn by Muslim women. In Islamic scholarship, hijaab is usually taken to take on the wider meaning of dressing modestly. The word used in the Quran for a headscarf or veil is khimar. The burqa covers the wearer's entire face except for a small region about the eyes. A full burqa or Afghan burqa is a garment that conceals the entire body. The full burqa includes a "net curtain", which also hides the wearer's eyes.

gave birth to her first child, Nabeela, at the age of eighteen, then two years later she had a boy called Asad. She was happily married and enjoyed a good life with her husband who treated her with respect.

Rabia's father wanted Sarfraz to become a doctor, so when Sarfraz left school, he moved to Lahore where he attended medical college. Whilst studying at college, Sarfraz met a girl called Nadia. At first they became friends, but their feelings for each other grew and grew until eventually they fell in love. Sarfraz never mentioned anything to Nadia about being engaged since the age of eight, but still asked her to marry him. He went along to meet Nadia's parents who knew that he was from a respected well off family. Sarfraz did not want to reveal his childhood engagement, so he merely told Nadia's mother and father that his parents probably would not agree to a marriage with Nadia because he was not allowed to marry outside of the family. Despite this, Nadia's parents gave their consent for him to marry their daughter for the sake of her happiness.

After a year had passed, whilst studying at medical college, Sarfraz married Nadia, even though he was still engaged to his cousin. His dilemma played upon his conscience, so he intended to tell his family shortly after the wedding.

Rabia and Sarfraz's father had a personal assistant who looked after the day to day running of the family's household. One day, shortly after the marriage, this personal assistant was due to visit Lahore. So, Sarfraz's father entrusted him with some money to pass on to his son when he arrived there. It was upon his arrival that he discovered Safraz and Nadia living together, so he naturally assumed they were married. He immediately returned to report this news to Sarfraz's father, who could not believe that his son had betrayed him. In fact, he decided to travel to Lahore to find out for himself. The news spread in the village like wild fire. Rabia's father-in-law and his brother were very angry at the neglect of their family and had already passed on a message to her father that Sarfraz had to divorce Nadia then return home to marry his cousin.

When his father arrived at Lahore, Sarfraz experienced his fury, his shouting, bawling and screaming once the truth was revealed. 'What have you done to my niece!' he cried, 'You're going to break our family up and bring shame on them if you keep this marriage!' As well as instructing his son to divorce his wife, Sarfraz's father even offered money to Nadia as an incentive to accept a divorce, then leave his son alone and act as if he never existed. Sarfraz and Nadia rejected his wishes. However, Sarfraz's father was not finished, he told him that if he remained married he would no longer be entitled to any inheritance, but Sarfraz replied that he was not bothered as he loved Nadia too much. Just before he left Lahore, his father stubbornly told his offspring that he was longer his son, no longer entitled to any of his wealth and no longer part of the family. He then travelled home and told the rest of the family what had happened.

Rabia's brother-in-law viewed Sarfraz's actions as an insult to his sister and family, so as an act of revenge he asked his brother to divorce Rabia. Fortunately, Rabia's husband was very loyal to her and replied 'I am very happy with my wife and children, why should I divorce her, it is not her fault'. Because of the different links within the whole extended family, they were all constantly fighting amongst themselves. Of course as Rabia's father and father-in-law were brothers it made matters worse because pride and honour were at stake. The situation grew more and more intense, becoming so bad that one night Rabia, her husband and children all left for Rawalpindi, four hours away from Peshawar, where they stayed with a friend. The family from her husband's side had threatened to kill Rabia if he did not divorce her. Rabia and her husband took the threat so seriously, that she sold the jewellery from her wedding along with other possessions in order to pay for the necessary documents to move abroad.

With the help of their friend, about seven months later, they moved to England. Rabia and her family are now settled here and are very happy. Rabia would like go back home and see her family in Pakistan sometime, but she is scared of what may await her. She has not contacted her family since she left home so she does not know what has gone on between them. She still cries because she misses them all very much.

Collated by Mussarrat Shafiq

It's My Body

(Anonymous)

I used to live with my parents in Mogadishu, the capital city of
Somalia, where the skyline of the buildings was not very high
at all, just on one level, with no upstairs. The houses were a
lot bigger than in the UK because every family had at least five
children. Including me, there were eight children in our family,
so our house had five bedrooms with two living rooms. Our
neighbours were more like brothers and sisters, because we
were so close to each other. There was at least one tree in the
front garden of everyone's house where families sat and drank
tea together after work. Our front door was always open; there
was no need to worry about people coming in to steal
anything. They could just pop into each other's house
whenever they wanted, without prior warning and whenever
someone needed some salt or sugar, it was just passed along
the row. Everyone trusted each other so much there was no
need to arrange baby sitters as mothers often asked 'Can you
just look after my kids whilst I go to the shops'. They just
expected this kind of favour from each other. We all shared
grief, sorrow and happiness together.

In between the months of March and May the weather is really
hot. It rains in the winter months, but it is still warm. When I
was only about six years old, one weekday morning in the
winter season I awoke to find my house empty. There was only
my older sister, Salma, sat outside in the front garden reading
a book with my younger sister next to her playing with her
dolls. 'Where's Mum?' I asked. Salma told me that Mum was
at my older sister Khadra's house. So I got ready, had some
anjera[1] with butter, sprinkled with sugar and a drink of tea[2] for
breakfast. Then I told Salma I was going to Khadra's house to
see Mum, a couple of streets away. Despite being only six

1 Like a pancake with yeast.
2 Similar to Indian tea with spices.

years old, it was quite common and safe for me to go off on my own as long as someone knew where I was. The weather was overcast, but it was still warm as usual. I wandered past some greenery adorned with white and pink flowers. Butterflies fluttered amongst them, a usual occurrence, even in these winter months. Eventually I arrived at Khadra's house and knocked upon the door. Surprisingly, she greeted me, looking extra happy to see me even though she did see me nearly every day. She invited me in. I couldn't see Mum and wondered where she was. Khadra said 'I have something to show you'. She took me to her dining room, so I thought we were going to get something to eat. However, on entering I was surprised to find there was no dining table, but a different kind of table in its place. In fact it looked more like a bed. A woman in a white coat stood beside it, appearing to be cleaning some small knives. There was a man, also wearing a white coat. From my experience of having vaccinations against malaria, I was surprised to recognise some injection needles on a trolley. I asked Khadra who these people were. She replied 'He's a doctor and she's a nurse'. So I asked her 'Who is sick?' She explained:

> They have just examined the children. Now, as you are also part of the family could you please climb upon the table. Everybody is here and they have all been very brave today. They are just in the bedroom taking their rest now. You're going to be really brave as well aren't you? You're going to be so much better than everyone else. I hope you're not going to cry like my youngest daughter.

Khadra used to take me when I needed injections against malaria, flu and chicken pox so I trusted her and replied 'I will show you, I'm not going to cry'. With a mark of acknowledgement she said 'Of course, I know you're brave. This doctor is really nice; he is going to take care of you'. So I went to the table and sat down waiting for my injection. 'OK lie down now' the nurse instructed. 'No' I replied. 'Yes!' she repeated. 'No!' I stubbornly refused. I thought the injection would hurt more if I lay down, so I continued to resist. My sister asked 'Why are you worried? I'm here to take care of you; it's not going to hurt'. I finally agreed as I always trusted her. As I lay down the nurse injected the needle into my arm. I began to feel a little drowsy. Then I noticed the doctor come to sit at the bottom of the table. He took my dress up. I began to feel there was something wrong. Nervously I asked my sister at the side of me 'What is he doing please?' She said 'Now don't worry. You can see later'. I said 'What later?' Attempting to reassure me Khadra stated 'Everybody has had this done at some time, the children and me'. I said 'What? What's that?' She could only say 'It's nothing bad, it's going to be OK, don't worry'. I was not listening, I was really upset, I started crying and shouting. 'Mum, Mum, please come, they're hurting me!' I cried. I was losing the feeling in my hands; they were getting heavier and heavier. I couldn't even lift my eyelids they were so heavy. I held onto my sister's hand for some sense of security. The doctor looked very mean with big strict eyes. He told my sister to stop my feet shaking as they were supposed to be still. I tried to kick him away with my feet as he wanted to keep them apart. This made him angry. My sister told me to stop. He suggested my sister hold one foot, whilst the nurse held the other. I just wanted to jump off the table and run away. Suddenly my trust in Khadra had evaporated. I felt betrayed as I thought I was only going to have an injection. The doctor now began to appear as many doctors, as I drifted out of consciousness.

I opened my eyes, a glint of light shone through a window in a small dark room. I was lying in a small bed, feeling very tired, my eyelids were very heavy. I was confused, not knowing what had happened. There was pain all over my body. I tried to find where it hurt the most. Then I realised that both my feet were tied together with a thin piece of cloth. I was shocked. This revelation made the pain feel even more excruciating. The cloth was tight. I did not have enough strength to move anyway and fell back to sleep.

I woke to find Mum coming into the room. I asked her why my feet were tied together. She said 'Don't worry honey, you're going to be fine. You've been a brave little girl today'. She picked me up and carried me to the bathroom, thinking I needed the toilet and sat me on the toilet seat. Nothing came out, but I felt like I was bleeding. She carried me back to a different room. There I saw my cousins, three girls aged nine, ten and twelve and two boys aged twelve and fourteen. They were all lying down, but did not have their ankles tied up, like mine. I began crying because the pain appeared to increase. 'Mum it hurts, it hurts, take this pain away' I begged. She tried to reassure me the pain would pass, but I told her it was never going to pass, it was too much. I felt there was no end to my cut, bleeding, tight flesh, throbbing on every pulse. Mum also began crying, saying 'Don't hate me please'. She told me I should not have come to the house. She did not realise when I had arrived, but since I had come, she said it was better this thing was over and done with early, than later on in life. Mum asked me if I was going to be a good girl whilst she untied my feet. First of all she made me promise not to move my feet around, otherwise I would damage myself. I agreed because I did not want any more pain. Mum untied them and laid me on another bed. She then came in every five minutes to check on me. Sometimes she gave me pain killers. Sometimes she dabbed antiseptic and rubbed oil on my mutilated flesh to increase the circulation. Whilst Mum was there to comfort me I did not feel the pain, but as soon as she left me, it hurt so much.

After a short while, a woman from the neighbourhood entered the bedroom and began telling us all stories, to keep our minds off the pain. The others did not seem in as much pain as me. I was still crying. Mum had to come back to comfort me, because every time I cried the story had to stop. She sat with me so I would not disturb the others. Then some aunties came with candies, told us all jokes and reiterated how we had been good girls and boys.

All of us stayed at the house for a couple of days. We were not allowed to move our feet, we could not sit, we had to lie down. If I wanted to go to the toilet I was carried. My girl cousins only appeared to be in pain after going to the toilet, but I was in pain all the time. There could not be any material in contact with the flesh in case of any bacteria or irritation. My back was aching because I was lying down all the time and the muscles in my legs ached because I had to keep my legs closed, together. Pain had taken over the essence of my being. I did not know why and how I was hurting. During these two days, we watched television and more visitors came around with toys and candy. Mum was there all the time to help look after me.

The pain did not start to go until I went home. After about a week, I could stand up and move around a little, in tiny steps, just to help with the circulation, then sit down again. However, I was not allowed to walk, run or play. After two weeks I began to itch, which was a sign of healing. I had to sleep in Mum's bed and tell her when this happened because she did not want me to scratch and cause any damage. I was back playing with my friends after about a month, but could not do things like climb up the lemon tree to pick lemons. It was not until about six weeks later until I asked Mum why I had this painful experience inflicted upon me. She said it was something traditional, done to all boys and girls, something everyone in Somalia has to go through. I told her that I now felt different from my friends, because we always did everything together, yet they were not at my sister's house that day to go through the same experience with me. Mum said I should not feel that way because if they had not already undergone the operation, they would one day.

If I hadn't gone to my sister's house on that fatal day maybe I would not have had the operation, as a few years later our family left Somalia. Personally, I do not agree with female circumcision, because it is not necessary. However, absolutely everyone in Somalia has this operation. If by chance someone does not have it, they feel outside of the culture, as happened to a teenage girl I knew, who only found she was different than the rest of her friends, through a discussion. She felt so excluded, she ended up carrying out the operation on herself. I don't believe in damaging yourself for the sake of your culture. If I had a daughter I would not let her go through the same experience. I underwent the second level of female circumcision[3]. Before the operation there should at least be an explanation of what is going to happen and the child should be much older. If I lived in Somalia all my life then I would no doubt have been influenced by the culture and agreed with female circumcision. However, since I am now here in the UK, outside of that culture I can see it from another perspective and know it is wrong to mutilate a young girl's body. All my Somali girlfriends over here also disagree with this tradition. People should have the freedom to choose for themselves.

Collated by Michael Carroll

---

3 Female circumcision generally has three levels of severity. The first level involves removing part of the clitoris. The next level, excision, involves removal of part or all of the labia minora. The most severe form, called infibulation, is the removal of the clitoris, labia minora and part of the labia majora, which are then sewn shut. Sometimes the families instruct the surgeon precisely on what they want to remove.

Childhood Imagination

(Anonymous)

This is a story about Aisha Khan. She was born in Sohawa, a small village in Pakistan. Aisha had four sisters and two brothers; she was the youngest child in the family. Aisha told me that when she was little, about seven years old, she used to see things in the dark. This made her very afraid when she used to go to bed because she never knew what she was going to see. In the summer, when it was really hot in Pakistan, Aisha and her family would sleep in the garden. The garden was an open space in front of the veranda with lots of dhreak trees. The dhreak trees were very big with thick branches and large leaves. They bloomed with lilac and white flowers producing small green berries. The berries were bitter and inedible, but the flowers produced a light musky smell. After darkness had descended and it was time for bed, everyone would drift off to sleep, except Aisha. Instead, she would gaze across the garden, seeing people and animals sitting on the trees.

Aisha's house was very big. It had a number of rooms inside and a big veranda on the side with stairs leading to the roof. One hot summer's night the sky was like a velvet blanket with small stars piercing through the blackness. The moon cast a dim wash over the house and garden. Everyone was sleeping inside the house, but Aisha could not go to sleep, because it was very hot, there were lots of mosquitoes and other flies buzzing around the place. No matter how hard she tried, Aisha couldn't relax and fall asleep.

As Aisha peered from her bed towards the veranda, suddenly something caught her attention. She spotted a figure climbing down the stairs from the roof. Aisha became really scared, she started to tremble and sweat. It was very dark so Aisha couldn't make out any features of the person, she could only see a shadowy figure. Aisha became more anxious and began crying loudly. Her mother was asleep next to her and Aisha's crying soon awoke her. She comforted Aisha and asked her why she was crying. Aisha described to her mother what she had seen. In an act of reassurance, her mother switched on the light to see if anyone was there, but as she expected, there was nothing. She assured Aisha that she would be safe and sound, then switched off the light and ushered Aisha to sleep. No matter how hard she tried, Aisha could not get rid of her fear and hid her face underneath the blanket. She was still curious though and just wanted to check if anyone was out there and slowly pulled the blanket off her face, turning her head towards the stairs. To her amazement, there was the same person walking down the stairs again, this scared Aisha even more, her heart began beating faster and her throat became dry. Through the pitch-black night, she could see the shadow of the person cast by the lights from the neighbour's house onto the veranda. Accompanying the scary shadow, Aisha could hear the sound of mosquitoes and dogs barking. She hastily awoke her mother to ask her for a glass of water, seeking sanctuary from her ordeal. Her mother switched on the light. Aisha wanted her mother to leave the light on whilst she went to sleep, but her mother disagreed because the light would attract flies and mosquitoes.

Disgruntled that her request had been refused, Aisha attempted to go to sleep for the third time. She felt a lack of support from her mother, making her feel more lonely and vulnerable than before. Aisha found herself going through the same motions, again hiding underneath the cover, becoming anxious, yet still curious to see if the stranger was there. She knew that if she looked towards the veranda and the figure was not there, then everything would be all right, there would be no need to worry. So again she pulled the cover slowly down, peering over it, looking across to the veranda. The stranger was there again! This time he was walking towards her. He was creeping at a very slow pace moving with the intention of harming her. The stranger must have hidden each time her mother had turned the light on; he was real after all. He crept closer and closer to Aisha until he was within touching distance. Aisha screamed out loud at the top of her voice. She screamed so loud, she woke up everyone in the house. 'He's here! He's here!' she cried. Everyone looked bemused, where was he? Aisha told her father that she had definitely seen a stranger in the house coming to get her. Her father switched on the light and went to check the stairs and the roof, but there was no one to be found. Her mother sighed deeply explaining to her father that Aisha 'saw' people that they could not see, that it was just her imagination. She comforted Aisha once again and let her sleep in her bed. Eventually, Aisha fell asleep with her mother, feeling a lot safer next to her.

Even now that Aisha has grown up, she still remembers that night when she was awake all night, terrified of the stranger in the dark and has nightmares about it. Aisha is still scared of the dark. She is scared to walk in a room alone and whenever she sees things in the dark, she tries very hard to convince herself that it is just her imagination.

Collated by Mussarrat Shafiq

First Love Never Dies

(Anonymous)

This is a story about Saida, who was a very young, loving and innocent girl of sixteen years old. Saida lived in Bharuch in India with her family who were a very big family of ten, including her middle-aged parents and her grandparents. Even though her brothers and sisters were close to her, she could not confide her true feelings to them because she feared how they would react to her.

Opposite Saida's house there lived a young boy called Javed who had a lot of respect from the other people in the village. Javed studied with a Pir Saab[1], listening and following his preaching on Islam. He enjoyed discussing Islamic principles and looked up to the Pir Saab as a role model. However, Saida's family did not recognise the authority and teachings of the Pir Saab. Saida would look out from her window at Javed in the courtyard and in turn, Javed reciprocated the odd occasional glance to Saida, followed by corresponding smiles. An attraction began to develop between both of them. Simple gestures and eye contact developed into exchanging letters of correspondence between each other. Everything was discreet, in secret, as Saida and Javed were both Sunni Muslims[i], but from different sub castes. Javed was a Syed[2], the highest-ranking sub caste of the Sunni sect. Saida's family had no idea of the love that was blossoming day by day between her and Javed.

One day, as usual, Javed paced up and down outside in the courtyard waiting for a glimpse of Saida, but Saida had not managed to come to her window as she was attending her

---

1 A holy pious man and spiritual leader, similar to a guru. People follow him and ask for his advice on social and religious issues, believing in everything he says. He may instruct people to recite certain prayers in order to accomplish specific goals in life.
2 The status of Syeds (or Sayyads), putative descendents of the Prophet Muhammad, has always been special and privileged amongst Muslims.
i See end note.

grandma who was busy praying. Javed often managed to throw a note or a letter to Saida, attached to a stone, whilst she was watching. She would then pick it up later when no one else was about. Javed had already been waiting a long while for Saida to appear, so he decided to throw his letter as usual, this time attaching it to a cotton reel, expecting Saida to find it later. The letter to his beloved sailed just into the open window where Saida usually appeared.

Whilst Saida expected some form of correspondence from Javed, she did not get any time to go and look for it, thinking her grandmother might become suspicious if she tried to leave her. All Saida could do was try to wait for an appropriate moment. However, it was soon evening and it began to get late. Saida decided to go to bed and wake up early in the morning to see if there was a note from Javed.

The next morning Saida overslept and before she could even begin to see if Javed had left her a note, she walked into the room where the rest of her family was seated. All their eyes bore down upon her, filling the room with an atmosphere of shame and disgust. She knew something was wrong. Her strict grandfather held a letter in his hand. He confronted her about it, in front of the entire family. Her worst nightmare had come true. In his other hand, her grandfather displayed a ring, as though exhibiting a piece of evidence to a jury. Javed had wrapped up the ring in the letter. Saida's grandfather mockingly read the words out aloud:

> Let us run away from home tonight. I will love and treasure you all of my life. I will never hurt you.
> You are my first and last love.

The words painted revulsion onto each face of her family. They proceeded to vent their anger on her for disgracing the family name and dishonouring their trust. Her grandfather ranted and raved with puritanical displeasure. Saida cried. She felt as if her whole world had caved in on her. She felt stripped naked having being exposed in front of the whole family. Saida was forced into her bedroom. As she lay crying on her bed, the door key turned and creaked, making her a prisoner.

Whilst everyone else in the house was fast asleep, Saida's grandfather crept up to the door of her bedroom. He turned the key, opened the door, and walked in wielding his walking stick, casting a dark shadow of intent upon the wall. Without warning, blows from his stick lashed through the air and his free hand battered Saida, beating her black and blue all over her body. He then left her alone, to wallow in her pain and self-pity with huge bruises on her arms and face. Again, the key turned in the lock, sealing her fate. Saida cried herself to sleep with aching limbs and an aching heart for her beloved Javed. A volcanic anger was raging inside her, fuelled by the punishment she had been subjected to.

Driven by uncontainable feelings of resentment, Saida devised a plan to poison her grandfather and grandmother. The other family members shunned Saida, whilst at the same time, watching her very closely. Her every move was observed, invading her privacy. She soon learned that her brothers had beaten up her beloved Javed, which only served to fan the flames of vengeance.

During the month of Ramadan, Saida decided to put her plan into practice. She made a mango lassi[3] for her grandparents. They always enjoyed this cool drink at night before going to bed. Saida laced the two drinks with rat poison from the kitchen cupboards, then presented them to her grandparents. She had planned everything carefully, but was shocked when one of the drinks came back untouched. Her grandmother had

3 Like a milkshake made with yoghurt, with a savoury or sweet flavour such as mango.

drunk her lassi, but her grandfather had not touched his. Saida's grandmother complained of stomach pains for the rest of the night. The doctor was called early in the morning, but after a few tablets, her grandmother soon felt much better. It dawned upon Saida that she had made a terrible mistake and she regretted it deeply. She realised that this was not the answer to her dilemma, it certainly hadn't solved anything. Now, she saw herself in the same light as her grandfather wanting to issue some kind of punishment.

Unknown to Saida, her grandparents had quickly been making plans to arrange her marriage and there had already been a marriage proposal from England. When they broke the news to Saida, she was heartbroken and deeply distraught at the prospect of being kept apart from Javed forever. She pleaded and begged her grandparents not to make her marry anyone else and not to send her to England. However, her grandparents no longer cared. They had concluded that this was the best solution to save their family from shame and dishonour.

There was nothing Saida could do, she was forced to leave her home in India and travel to England to satisfy her grandparents' wishes. She had some unknown life planned for her in a foreign country. Saida began to lose a lot of weight from all the worry. She had no appetite anymore and could not bear the thought of being away from home and her beloved Javed. However, her life was out of her own hands and Saida finally had to concede that it was not her fate to marry her own true love. She reluctantly complied with her grandparents' wishes.

Saida left India and was quickly married within a month, whilst trying to suppress her feelings for Javed. First of all, she moved in with her husband and her in-laws, trying very hard to adapt to her new life. Now she is living with her husband and their two young children, but finds it very difficult to sustain her marriage, especially when she still possesses feelings for Javed. Her biggest regret is that she never had the opportunity to say goodbye to him. However, she will never forget her first love. He will always remain in her heart and her feelings for him will never die.

Collated by Tahira Patel

i Sunni and Shia are the two main sub-groups within Islam. Sunni and Shia Muslims share the most fundamental Islamic beliefs and articles of faith. The differences between the two initially stemmed not from spiritual differences, but political ones. Over the centuries, however, these political differences have spawned a number of varying practices and positions, which have come to carry a spiritual significance.

The difference between Shia and Sunni dates back to the death of the Prophet Muhammad, and the question of who was to take over the leadership of the Muslim nation. Sunni Muslims agree with the position taken by many of the Prophet's companions, that the new leader should be elected from among those capable of the job. This is what was done, and the Prophet Muhammad's close friend and advisor, Abu Bakr, became the first Caliph of the Islamic nation. The word 'Sunni' in Arabic comes from a word meaning 'one who follows the traditions of the Prophet.'

On the other hand, some Muslims share the belief that leadership should have stayed within the Prophet's own family, among those specifically appointed by him, or among Imams appointed by God Himself.

The Shia Muslims believe that following the Prophet Muhammad's death, leadership should have passed directly to his cousin/son-in-law, Ali. Throughout history, Shia Muslims have not recognised the authority of elected Muslim leaders, choosing instead to follow a line of Imams which they believe have been appointed by the Prophet Muhammad or God Himself. The word 'Shia' in Arabic means a group or supportive party of people. The commonly known term is shortened from the historical 'Shia-t-Ali' or 'The Party of Ali.' They are also known as followers of 'Ahl-al-Bayt' or 'People of the Household' (of the Prophet).

Sunni Muslims make up the majority (eighty-five percent) of Muslims all over the world. Significant populations of Shia Muslims can be found in Iran and Iraq, and large minority communities in Yemen, Bahrain, Syria, and Lebanon.

It is important to remember that despite all of these differences in opinion and practice, Shia and Sunni Muslims share the main articles of Islamic belief and are considered by most to be brethren in faith. In fact, most Muslims do not distinguish themselves by claiming membership in any particular group, but prefer to call themselves simply, 'Muslims.'

Source: http://islam.about.com/cs/divisions/f/shia_sunni.htm

Bombay Riots

(Anonymous)

Shenaz was born in India in 1978. She lived in Bombay until she was three years old, then her family moved to a village near Bharuch, in the district of Gujarat. Though she was very young at the time, she remembers the quietness, the space and clean air, which was such a stark contrast to Bombay. Here there was a clear blue sky and breathing appeared so much easier. Shenaz's house was very big, the only one around in a rural area which mostly consisted of farms. There was land all around her house. There was a lovely garden at the front with some beautiful flowers and a sprinkler system in the middle, to make sure the grass and the flowers did not dry out, as it only rains in India during the monsoon season, between June and August. Right outside the house there was a mango tree. Shenaz used to love the sweet taste of the mangoes. She wasn't allowed to climb up the tree in case she fell and broke her arm or leg, but she used to climb it anyway when no one else was around to tell her off, then eat the mangoes in the secrecy of her own bedroom.

When Shenaz was thirteen years old, her parents sent her to Bombay, to an English speaking school to develop her English through traditional subjects such as maths and science. She also studied Hindi. Shenaz wasn't upset at the prospect of leaving her family as she knew they would come to Bombay to visit her. She could always visit them and her friends, when she returned home during the holidays.

Shenaz moved to Amboli Naka near Andheri in Bombay with her aunt and lived on the first floor of a block of flats, situated on a main road. Bombay was just as Shenaz had remembered it when she was younger. It was noisy, smoky, with traffic jams and was very crowded with lots of people. She was immersed in a congested, polluted and humid atmosphere blaring with car horns. In India there are no regulations about sounding car horns on the roads. This time round she was considerably older and so was more conscious of what was going on around her. One of the first things that drew her attention was the street beggars. There were lots of them placed at strategic vantage points, but Shenaz couldn't tell the real beggars from the professional ones. They were all so persistent, sometimes there was no escaping them. If she was riding in a taxi, beggars would knock on the windows asking for money. There were also children, even girls as young as ten years old with babies in their arms attempting to obtain money by appealing to people's sympathetic natures.

It wasn't long before events elsewhere, in the north Indian state of Uttar Pradesh, were soon to affect daily life in Bombay and other regions of India. On 6th December 1992, the sixteenth century Babri mosque in Ayodhya was demolished by Hindus. Ayodhya is more than a twenty-four hour train journey away from Bombay. The incident stemmed from a growing dispute between Hindus and Muslims over who actually owned the religious site where the mosque was built. Hindus believed that originally a temple was situated on the site and that it was the birthplace of one of the most revered deities in Hinduism, Lord Rama. Therefore, a movement of Hindu political parties, religious groups, and cultural organisations, including the Bharatiya Janata Party, Rashtriya Swayamsevak Sangh, Vishwa Hindu Parishad and Shiv Sena, instigated the move for the construction of a temple on the site of the mosque. Over one hundred and fifty thousand supporters known as Kar Sevaks[1] converged on Ayodhya, where they attacked the three-domed mosque with hammers and pick-axes, reducing it to rubble. The incident was widely covered by the Indian and international press and the BBC. Images of the destruction spread throughout India and soon had an impact on Bombay where Shenaz was staying.

---

1 Voluntary workers.

As soon as news of the demolition spread, Muslims in many areas of Bombay came out onto the streets and expressed their anger against the government for failing to prevent the destruction of the mosque, by attacking buses and other public property. One day Shenaz's school received a phone call telling the staff to send the children home because word of mouth had reached them that there was going to be trouble on the streets. The teachers didn't want to risk the children being caught up in potential violence, so they arranged for all of them to be taken home on buses and to be provided with a police escort. It turned out to be a wise move, for during the demonstrations, government property, including public transport facilities and police stations, were attacked. Even some temples were attacked and partially damaged. If the police had acted with tact and imagination, the violence could have been contained and the miscreants arrested. Instead, in many cases, the police opened fire indiscriminately and many innocent people were killed. There were many complaints that the police were firing only at Muslims.

From this point on, relationships with some of the girls who Shenaz had made friends with at school became strained, they appeared more distant. During the following days and weeks, Shenaz and other Muslim girls began to hear derogatory remarks about their religion on the streets. Muslim women were sworn and spat at. Shenaz witnessed women having big stones thrown at them and being verbally abused in front of their young children. It was easy for the Muslim women to be picked out as their dress consisted of a headscarf and a salwar kameez[2]. The men too, also stood out as they wore topis[3] and grew long beards. She witnessed Muslim men being beaten in the streets by the police. Bearing all this in mind and fearing they would be targeted whenever they went out shopping, Shenaz and her auntie disguised themselves as Hindu women by marking a bindi[4] on their foreheads and wearing saris.

2 Salwar are loose trousers and the kameez is a long shirt.
3 Small white, usually crocheted, circular cap.
4 Hindus wear a tilak (a red dot by women and an elongated dot by men) on their foreheads, between the two eyes. This point is known by various names such as Ajna chakra, Spiritual eye, Third eye and was said to be the major nerve in the human body, in ancient times.

The situation grew worse day by day and Shenaz began to feel isolated. From her bedroom window at the front of the flat, she was able to observe everything that happened outside in the street. Her aunt banned her from going to the window, as she didn't want her to become traumatised. However, when Shenaz was alone, she would stand there, gazing at isolated incidents. She saw a gang of men picking on a single man, then kicking him in his stomach. She saw a Muslim rickshaw driver being pulled out of his rickshaw and pushed around by a group of Hindus. They pulled down his dhoti[5] to see if he was circumcised. Seeing that he was, they beat him severely and took his rickshaw. She stared in dismay at gangs of rioting Hindus and Muslims fighting each other with knives, stones, hockey sticks, coke bottles; whatever they could get their hands on. In all the men's eyes she saw hatred and a fear of what lay ahead. Even refuge waste was recycled to make homemade bombs. Shenaz's eyes followed the trails of the bombs heading towards their targets, exploding into the dispersing crowds, like stones displacing water. The sounds of smashing glass were followed immediately by the injured, screaming and crying with pain, unveiled beneath the black cancerous smoke, leaving a charred taste amidst the polluted air. At the window, Shenaz felt very helpless, she could not bear to see people dying right in front of her eyes and prayed for the bloodshed to end. She could not eat her food, as her taste buds were numbed. Her sense of smell was frail due to the constant bellowing pollution. All she could hear day and night were the petrol bombs going off, intermingled with police gunfire.

Amongst the lingering burnt air lurked a tremendous stench from the dead bodies on the streets. Sometimes Shenaz found herself literally having to step over lines of bodies, whenever she went shopping, outside the hours of curfew. She had to be careful because even if anyone was just walking and going

5 Loose pants.

about their own business, it was so easy to get caught up in a spontaneous tide of fighting and bloodshed.

Many deaths were incurred from both sides and many Muslim families moved out of the area, as they feared for their lives. As Muslim stores, restaurants, and service centres were destroyed, tens of thousands fled to refugee camps and to areas surrounding Bombay.

In the midst of the rioting Shenaz still went to school. Her uncle would drop her off and pick her up. Once in school, if the teachers thought that the riots were going to spark up again, they phoned the pupils' parents and asked them to come and collect their children. At night, whilst Shenaz was in bed, she couldn't sleep. She would lie there thinking about the day's events and analysed which day was better and which day was worse. Shenaz dreamed of going back home to her village, but all forms of transport had ground to a halt; trains, buses, taxis and even rickshaws.

The riots carried on for three months. In total three thousand people died nationwide. Towards the end, the police managed to control the people and suddenly the fighting stopped. For a few days, Shenaz listened out for bombs exploding and the accompanying screams, which she had become accustomed to, but now there was just a calm, eerie silence.

When the transport services resumed, Shenaz was extremely glad to go home for a month and leave Bombay for a while. She felt fortunate to be alive and was very happy and emotional upon meeting her family. She was relieved to be back in a secure place of peace and tranquillity, but knew that before long she would have to return again to the hustle and bustle of Bombay.

Shenaz went back to Bombay for three more years to finish her studies, then returned home to her village for further study nearby. She is now living in the UK and is married with young children. She couldn't go into too many details of how women were treated during the riots, as it is too painful to recollect, suffice to say that many of them were raped. It was a very dangerous time for Muslim women who were generally bullied to the point of despair and only the thought of their children kept them alive. Despite what happened all those years ago, like the vast majority of people in the community, Shenaz embraces people of diverse faiths and cultural origins. She would not wish her experience on her worst enemy and says that at the end of the day, it all boils down to innocent people getting caught up in politics.

Collated by Selma Kadva

Polish Roma

(Anonymous)

I am a fifteen year old girl and have six brothers and sisters. My father is Polish and my mother is a Polish Gypsy. I used to live in the city of Tarnow, Poland, with my family. Many of our relatives still live there. We always spent a lot of time together and attended events such as Tabory in the month of July where we remember the Roma[1] people who were killed by the Germans during the holocaust in World War II. On this day the caravans are brought out of the museum and driven down the main street passing war memorials and monuments. We dance in each of the towns along the route for the Polish people, as many helped to protect us from the Germans during the war. Some families actually hid Polish Roma children. The procession begins at the Muzeum Okregowe W Tarnowie, then to the middle of the city of Tarnow past the Town Hall to Niedomice, the last place where the Gypsies visited before they were captured by the Germans in World War II. Here lots of dancing and singing takes place. The day after this procession, the cemetery is visited, where candles are lit and melancholy music is played for the Gypsies buried at their place of rest. Many people attend the event which is covered by television and radio.

In 1964 a law was passed forbidding Gypsies to roam within Poland, meaning that Gypsies had to find a place of permanent residence. Most of the caravans ended up in museums and are just used on special occasions. This law caused problems because the government had to house us and people became resentful whenever Gypsies moved into the provided accommodation.

Lots of people from Poland don't like Gypsies because of their

---

1 Roma is the preferred name as the term
Gypsy is viewed as derogatory.

skin colour. The vast majority of the people in Poland have very white faces, but my mum's skin is a dark oily brown. If anyone looks at her face, they realise she is a Gypsy straight away. People try and put us down by saying we do not have our own country, therefore we do not belong anywhere. We don't like being called Gypsies because in Poland, if someone tells a lie, people say 'Don't be a Gypsy'. If someone steals in Poland, they say 'Don't be a Gypsy'. Mum could not go into restaurants and pubs in case skinheads found out she was there and started to cause trouble. My eldest brother played professional football for fifteen years at Blekitni Stargard Football Club, but Mum never attended any of his matches because she did not want to cause any trouble for him.

As a little girl in Poland, I went to school regularly and got on well with the other kids. For a long time Dad came to school whenever he needed to attend for parents' evenings and other special events. My mother did not attend on purpose because she knew life would become difficult for me if my friends and teachers found out that I was half Gypsy. However, one day Dad could not come to school for some reason, so Mum had to take his place. She was so afraid. When she arrived everyone looked her up and down, in a funny way, at her face and long black hair. When the kids found out she was a Gypsy it caused me, my brothers and sisters many problems. They called us all the names associated with Gypsies, such as black pigs and said that we should go to the gas chambers along with all the other Gypsies. They said we were dirty people because of our skin colour and tried to start fights with us.

A group of boys gathered in the classroom one day and one of them spat out of a window. As my brother was stood near the window he got the blame. The teacher followed him to his next class, where he informed my brother that he was wanted by the head teacher. As soon as my brother stepped out into the corridor, the teacher beat him up. After a while my brother managed to escape and run home. He ended up lying on the sofa suffering from concussion. We had to phone for an ambulance to take him to hospital. The police went round to the school and actually found that the teacher was drunk. He was never reprimanded for his actions even though the whole incident was reported in the newspapers and on television. Because we are Gypsies no one else believed our side of the story. My brother had to stay in hospital for two weeks. None of the teachers visited him whilst he was there. The teachers always blamed us if a fight started; they always said it was our fault. They never defended or spoke up for us, it was as though we didn't matter. The most help we ever received in Poland was actually from English people.

We decided that it would be much better for our family if we went to live in England. This way we would not have to put up with the discrimination that had become part of our everyday lives. Mum and some of my brothers and sisters went to England first, as asylum seekers. They were given a house in Liverpool. They phoned the rest of us in Tarnow and told us life was much better there. I missed my Mum and brothers very much and could not wait to join them. So the rest of us saved up some money, with kind contributions from friends and relatives. We promised to pay them back as soon as Mum and Dad found employment and earned some money.

Eventually, when I was about twelve years old, I came to England with my Dad and older sister, by plane. It was the first time we had been on a plane. I liked it, but my Dad was scared, he was sweating as he was thinking of the terrorist attack on 9/11 when the planes had crashed into the twin towers in New York. I liked seeing the clouds close up, but Dad wouldn't let us open the window blind because he didn't want to see outside. He took some travel sickness tablets and the woman next to him advised him to drink a glass of wine.

We arrived at Heathrow Airport, London and told the officials there we wanted to seek asylum in England. Then, we were informed that our luggage had been lost. They found a suitcase containing our food, but the cases containing our clothes could not be traced. They took all our fingerprints and our photographs, even though I was only a child. I thought it was funny, but Dad felt like a criminal. The officials took our belongings such as personal stereos and cigarettes. We stayed at Heathrow Airport for one day and one night in a big waiting room. There were no beds, just the waiting room seating. I slept on the floor with some other Polish Roma girls who were on the plane with me. It became apparent that the officials were trying to keep everyone there for as long as possible in order to deter them from staying in England. Some people, who had been living like this for weeks, gave up and went home.

The next day we were taken to a special room for an interview. My sister could speak a little English and she asked for an interpreter to help us. They asked us why we wanted to come here, so we told them about the racism and the discrimination we suffered in Poland. They asked us where my Mum was and if we planned to live with her. After the interview we were driven in a big coach to an asylum seeker reception centre in Oakington. As we approached the centre, it was two o'clock in the morning. I was very worried because it looked like a prison, but another Polish woman with previous experience of the centre told me not to worry, it was OK inside.

On arrival our personal items were taken from us again. We were all scanned by a metal detector. They felt the skin up and down my arms and legs to make sure I was not hiding drugs or anything. All the children had to undergo this procedure. As our luggage had been lost, we were provided with some second-hand clothing. There was quite a friendly atmosphere. One of the security guards was Polish so he would often talk to us. There was a shop inside the perimeter of the complex, but we had to wait for hours for an official to take us there. Other buildings within the complex included a dentist's and a doctor's surgery. We had to obtain passes if we wanted to go to any of these buildings. There were smoke alarms everywhere and they were always going off because of people smoking in their rooms. When the alarms went off in the middle of the night we had to congregate outside every time. We didn't get much sleep.

After four or five days we had another interview with a solicitor and an interpreter. They just asked the same questions as we had been asked at the airport. Every day we asked them when we could see our family. Every time they just kept saying tomorrow, tomorrow, tomorrow. At least the day after we had arrived we had been given a telephone card so we could contact Mum to tell her we were in England. Mum then phoned us at the centre more or less every day.

It was not until three weeks later that we were able to leave Oakington and see Mum, which was a very long wait for us. When we arrived at Mum's house in Liverpool I was shocked because she was so thin. She had not taken a liking to English food and was suffering from stress because she did not know when she was going to see us. She could not believe we were here and cried with relief. Everyone was crying. Seeing Mum again was so emotional. Shortly after all the tears had subsided, I went straight to the fridge because I love bread and butter and there had been no butter or margarine at Oakington. The house was too small for us now that Dad, my sister and I had arrived. So after one day, NASS[2] found a bigger house for us in Birkenhead. It was big enough for us all to live together, with five bedrooms, but it was very cold. There were no other immigrants in this area. Most people treated us nicely, but there is always a small minority that wants to cause trouble. A teenage boy urinated on our window and some other people threw eggs at our house.

2 National Asylum Support Service.

I attended the local school and made some good friends. However, after only six months we had to move to different accommodation because the contract between the landlord and NASS for lease of the house had expired. This resulted in us moving back to Liverpool where we had to start all over again, changing schools and making new friends. Then a letter from the Home Office arrived stating that our application to stay in England had been refused. Mum and Dad went to see a solicitor who had been recommended to them. He said that he could put forward a good appeal, but it would cost five hundred pounds. So Mum and Dad had to borrow some money to pay him.

A month later at about five o'clock in the morning, I was asleep downstairs dreaming about my uncle having an argument with my auntie, when I was woken up by knocking at the front door. Through the glass window I could see the shape of a man. He vaguely looked like my uncle Robert from my dream. I looked through the spy hole in the front door, then opened the door. Before I could blink my eyes, loads of people barged their way into the house. One of them said 'Go and wake your family!' I ran upstairs screaming, 'Mum! Mum!' I was very scared. Mum and Dad could not believe that they were trying to put handcuffs on me. Mum was shouting at them, she told them to stop because I was only thirteen years old. Dad showed the immigration officers the letter from the solicitor, but they would not listen. They said 'You are going to Poland!' They told us to start packing our clothes. A lady got some bags from a car. We had bought extra things for the house to make it a comfortable home, but we were not allowed to take any of our possessions. Mum was very distraught. She did not know what was going to happen to my older brother in Birmingham or my older sister who was living with her boyfriend.

We were taken to the Home Office in Liverpool, then we were moved into the centre down at Oakington once again. We asked for an interview, but they just told us we were going to

Poland. We asked them when, but they just kept saying tomorrow, tomorrow, tomorrow. This time the centre was not so accommodating. At around three o'clock one morning the fire alarm went off. Everyone had to congregate in the yard outside where it was freezing cold. We all just wanted to go back inside to sleep. We were then moved into a room where the officials told everyone they could go back to bed apart from rooms one, two and three. As we were staying in a couple of these rooms, we had to remain behind. Then they accused Mum of smoking in her room and setting the alarm off. She told them it was not her and a big argument erupted. One of the security guards called Mum a Polish bitch. My brother had to be restrained from fighting with him. We had no interview there and after two and a half weeks we were sent back to Poland.

We arrived back in Poland at Easter time. My auntie came to meet us at the airport in a minibus. We were very happy to see her and she was happy to see us. It made us cry. My dad got a job and we began to save up enough money to go back to England again in three months. We received a letter from a friend in England, inviting us to visit and stay with her. Because of this letter of invitation we were confident that things would work out well this time. We bought tickets for the bus to England.

We had travelled as far as France on the bus, where customs officers checked our passports. When they asked why we were going to England, we showed them our letter. They did not believe us and said we couldn't travel any further. They ordered us back to Poland. The bus just had to leave us there in France, as it was about to board the ferry for England. We were left to sort our problems out with the police. They refused to let us go to England. We had to stay in a hotel for the night then wait for a bus back to Poland. We didn't know when the bus was coming and waited at the station all throughout the next day. Finally it came, the same bus that left us the day before. Once again we arrived back in Poland.

Dad managed to buy a ticket for a boxing match at the MEN Arena in Manchester, to see a female Polish fighter called Agnieszka Rylik, fighting Eliza Olson of the United States for the WIBF and WIBO Junior Welterweight titles on 10th April 2004. This provided him with a good reason to enter England. There were no problems. After the boxing match Dad just went to live with my older sister who already lived in England. He got a job and started to save his money for tickets so the rest of us could join him. It was about a month later before the rest of us arrived in England again, shortly before Poland became part of the European Union in May 2004.

All of our family are now living in Bolton because we know an aunt who lives here. Life is now very easy for me. I have managed to learn the English language and translate information for the rest of my family. I do not have to be scared about being sent back to Poland anymore. I miss my relatives, but we can travel freely between England and Poland whenever we wish, now that it is part of the European Union. It is good to know that Poland is now taking steps to alleviate racism and that the quality of life for the Polish Roma community there is beginning to improve.

Collated by Michael Carroll

Rubina's Diversion

(Rubina)

Rubina lived in a small village in India. She had a small family, including her grandma, mum, and her brother. Her house was situated at the end of the village next to a beautiful tamarind tree. One delightful morning, Rubina was playing under the tamarind tree whilst the birds were flying and singing amongst its branches. Near Rubina's house, there was a well where water was drawn through a connected pipe into a very big water tank on stilted legs. This was common in the villages of India at the time. The water tank over-looked the villagers as they filled their buckets with water. It acted as a local meeting point where gossip could be exchanged. As Rubina's grandma was waiting to fill her bucket, she suddenly called Rubina across. Rubina noticed immediately that her Grandma's face looked tense. She soon discovered why, when her grandma told her to quickly call the midwife as her mother was having a baby. Rubina stepped into her house, catching a brief glimpse of her mother. She could see that she was in a lot of pain, so with great urgency she ran out of the house to call the midwife. She was so scared and worried about her mother, that her legs carried her as fast as they could.

On her way through the village she saw a big crowd of people gathering, which diverted her attention. She ran towards them to see what was going on and noticed a man amongst the crowd with something in his hand. She asked another man what all the fuss was about. He replied 'Someone has shot our Prime Minister Indira Ghandhi!'[1] Rubina then squeezed through to the front of the crowd, where she saw her uncle holding a portable television. The coverage surrounding Indira

---

1 On 31st October 1984, two of Indira Gandhi's Sikh bodyguards Satwant Singh and Beant Singh assassinated her in the garden of the Prime Minister's Residence at No.1, Safdarjung Road in New Delhi. As she was walking to be interviewed by the British actor, Peter Ustinov, she passed a wicket gate, guarded by Satwant and Beant; when she bent down to greet them in traditional Indian style, they opened fire with their semi automatic machine pistols. She died on her way to hospital, in her official car, but was not declared dead until many hours later.

Ghandi's death was being shown on television, everyone was watching it, shoving and pushing to get a view. More and more people were gathering round all the time, trying to watch the news. They were all shouting and screaming at each other complaining that they could not hear the television. Much to everyone's dismay, Rubina's uncle became very angry and switched the television off, took out the plug, picked up the television and walked towards his house. He took the television inside and began watching it on his own. His wife would not dream of letting anyone inside the house, as she wanted to keep it clean and tidy. However, people outside were banging on the door and shouting 'Open the door! Open the door!' His wife became very angry and forced him to take the television back outside, so he began to walk towards the new house that he had nearly finished building.

Rubina was still amongst the crowd. Amongst all the furore, she had forgotten all about calling the midwife for her mother. The crowd was now moving in the direction of Rubina's house, pulling her along with it. Her grandma was standing outside looking to see if there was any sign of Rubina. She was shocked when she saw Rubina's face in the crowd and briskly walked towards her to drag her out. Her grandma desperately wanted to know where Rubina had been, she had been looking for her for the past three hours and wanted to know where the midwife was. Rubina's whole being experienced a shrinking and sinking into the ground sensation as she realised she'd forgotten to call the midwife. Her grandmother could not believe Rubina had behaved so irresponsibly.

Rubina's mother had lost a lot of blood and had to be taken to hospital. The doctors at the hospital said she that she needed more blood to keep her alive, but didn't have any at the hospital to match her blood type. It was difficult to obtain the right blood because there was a curfew in most of the towns. Her condition was getting more serious and the doctors said that she would not live if the right blood did not arrive quickly.

Rubina felt extremely guilty and personally took the blame for her mother's condition. She could not even bring herself to visit her mother in hospital. She was scared that her mother and the baby would die and it would all be her fault. Every day Rubina wallowed in her guilt and every day seemed like forever. Fortunately, the right blood type arrived from Ahmedabad in time, and Rubina's mother was immediately given a transfusion.

After fifteen days, Rubina's mother came home with the newborn baby. Rubina cried with remorse and begged her mother for forgiveness. Rubina's mother could see that her daughter was extremely upset and gave her a big hug, telling her not to blame herself, that it wasn't her fault. Rubina had a long cry in her mother's comforting arms. She was so relieved that her mother and newborn baby had survived their trauma. Even now, Rubina cannot forget the day that she was irresponsible.

Collated by Samim Vali

Mahdi

(Anonymous)

Mahdi was born in Baghdad in early January, 1967. He had a normal and common childhood, growing up with three brothers and four sisters. At the secondary school he attended in Baghdad, he graduated as a top student in 1983. In 1984 he joined medical school, where he graduated as a qualified doctor in general medicine and surgery six years later.

In 1991 after Iraq had invaded Kuwait, Mahdi was working in a pediatrics hospital. He remembers vividly being on duty there at exactly at two o'clock in the morning on 17th January that year. He was on call and had been finally able to get some rest after a very busy day attending to many patients. However, Mahdi was suddenly awakened by a loud earth-shattering noise. He shot up and dashed into the corridor to see what it was. There was an array of shattered pieces of glass covering the floor, then bang, there was another explosion, then another. The hospital shook and Mahdi was transfixed for a moment. Through the shattered window panes, he gazed at the dark sky, flickering with a blaze of colours from the surrounding demolished buildings. Trails of anti-aircraft fire shot across the sky, petering out and bowing to the marauding flashes of bombardment by enemy aircraft. Hundreds of aircraft had struck the capital of Iraq and other parts of the country.

Initially, the whole hospital was in a state of shock, but there was no time to waste. The doctors acted on impulse and adrenalin. The corridors became frantic hives of activity. In-patients, some of them incurring injuries from the blasts, were being transferred to safer areas of the hospital. They included children who were already under treatment for serious illnesses and casualties. Mahdi was overwhelmed by distraught parents holding their loved ones, not knowing what to do, not knowing which way to turn to ensure their safety. In the chaos, some parents carried their loved ones out of the hospital, looking for a safe place, but were then thwarted in their tracks by further explosions. Some of them were holding premature newborn babies, which had been taken out from the incubators, crucial life support mechanisms.

The entire experience was about survival. Each fraction of each second became the most immense and fullest fragment of time experienced by Mahdi's hyper alert senses. The sounds of explosions, shattering glass, the cries of parents and children, the images of bleeding wounds, the smells of antiseptic, the taste of dust on the tongue, the touches of care and consolement all converge together in Madhi's memories of that morning, eluding his attempts to compartmentalise and describe each incident. After the battlefield of that night, in the sunrise of the day, Mahdi observed the surrounding carnage that had been inflicted on a massive scale. Victims of the bombings were literally being treated amongst the dusty rubble.

It had been the beginning of the offensive by the US led allied forces, code-named Operation Desert Storm. The missile strikes continued for forty three days, with sustained attacks on supposedly 'military targets', not hospitals. The city of Baghdad was reduced to ruins. All infrastructures were damaged. There was no electricity, no water, no fuel. Worse was to come as cholera flared up because of the conditions, causing lots of children and newborn babies to die. The continuation of the war caused health and education services to collapse. The community was crippled and the future was very bleak.

After the Gulf War, Mahdi worked as a junior house officer in different medical and surgical departments for two years. He then worked as a Senior House Officer in a gene obstetrics department. Mahdi was very interested in gene obstetrics and in 1998 undertook postgraduate study in this field. Unfortunately he couldn't finish his research as a result of his opposition towards the dictatorship governing in Iraq. Therefore, he was obliged to leave his country.

Ironically Mahdi now lives in England, where he feels he can start a new life away from government harassment and such atrocities. He has found a lot of people here very friendly and quite hospitable. They are helping him to take steps forward again for a good and productive future.

Collated by Mariam Salimi

Taking the Snake for a Walk

(Summaiya Kadva)

Summaiya and her family lived in five apartments on the ground floor. There were also five apartments above, which housed another family. Summaiya's flat was on the corner with stairs leading to the top floor. Alongside the main entrance there were smaller houses where the hired help lived. On the opposite side of the apartments were pens where the cows and buffalos were kept. From here, grunting and mooing could be heard throughout most of the day. In the middle of the pens and the apartments was a substantial garden containing a mini park for the children.

One hot summer's afternoon everybody had just woken up from their siesta. In India, most of the population has a nap for a couple of hours after lunch, which is mainly due to the extreme heat in the afternoon, but the weather begins to cool down towards the evening. Summaiya, about fifteen at the time, awoke to the grunting of the cows and buffalos from across the way in the pens around half past four. She got up and made tea for her family then wandered off onto the porch where she sat on the hichko[1] outside and enjoyed her cup of spicy massala tea with her mother. It was a very peaceful afternoon. The clothes were hanging on the washing line, the children were playing with their toys and the tea tasted excellent.

Women from the other apartments soon emerged and came over for a chat and a gossip. Summaiya's mum offered them tea, but they refused as they had some a little earlier. As the men chatted away on a bench outside, the smell of cigarette smoke drifted across through the air. At this point the children decided to go and play in the park. They all ran for the swings.

1 Like an upright cradle attached by a chain above, very common in India.

One of the women yelled at her young son for not wearing any slippers. All was well as the women gossiped away, all talking at once as usual. The laughter from the children in the background sprinkled a sense of comfort and well being on the lazy afternoon.

Suddenly the children screamed an almighty scream, causing the men to jump up together and run to see what had happened. The women panicked and became hysterical grabbing each other for comfort. Tears rolled down some of the children's faces as they screamed and ran towards their homes as fast as their legs could carry them. In turn the women screamed egging their children on to run and get inside quickly, knowing there was some kind of danger. They then bolted their doors behind them. Bang! Bang! Bang! Summaiya's father had ordered the children inside immediately as a long big black snake was slithering about in the park. Summaiya and her friend both felt scared and could feel their stomachs quivering inside, but stood on the porch watching curiously. They were eager to see if the snake would get caught.

Though the men approached the snake cautiously they appeared to be running across from one area of the park to another with their sticks in hand as they attempted to catch the snake. The snake kept wriggling away from them, shooting fast in a straight line, hissing at them every time it was touched, causing the men to jump back. It was really trying their patience. It seemed as if the men were just running around in circles and as if they had been trying to catch the snake for a lifetime. They became tired and breathless. Just as it seemed they would never catch the snake; it became tangled in the wire fence surrounding the park. It struggled very hard to wiggle its way out, but it could not escape. Then with a swing of a cleaver, one of the men sliced the snake's head off. This made Summaiya and her friend cringe sending shivers up their spines; covering their mouths with their hands in disgust. Poison drizzled off the snake onto the ground, drip... drip... The hired help were then summoned to clean the area thoroughly and make sure that no traces of poison were left.

A sense of relief encompassed the families, now the park was safe and the snake was dead. Yet Summaiya and her friend couldn't help but feel a little sad at the snake's fate. However, worse was to come as her father ordered the snake to be washed and prepared for a barbecue. So, later that evening the snake was cooked over a fire. As it sizzled, it smelled like burning rubber. The men who had caught it, each ate a piece of the snake. The slightest thought of eating it made the women's stomachs churn, even though the men insisted it had a very moist texture. Summaiya wanted to vomit. Her mother complained to her father, telling him that they should have thrown it into the bin. Her father just laughed saying that it was harmless and edible. However, soon after dinner, the garden filled with hysterical laughter as everyone reflected upon what had happened during the course of the day.

Collated by Rehana Makkan

The Bantoue Ceremony

(Kalomba Kanda)

I used to live in the Catholic Missionary village of Ndekesha situated one hundred and twenty kilometres from Kananga in the province of Kasai, the centre of the Democratic Republic of Congo. It was founded by the Belgian Catholic missionaries at the beginning of the 1900s. The area consists of bushy terrain with trees, but not like in the equatorial forests. This province is known for being rich in diamonds and it is a province where the inhabitants follow the traditional rules handed down from generation to generation. The village of Ndekesha is very rural. There aren't any proper roads like here in the UK, just dirt tracks. There are no cars, though maybe an occasional coach will turn up from time to time for people who want to visit bigger towns or other villages. The weather is very tropical, very hot with a dry season and a wet season.

Originally, within every village in the province, there was a tribe and every tribe had a chief. When the Missionary was set up, people from the neighbouring villages began to move into Ndekesha because they had heard about the hospital and schools that the Missionary was building. These people wanted work, access to education for their children and better health care. So the village expanded with an influx of people from different tribes each comprised of their own families or bloodlines. The chief of each tribe remained in their original village, but had a representative in Ndekesha who would contact them if there was an important meeting to attend. Apart from this, they all basically had the same beliefs. They worshipped various gods and had statues of them, such as lions. However, sometimes people were confused about who to worship because of the traditions handed down from generation to generation and the presence of the Christian church. Some were Catholic, some were Protestant. The Missionary had two convents, one for the Fathers and one for the Sisters of Charity.

I invite you to read my story with care and attention as it is a true story that I personally experienced at the beginning of the eighties when I was only about ten years old. I am from the Bantoue tribe, the original and main tribe in the village of Ndekesha. I lived in a mud brick house with four rooms all on one level. The cooking was always done outside. There was no electricity so we used oil lamps. There was no running water, not even a well. Water was collected from the forest at its source, although some inhabitants were able to collect water when it rained on their metal roof. Life was quite basic and simple.

I remember it was the wet season, one afternoon as I sat with my family. The rain was crashing down hard on the corrugated metal roof. Everyone in the village was taking shelter inside, resting on the rural wooden furniture and cushions. As if determined to find a way through the metal, the rain summoned an accomplice. Hard balls of sleet attempted to bash their way through the roof, pounding our ears for some time. Then, as if frustrated and angry, the rain called upon its big brothers, whip-lashing lightning and ear-cracking thunder. Perhaps someone had angered one of the gods or had dabbled in witchcraft. From outside, I heard the faint velvet screaming of human voices in the background. There was some kind of commotion. I walked onto the covered terrace. Under the darkened sky and drenching rain, villagers were gathered around a spot on the ground with deep concern. A wailing of voices ensued. The thunder had stopped; someone had paid for nature's anger. A small body was lifted amongst a group of villagers and carried towards the Missionary hospital four hundred metres away. Word filtered through from one of the other villagers that it was Bilonda. She was the eight-year-old daughter belonging to the second wife of the government representative in the village. She was a very pretty girl, a fairer black than the rest of us. Bilonda had been struck by lightning whilst playing outside her house during the thunderstorm. She lived quite near to me. We used to play together sometimes as I was a close friend of her elder brother.

Like the dark clouds, a sombre mood had descended upon the village as we awaited news from the hospital. I knew in my heart it was not good news, when some of her relatives drifted back from the hospital in tears. The doctors had tried to resuscitate her, but had failed. I was numbed by the temporality and mortality of life, the random blow nature dealt to such youth, beauty and vibrancy. Now there was no angry storm or battering icy hail, just a calm light rain as Bilonda's body was carried to her house by the rest of the family. It was as though her body had consumed the rage of the storm. This day was the beginning of a three day mourning period. Bilonda was shortly laid upon a bed on the terrace of her house, so that everyone in the village could pay their respects. Many people began to arrive there, crying rivers of tears. Her mother was distraught, haggard, not dressed properly, with her wiry hair all straggled. She did not care how she looked, nothing mattered anymore.

Even the next day people kept arriving so the family left Bilonda's body on the terrace. I saw her on this second day of mourning. It was a fine day. She lay in an open coffin, covered in a white sheet, except for her head. A bandage had been tied around her open mouth to prevent flies and insects entering. All the women of the family were sat around her head. The men were sat further away from the feet of her body. According to tradition, during this mourning period, Bilonda's mother could neither drink nor eat in order to express her love for her daughter that had left this world forever. Tears streamed down the cheeks of her brothers. Everybody began to sing traditional heart wrenching songs of mourning, wringing out their anger with specific outpourings of emotion where villagers cried out against the perpetrator 'Bilonda, because you are leaving us, do not spare the person that did this to you!' then the singing resumed. There was a variety of songs, some directed at the perpetrator, some to honour Bilonda. Everyone sang what they wanted, crying out and creating a discorded harmony with a steady clap of their hands. The sadness was present in everyone's face and in each note of their voice.

The burial usually takes place on the third day, but in this case the body had begun to smell, so it was taken to the cemetery on the second day for burial. After the burial, everyone went back to the place of mourning before going home. That evening a group of singers organised themselves with traditional instruments, including the tam-tam[1], empty bottles and tonal wooden sticks. They sang, danced and played music to lift the spirits of the grieving family affected by this tragedy, to make them forget, to make them laugh. There was a mixture of songs, the slower songs were Christian. Villagers came forward and sang their own chosen impromptu song with no connection to death. I left as other people did when I became tired, though the singing carried on long into the night.

During the evening of the third day, a celebration was organised to thank the people who had attended and mourned for Bilonda and to officially close the three day mourning period. There was lots of food, such as pork, goat, beef, and wine to drink. Some people also brought their own food to share. After this mourning period, villagers could then choose their own moment to privately console the family.

Everyone shared the sadness that had enveloped the community. They asked themselves why this tragedy had occurred. A few days later some wise people, young and old, were discussing Bilonda's death. They all blamed themselves and could not trust each other. Some believed the tragedy had descended upon the village from afar. Some believed it was a

1 Tom tom drum.

traitor from amongst the tribal representatives, or maybe from a neighbouring village unhappy with the authority Bilonda's father possessed as a government official, for he was also the representative for all the surrounding villages. This meant there had to be a traitor amongst our own village, because in order for someone to carry out evil from another tribe, they had to have a pact with someone from within our own tribe to provide them with authorisation. Some people thought Bilonda's father was abusing his authority as he was applying the law of the government which sometimes conflicted with the way people were used to living their lives as part of the culture. Therefore Bilonda's father made a decision to organise a traditional ceremony aimed at protecting the inhabitants of Ndekesha and the neighbouring villages. Through the representatives of the tribes that had moved into the village he summoned all the chiefs together from the surrounding villages to discuss how they could prevent such tragedies occurring again and to unite everyone through a protection ceremony.

The ceremony began at nine o'clock on a Friday morning. A traditional folklore group played non-stop music attracting more and more villagers to gather round. Everybody from the neighbouring villages congregated at the crossroads in Ndekesha. By about ten o'clock all the chiefs from the neighbouring villages were assembled, dressed in their traditional clothes, leopard skins, with birds' beaks strung around their necks and headdresses made from animal skins. A few minutes later, Bilonda's father arrived and the ceremony began.

At the centre of the crossroads, a group of men dug a hole in the ground. A live sheep, a live dog and a leopard skin were lowered into the hole. The eldest chief shovelled some sand into the hole to initiate the burial. The rest of the hole was then filled in by villagers. Once these animals were buried, the chiefs from every village held hands around the freshly filled hole. They spoke in turn, in front of the assembled villagers and swore an allegiance to work together, that there would be no treason and no back stabbing of each other. Everyone then began singing, shouting and dancing, rejoicing and expressing relief that the village could now move on with a sense of protection from tragedies such as the one that took Bilonda away from us.

This particular ceremony is linked to the ceremonies of the distant past narrated to us by the elders of the village. As children, we learned about the burial of a king where strong healthy men and a virgin bride were chosen to be buried alive to accompany him on his journey, carry out their duties and help protect him in the afterlife.

In the light of this story, I can say that nowadays there is a conflict between the old and young generations about traditional beliefs. Where this story is concerned, the traditional belief is that we are subject to a number of unseen agents and forces. Unlike in the West, accidents are virtually unheard of and there is always a cause behind any misfortune. In many indigenous societies, for example, a death is always followed by an inquest where the cause of death and the identity of the killer are determined. Measures are then taken against the alleged miscreant, even when someone dies of disease in bed at an advanced age. Some still believe traditional practices have a great impact on the village. Some say the ceremonies no longer have any effect because tragedies strike in one way or another regardless of what people do. The younger generations are beginning to think more about things and are making informed decisions due to the mixing of cultures from towns and cities. Everything is becoming more modernised and education is teaching concepts that sometimes contradict traditional culture. The state will now not allow certain practices especially relating to any kind of sacrificial offerings. Now, only the first wife of a husband is recognised by the state, whereas other wives are not recognised by the state, but are still recognised by the village.

This childhood story is very significant to me and has had a great impact upon my life. It was the first time I experienced the death of someone I had known and all the traditions associated with it. It is strange to think back and reflect upon the atmosphere and imagery from the village at that time, especially the living animals being sacrificed. When my children grow up, I shall narrate this story to them so they know about the traditions attached to Ndekesha and how we have arrived at who and where we are today in the United Kingdom.

Collated by Michael Carroll

Honey Bee

(Virginia)

My name is Virginia and I was born on 13ᵗʰ June 1964 in the city of Cebu on the beautiful islands of the Philippines. I have two brothers and one sister, but my father died when I was eleven years old. My father and mother had a small business in the city of Cebu, where we lived. After the death of my father, my mother could no longer afford to keep running the business and look after us at the same time. So I moved with my brothers and sisters to a small village to live with our grandparents. We enjoyed this very much because our grandparents lived on a farm. However, the house didn't have any running water so we would often have to gather together to fetch drinking water from a well about one kilometre away from the house.

I always headed off early to school with my two cousins. On our way we used to pass an old abandoned farm where some wild animals lived, including some smelly pigs. We had to listen very carefully around the farm as sometimes there were hissing snakes slithering around in the grass. They gave us a fright on more than one occasion. Our favourite pastime on the farm was picking the berries from the wild brambles. They tasted quite like plums, very juicy and sweet. Passing the farm was a great distraction, we often spent time chatting and playing there with friends. Sometimes we climbed the coconut or mango trees, even though we had been warned not to, but the warning just made us want to climb them even more.

There was one particular tree that I was constantly told not to climb by various members of my family. It grew on a field near the house. It was my favourite tree, the grapefruit tree. One day whilst I was out playing, despite the voices of my grandmother, uncles and aunties echoing in the recesses of my mind, I could not resist the temptation to find out why I should not climb the grapefruit tree. Besides, it looked easy enough to climb and its branches seemed sturdy. So, off I went. I discovered a winding part of the root, stemming from the base of the tree, leading into the ground. This provided a great platform to place my first foot. Then I was able to stretch an arm up to the first branch. I put my hands around the dry bark of the branch and scrambled my feet up the trunk until they found a natural recess, where I could push myself further up the tree and grab another branch. I was then able to pull myself up and actually sit on the first branch. It was easy! I wedged myself in between this and the trunk of the tree. I sat there for a short while, enjoying my little tree house, adorned with green leaves and small planets of grapefruit. It was pleasant viewing life from this level, spying from within my shelter. I felt content and secluded as I looked across the way, towards my house.

I decided to be bold and venture towards the top of the tree. Now there were a lot more branches to grab hold of for support, but as I clambered higher up, the branches were thinner and things started to get a little shaky, including my legs. I noticed a curiously shaped object, neatly camouflaged within the tree. 'Wow!' I thought; 'I bet this is a hive'. I stretched over, eager to see if there was any honey inside. I cautiously began to move my hand into this strange object, then felt around inside. I could feel a gooey substance on my fingers and the palm of my hand. Sure enough, when I withdrew my hand, there was my golden syrupy prize. Mmmmm, I began to lick it off my fingers, savouring every moment. The honey was sticky, but deliciously sweet. I was so pleased with myself and revelled in my own secret discovery. I inserted my hand into the hive for some more, what a treat! Just then, a small dark cloud in the sky caught the corner of my eye. I turned to see what it was. It appeared to be travelling towards me. I saw another one. They seemed to be appearing from every direction, drawing closer and closer, growing bigger and bigger. They were heading right towards me. Oh no!

Suddenly I froze. They were swarms of bees! What was I going to do? There were so many angry bees, there wasn't anything I could do, except panic and scream as loud as I could!

I scrambled down the tree as fast as I could with my honeyed hands rasping against the bark like a striking match. I had to make a dash for home, but the raging bees began to chase me. I let out a big scream, with fear driving my legs like a steam engine. I could hear the buzzing becoming louder and louder as the bees began to catch up behind me. I couldn't run any faster, I couldn't scream any louder. The big, buzzing blanket of stinging bees engulfed me. They crawled in my ears, around my eyes, stinging me all over my face, legs and arms. I waved my arms around in a drunken daze as they clung to me, exacting their revenge. I was hysterical, screaming and crying, then I heard the voice of my uncle shouting. He and the rest of the family were running towards me, but by now most of the bees had already stung me and were beginning to drift away.

After my family had seen what had happened, they all helped to carry me home. My skin started to swell up all over my body. My face was so swollen that I could not open my eyes. My whole body felt like a sore balloon. Meanwhile, my grandmother had mixed together some herbs in a potion. Every so often she applied the potion to my swelling to relieve the pain.

I stayed in bed for the first three days because it hurt to move and I still could not open my eyes. Slowly, with the aid of my grandmother's remedy, the swelling began to decrease. Soon, I was up and about again. Before too long I was playing outside, but found myself constantly keeping a look out for bees and I certainly wasn't going to climb the grapefruit tree again. Now I knew why I had been warned about climbing the tree. I will never forget this moment in my childhood, whilst growing up in Cebu.

Now, I am living in the Deane area of Bolton, married with two daughters after meeting my English husband whilst working at a hotel in Cebu. First of all I didn't like it here because of the cold and things were so different. However, I have now adjusted to life here and like it very much.

Collated by Nyla Anwar and Nusrat Rafique

Street Life

(Jayne Hargreaves)

[Setting: Manchester Palace Theatre, Oxford Road. It is evening just after seven thirty. Doors are just opening inside the theatre as the final bell announces that the evening's performance is about to start. A few stragglers are showing their tickets and a well dressed couple is hurrying to make the beginning of the show. At the bottom of the steps in front of the theatre to the left stands a girl holding copies of the Big Issue in each hand. Apart from an occasional response to the front of house staff she is silent. Stretched on a blanket to her right sleeps a large brown dog. The doorman comes down the steps to ask her if she would like a coffee. She nods and thanks him, her eyes following him into the theatre. When the doors close behind him she glances to her right and sits down on the blanket beside the dog. She feeds the magazines into a clear plastic bag and slaps them down on the ground to her left. She sighs heavily].

[*To dog*] Crap night tonight darling. We've only sold two and one o' them was a regular. I knew this show would be bloody useless, bloody Guys and Dolls! Oh well, I suppose they didn't put us 'ere. They're probably sick of havin' Big Issues shoved in their faces day after day. Feel they don't want to know when they are on a night out. Not a bit like the opera crowd. Sell out every time there's ballet or opera on here. Shame I've never got enough money to buy loads o' copies, I'd be back on my feet in no time. Or if I could get another daytime pitch to get the money up before the Issue office shuts. I miss Marks; miss the regulars. Just getting to know people, when they blew the bloody place up. What a day that was eh? Miracle no one was killed. Bloody fools trying to get back into town every time the policemen's backs were turned. As if it's normal to have cops everywhere, evacuating the city centre. I mean, I've seen Marks during the usual bomb scares. The security just push 'em all outside and there they stand like a flock of lost sheep, waiting for the all clear so's they can get back in and shop till they drop. But not that day.... Policemen everywhere, rounding up all the city shoppers. 'Out of town!' they shouted and out of town they meant! Not 'See if you can wander down a side street back towards the town and find an open shop!' Or even 'Why not stray in that direction to see if you can find your car'. Bloody fools. Police did a good job that day. It really was a surprise nobody was killed. Too stupid to live, half of 'em, or perhaps tired o' life. Good job I'm not. Wouldn't last five minutes out 'ere if I was. Nope, you've just gotta fight to survive, fight for yer pitch, fight for a brew at the soup van, keep yer eyes on yer stuff at all times and fight the Tetley Bittermen falling out of the pubs at the end of the night. That's what I call them, after the advert. 'Tetley Bittermen, you can't beat 'em' it used to say. 'cept with a big stick that is... Or a big dog and a dog lead. That's what I've found anyway. Had to jump in just the other week. Tetley Bitterthug would've killed the guy if I hadn't. Bit of a weirdo, the bloke, like. Looked like a Goth, long black hair and a top hat. Comes past me every week, Thursday nights, on his way to some Goth night. Always tips his hat to me as 'e goes past. Never given me a penny like, but at least he's polite. At least he can 'see' me, so I always smile. Not that I like him that much, but manners cost nowt, so I smile to acknowledge him. He doesn't always see me on his way 'ome. He's usually a bit worse for wear by then. He was on his way 'ome the other week, reeling down the road towards me, when I heard a cry from behind 'im. 'Oiy! Top 'at!' and a Tetley Bitterman came pounding up the pavement behind him. Massive bloke 'e was, like a giant Buster Bloodvessel. Top 'at didn't stand a chance. Doubt he even knew who or what 'ad hit him first. Just came thudding up from behind and decked him. But the thing was... he didn't stop... just kept on punching and punching. I thought Christ 'e's gonna kill 'im. And all the clubbers, the homeowners, the home goers, big men some of 'em, just looked on and kept walking. So what could I do? I tried to reason with 'im first. 'Here y'are mate, you're gonna get nicked for GBH if yer don't stop. You'd best do one before the Old Bill turn up'. But he just turned on me, snarling, spoilin' for a fight he was. So Jody started screaming, tried to bite him. So I grabbed her collar. But he just lunged at me. So I let 'er go and slapped him in the face with her chain lead. That slowed him up all right and I used that time to get help from a couple of passin' students. Buster started backin' off then, back in the direction he'd come from. And one of the students phoned an ambulance. Top 'at was in a bad way all right. Clean unconscious. But at least he wasn't dead. Came past me last week and gave me a fiver, thanked me for savin' his skin. That's all right, I said, it's what bein' human's all about. He smiled and tipped his hat.

Lotsa Tetley Bittermen at weekends. Jody 'ates them, she does. 'Can I stroke your dog, luv?' they ask, stumblin' up, fallin' into us. 'Only if I hold its mouth shut', I tell them. Can't blame her really. And I don't, not a bit. Watches me back she does, and me gear too, if I go inside somewhere to use the loo. That's if they let me in of course. Snobs some of them, not like this lot in 'ere. Which is odd really, you wouldn't think they'd like 'avin' me outside, 'specially when the opera's on. But they're great, bring me coffee every night after the show's started. They've even shooed other Issue sellers away for me, when I've been sat 'ere beggin. 'smy pitch and just cause I can't afford the Issues why should I lose it? It's nice to be liked. But I don't pester people, you see and I watch out for dippers[1]. One of 'em called me a grass, just 'cause I warned this lady that he was tryin' to steal her purse. 'Who you callin' a grass?' I asked him. 'A grass informs the police on somebody, I'm just protecting me own interests. And I'm not bein' blamed for sommat you've done, just 'cos I'm still sat 'ere wi' nowt while you're long gone up the road wi' someone else's money in yer pocket. Now bugger off!' And 'e did.

Oh no! Rain! That's all we need! Stuck under 'ere 'til it stops.

1 Pick pockets.

Can't go out there and risk being wet all night. Good job I'm getting a brew. 'Thanks Daniel'. I'd better keep an eye open f' t' begging squad while I've a cup in me 'and. Don't need that tonight. Plain clothes they have, proper job it is. It's all they do all day, nickin' beggars. But I'm not even 'asslin' anyone and me cup's still got coffee in it, I protest. 'Come on Jayne! You know the rules' they tell me. 'Placing yourself in a thoroughfare in order to collect moneys or alms, that's alms with an L not an R'. They always say that, like they think it's funny or something. It might be if I only had one arm. 'You're in contravention of section 47 of the 1842 Vagrancy Act', they tell me. 'Eighteen hundred? You're so out of date!' I always say. Something like it anyway. Trouble is, you get an A3 ban, until the date you're up in court for the beggin' charge. It means you can't come near the town, no soup runs, no Issue office, no nowt. Course, I always break it, then they nick you for breach of bail conditions, so I get a bed for th' night. Plus when I'm up in court the next morning, they always bring the begging charge forward, so then I'm not banned anymore either, pisses the beggin' squad off no end. Bit tough on me dog though. If I can't get anyone to take her, she has to go to the pound. Which she hates and which is why I'm watching out for 'em really.

Lots of people have a go at me for havin' a dog. Say it's cruel. Should have seen her when I stole her, all covered in mud, and grease, and engine oil she was. Thought she was black, not brown, six feet of chain. Now, that's cruel. As far as she's concerned, she's much better off, thinks the sun shines out of my arse she does. And it's not like I was homeless when I took her, as if I thought 'I know, I'm homeless, let's get a dog! And just to make things harder, I'll get a big one that doesn't like people and loses me money all the time'. 'snot her fault though. She just doesn't trust people. Neither do I. As long as they leave her alone, she's all right, quiet as a mouse. But there's always one. Some dog expert who wants to wake her up and stroke her. I'm sure they think I superglue her to the floor so she has to stay by me. Look! No strings!

I used to think no one who sat out in the rain could possibly be homeless. If you can't get dry afterwards, then don't get wet. Makes perfect sense to me. And then I met Mad Lee. Shut in a cupboard for years, Lee was, and yer can tell 'e's not lying. I don't think 'e knows it's raining, never seems to care how wet he is, until it's time to sleep. Then it's 'Auntie Jayne! Me beddin's all wet!' And I give him one of my blankets. After all, I've got me dog t' keep me warm... 'How can you afford to keep a dog when you're homeless?' How can I not?

Collated by Michael Carroll

Voodoo Auntie

(Anonymous)

I'm from a Hindu family and have lived in a normal terraced house in Bolton since 1985. Though my son has now grown up, I remember when he attended Smithill's school around 1989. There was one particular incident that sticks in my mind from when he was eleven years old. He was going to school as usual, passing the park, behind our house, when he glanced over at a park bench and noticed a black sackcloth image sitting there resting on it. He tried to ignore it, but as he walked on, he noticed the top of the sack turning and following the direction of his walk. He became really scared, he could not make out whether it was a man, a woman or even a human being. He began to increase the pace of his footsteps and kept on looking back, but the image was still there looking at him. Manesh was afraid the image might start following him and was confused wondering whether it was real or just a figment of his imagination. His heart was racing, he felt sick inside as if he had caught a fever and rushed past the park. As he approached nearer to school, he managed to calm himself down. Once he met some of his friends there, it took his mind off the whole experience.

Later, on his way back from school, he wanted to make sure that what he had seen in the morning had just been an illusion. So he went home the same way, passing by the park, but was shocked to see the image of the black sackcloth sitting there again. He was speechless and trembled like a leaf, rushing towards home. He still kept his feelings to himself, hoping that he would never see it again. However, this was just wishful thinking as the next day he encountered the same experience only serving to cement in his mind the reality of the image. Whilst in school this played increasingly more and more upon his imagination, causing him to worry and even think he was beginning to lose his mind. He could not pay attention in class at all. He needed to talk about what he had seen, but felt he could not trust anyone, fearing friends would just laugh at him or maybe think it was just a joke. He could not even tell me, his mum, his dad or his little brother. Throughout that day Manesh could not eat anything such was the sick feeling of anxiety running though his body.

The next morning Manesh could not get up from his bed. He was burning with fever, soaking with sweat and as pale as a ghost, so he did not go to school. He completely lost his appetite. I assumed Manesh was suffering from flu or had picked up a virus from school like kids do. He murmured 'I don't want to go to school, don't send me to school again'. I wondered why he was saying this and asked him what was wrong. Maybe someone had been nasty to him, maybe he was being bullied or even one of the teachers was being hard on him. Manesh then began to explain to me all about the image he had seen. I was concerned that a stranger might be stalking my son. That night Manesh had nightmares of the image chasing him, he woke up screaming 'Go away! Go away!' and yelled 'Mum he's following me! Help me!' Upon hearing this I rushed into his room anxiously concerned. I shook him, asking 'What's the matter beta?'[1] Shaking his head vigorously, with his eyes closed tightly he shouted 'Go away! Go away!' Then I raised his head and placed it on my lap, running my fingers through his hair, trying to calm him down, saying 'It's ok beta, it's ok, don't worry Mummy is here'. Slowly he opened his eyes and hugged me tightly, relieved he was just dreaming.

Manesh's nightmares continued, he was even too scared to enter the sitting room, telling me that the black sackcloth was sitting on the settee. He had lost interest in everything, he did not watch television, listen to music or go out to play in the park with his friends. I tried to take him to the doctors, but he was never ready to come along with me. He was so rude and

---

1 Son.

loud, he kept on shouting at me, being vicious and violent, throwing objects at me, kicking and being aggressive. I was too scared to call the doctor to come and see Manesh at home because of how he might react to a stranger. All I could do was to give him paracetemol syrup. Soon letters began to arrive from school asking why Manesh was not attending. Manesh had a high temperature for three weeks. Once his temperature had cooled down I decided it was best for him to go back to school. However, I knew he was still scared about leaving the house, so I rang a neighbour of ours called Shan and asked him to send his son round each morning to accompany Manesh to school. Of course, when Manesh walked to school with his friend he no longer saw the dark sackcloth image in the park, but as soon as Manesh tried to go out on his own again, the image appeared. He had to live with the idea that the sackcloth would always appear whenever he went out alone. All the while, I never revealed any of this to my husband, if ever he asked what was the matter with Manesh, I just said that he had a fever.

My husband and I used to work in a textile factory in Swan Lane. Shan, whom I had known for about a year, worked there as well. I was closer to his wife as a friend. We used to take our children to the park together. Because Manesh was worrying me so much, I decided to confide my concerns to Shan. As a friend I asked him for his advice. Imagine how I felt when, with a sheepish look on his face, he then began to tell me that he had performed black magic on Manesh because he liked him very much. I could not believe what I was hearing and the anger began to build up inside me. 'Why my son?' I cried. 'Why do this to him? Do you not know what he is going through? I've just confided all this to you thinking you are a family friend and now I find out it is actually you behind all this harm'. Shan began to explain that he liked Manesh more than his own son because he was more intelligent, diligent in his studies and looked cool with his slicked back hair style. He wished he was his own son and wanted to own him. Because there was no possibility of this, he became jealous and could only think of hurting him. I asked him how and where he carried out this black magic. Shan could only helplessly apologise, explaining that he could not reveal anything as his power of creating spells would be taken away by God. If he revealed the spells to anybody, then others might learn them and start misusing the power, despite himself misusing it. I took a little solace from his guilt. As he had caused so much distress, he began to tell me about a remedy that would cure Manesh. He advised me to take salt and water in a glass and rotate the glass over his head seven times to get rid of the spell.

Later that evening whilst Manesh was sat up in bed before going to sleep, I followed Shan's instructions. Manesh started screaming and banging his head against the headboard. I could only attempt to hold him tightly, trying to calm him down in vain. I rushed straight to Shan's house a few doors away. He advised me to put dry salt only in a bowl and keep it under the bed when Manesh slept. I rotated the bowl over his head seven times chanting the mantra 'Sai Ram' then put the bowl under his bed. I began to hear noises from downstairs, so I rushed down to check where they were coming from. All the rooms looked fine. However, I could hear thudding noises coming from the storeroom. I started shaking, wondering if there were thieves in there. My heart was pounding as I hesitated to open the door. I started chanting the Sai Ram mantra again as I slowly pulled open the door. My eyes stared wide open in shock, I felt as if I was having a heart attack. Rice, chilli pepper, lentils, oil, flour, spices were crashing down to the floor of their own accord. I cried and panicked. I realised that the evil spirit must have left Manesh's body after I chanted the mantras, then escaped to the store room. I opened all of the windows and patio doors hoping that it might escape and leave the house. Bottles were opened, jars were opened, lids off tins were lying on the floor. I threw them all away, destroyed them all because I was very superstitious about what had happened.

One hour later Manesh became calm and he dozed off. When he woke in the morning too, he appeared calm. I recollected that my mother in Kenya used to burn some ingredients on a piece of paper to check if a person was under a spell or not. If a strong smell emanated after burning the ingredients, this signalled that there was no spell. If there was no smell then the spell existed. So to check if the spell had disappeared I took five tablespoons of red chilli powder; one tablespoon of oil; one tablespoon of salt; and a lock of Manesh's hair. All of this was burned on a piece of paper. Much to my delight, a strong pungent smell wafted through the air. I coughed as it entered my nostrils and throat, but sighed with relief that the spell had vanished.

Manesh behaved normally after that whereas before he was very vicious and restless. He became calmer and calmer day by day and began to settle in once again to his daily routine, eating meals and watching television, agreeing to go out with me for a walk. He did not recover fully until three months later. I could no longer look Shan in the eyes without a feeling of hatred and tried to avoid him. However, I became afraid that if I broke the friendship, he would hurt us again some other way. So we carried on being friends for the next two years until he moved house.

Collated by Monica Ballani

The Blundering of the Lover Boy

(Kennedy Mupomba)

With a road running before it, the bottle store, just like a UK off-licence, except that it only sold alcohol and soft drinks, was quite a hive of activity as the boozers took swigs from beer bottles outside in the evening sun. It was a Friday leading into the weekend and it seemed the affluent males of Magunje Growth Point[1] in Zimbabwe were all there, with ladies of the night in attendance. Mbigo had boarded a bus to get to the growth point, ten kilometres from the school where he taught and lived in staff accommodation. It was illegal to drink alcohol outside the bottle store and despite numerous police raids on the patrons, a barbecue fire was blazing at the end of the building to complement the drinking, with the aroma of roast beef appealing to Mbigo's nostrils. The boozers had bought beef from the butchery, doing brisk business, across the road. The barbecue was the idea of the bottle store proprietor who knew that cold beer and roast meat go hand in hand, though he was careful not to make any seating provision for his customers, otherwise he would be arrested for aiding and abetting the illegal drinkers. In any event, the boozers preferred to drink whilst standing, therefore gaining an advantage if they had to scarper, from a standing rather than sitting position, should the police arrive. Such are the ordinary sights at Zimbabwean growth points where the government thought such centres would bring services nearer to the rural folk, so they would not have to travel to the major towns.

Standing outside the bottle store, the taste of Mbigo's favourite Castle Lager beer was forgotten as his thoughts were elsewhere, thinking of the greater and bigger things set for that night with his girlfriend. He failed to take note of the

---

1 A location built far from towns in a rural area where services such as banks, the post office, chain stores, government services (birth & death, education offices etc) are situated. The plan was to bring the services to the rural community, to create employment, stop the drift to towns for jobs, bringing the town to the doorstep of the locals.

young, hour glass figured prostitute in a tight mini skirt leering at him. Even a recent pin-up of the model Jordan in the bottle store had not caused his thoughts to wander off, or the topical issue of Zimbabwean footballers who had dissolved into the UK after playing in a football match, rather than returning home. Instead, he reflected upon a cherished moment three months ago, when on a bus from the capital city, Harare, he had sat next to a beautiful girl named Mazvita[2]. Engaging her in conversation, one thing led to another culminating in both of them falling in love. Here he was now at the growth point, a kilometre away from her village. Time had dragged slowly for him that week during his teaching job. Now, he intended to throw caution to the wind, but was biding his time till darkness, for what they had planned was against their custom. Mbigo could lose limbs if he was found to be behaving in a clandestine manner with Mazvita, by any of her kinsmen. The customary laws dictated that he should openly approach her aunt, make his case before her and if she was impressed, she would then make contact with Mazvita's father to arrange a marriage. Before that, there could be no talk of sneaking into her bed. Despite her initial reluctance, Mbigo could not stop imagining his arms holding the tall, light-skinned Mazvita upon whom the gods had bestowed a beautiful slim figure. Her character was laudable and being softly spoken made Mbigo feel weak at the knees.

Sporting a black double breasted jacket, a white shirt, a good quality black pair of trousers and a pair of Hush Puppies, Mbigo felt on top of the world. For a bachelor of thirty-five years old, of short stature, dark skinned, with a bald head and nothing to write home about his face, his expensive attire compensated for his ordinary looks. The plan was simple, come darkness he was to sneak into Mazvita's hut and the world would be theirs. She had previously pointed out her hut

2 Meaning 'Thank you'.

in daylight, asking Mbigo to meet her there, but to be careful as it was next to her parent's hut. All the huts were a natural brown colour of mud. They contained only one bedroom, were rectangular in shape, with one door, a small windowpane and a thatched roof.

Sharing a mug of recently commercialised traditional beer with his friend in a beer hall, a hundred metres from the bottle store was Mazvita's father. Not boasting of any great height, bald headed and looking like one of the ordinary village folk, he drank with his old friend in silence, for all their stories had been told and exhausted. The beer hall specialised in traditional beer and was frequented by the elderly and the not so well to do younger people. At least it had walls surrounding it, therefore prying eyes could not see the poor from the public road and because it was a lawful place to drink, everyone had a seat. His loving, dutiful wife of more than forty years had of late been nagging him about his daily drinking bouts and longed more for his company. Both were around sixty years of age. At least she had company in the form of their lovely daughter, Mazvita, who took after her. Cultural tradition had been drummed into Mazvita from childhood and now that she had grown to seventeen years of age, she was in her prime time of life to get married. With word abound of her impeccable reputation, it was certain she would be snapped up soon. This her father hoped for, as he wiped his bald head, taking another swig of the opaque beer made from maize, yeast and water. It contained an unpleasant smell and also caused tooth decay. No wonder his wife was not amused with his drinking habits.

Having had one too many, as he had been drinking from four in the afternoon until about ten at night, Mbigo began to make way towards his girlfriend's residence. He had taken fifteen pints of the holy waters that day, not that it was such a great feat, as many were known to knock back a crate and still walk in a straight line. He could imagine himself already, with

Mazvita in his arms, just like the last time she had visited his school when he wanted her more than ever. This motivated him to quicken his pace towards her residence. Drawing upon the night as his cover, Mbigo attempted to walk upon the path, but kept stumbling onto the verge. Staggering from one side to the other, he nonetheless entered the perimeter of the homestead. Stopping to assess the dwellings, he was satisfied, as no eerie sounds emanated from his target, except noisy crickets calling to each other in the surrounding bush. There were no lights showing, which was a good omen. This meant his lover had disengaged herself from her mother and had retired to wait for him in her own hut. Barely able to distinguish between the dwellings due to the darkness, Mbigo prowled like a lion and stealthily moved towards Mazvita's place. So intent and anxious was he to claim his prize, Mbigo stumbled into a metal drum which began to roll and clatter towards the hut. Taking ages to grind to a halt, the drum's momentum finally faded, with Mbigo, having lost his balance, lying on the ground, surveying the situation. A dog began to bark from a neighbouring hut and worried by the prospect of more dogs joining in, Mbigo rose and rushed to Mazvita's door. Pushing the unlocked door open he quietly felt around for Mazvita's bed in the dark room. Hastily removing his clothing, he slipped under the blankets and commenced to caress the warm body within it. Indeed Mbigo was so knowledgeable in erotic matters, no sooner than he had started, she responded and he quickly gave her a French kiss. Startled by this she stopped him in his tracks, awakening from her slumber. Despite the darkness she could feel Mbigo's bald head, but a sixth sense told her that something was wrong. She screamed her lungs out, piercing the tranquil night! It was Mazvita's sixty-year-old mother! Mbigo had entered the wrong hut.

Sobering up instantly, Mbigo jumped from the bed and made off in his birthday suit. Following the alarm raised by Mazvita's mother, Mazvita herself rushed to her mother's aide crashing head on with her boyfriend as he dashed out of the hut. Her father, who was on his way home, heard the shrieks from his wife and quickened his pace. Mazvita quickly realised what had happened. Feeling quite shocked and embarrassed, she entered her mother's hut, where she was still wailing the place down. In the meantime Mbigo made his escape good by melting into the pitch black night. Neighbours rushing to the homestead to offer help were astonished to find an expensive set of clothing in the elderly woman's bedroom. With no harm having visited the woman, the villagers became engrossed in trying to identify the intruder by his clothing, whilst others thought of various punishments like cutting off his manhood. Mazvita was the only person who knew the owner of the clothing and she was not about to volunteer any information given the inherent consequences to her person. Meanwhile, lover boy, stark naked could not keep to the public roads as he headed a good ten kilometres towards home. Moving into the dense forest, thorns tearing into his flesh and often stumbling into pits, Mbigo made haste in putting distance between himself and the chasing angry mob, for looking back, he could see torch beams stirring the darkness, searching for their prey's footprints. However, Cupid saw him safely home that night.

Despite exhibiting Mbigo's garb in and around the village as well as the growth point, in an attempt to sniff out the assumed would be rapist, the bid was unfruitful for he lived too far away. It was not until a full month after his drunken blundering, when the various injuries incurred had healed, that Mbigo summoned the courage to visit his girlfriend. After receiving a chiding over his drinking habits from Mazvita, their love grew stronger and blossomed into marriage. The only catch was that Mbigo had to forego the brown bottle, nor was he the only one, as his father-in-law also threw in the towel and quitted drinking his opaque beer to be near his wife as much as possible.

Collated by Michael Carroll

Shah Ji

(Nusrat Rafique)

I was born in 1958; I have three sisters and one brother. I come from a long line of law abiding, upstanding citizens of the community. As we were landowners in Pakistan, we made a profitable living from our crops of wheat, barley, corn and lentils. My father worked hard all his life to provide for his family. We lived in a village called Mattu near Gujar Khan in Pakistan. Next to our home was my uncle Ibni's house and on the other side was my uncle Abdul's house, which was a bigger house with more rooms, because he was the eldest. The corn grew at the back of our house. In the front of all the houses was a huge area with trees and plants where we could play all day. Sometimes when it was Eid[1] we tied a rope onto a branch of one of the trees and made a swing. I remember only two types of weather. In the summer we used to have siestas when it was too hot to do anything. It got so hot you could not put your feet on the ground, as they would get burnt. During the monsoon season, when it rained, huge puddles appeared tempting my cousins and me to jump in them and splash each other. As soon as the rain dried up, we were able to catch frogs and beetles. Sometimes the rain lasted for days on end, even months, with only short breaks in between.

My grandfather was a journalist, my uncle was a policeman and my father was a farmer. My dad left his country, Pakistan, to fight for the British army when he was very young. This enabled him to get a visa pass to reside in England, one of only a few Pakistanis to obtain one at that time. When he left for England in 1965 I was a young girl of seven years old. My dad came back to Pakistan to visit us in 1968, but only stayed for

---

1 An Islamic holiday marking the end of Ramadan, the month of fasting. On the day of the celebration, a typical Muslim family gets up very early and attends special prayers held only for the occasion in big mosques, in large open areas, stadiums or arenas. The festivities and merriment start after the prayers with visits to the homes of friends and relatives and thanking the Creator for all blessings. Eid is a time to come together as a community and to renew friendship and family ties. This is a time for peace for all Muslims in the world to devote to prayers and mutual well-being.

three months before going back to England. Everyone else in our village thought we were very fortunate to have a father who travelled back and forth between two continents, but we were always very sad to see him go, especially my mother.

In England, my dad worked very hard in spinning and carpentry, but earned just a few shillings a day. With these few shillings he used to buy food, pay his rent and still managed to save some of his income. Every time he had saved up a few pounds, he sent it to his mother in Pakistan. Slowly he built his fortune by sending money home and encouraging members of his family to come to England so they could make a better living, as our country was poor. His own father had died when he was only two years old, but his mother remarried a cousin because she was still very young and it was not easy for her to bring children up on her own. My grandfather, or technically, step-grandfather, instilled the ethos of not squandering money, into my dad whilst he was very young. There was never a time when anyone went hungry in our family, but there were no luxuries either.

I arrived in England for the first time in 1977 to join my husband, who was my first cousin. We were married the year before and also had a little girl. In those days people were interrogated in great detail to see if they were sincere about why they wanted to settle in England. The experience always left me exhausted, anxious and terribly upset. It was very personal, but fortunately I received the visa and came to England with my daughter as soon as I could. My plane landed in England one evening at six o'clock. My first thought was 'Where am I?' It was so cold. My daughter and I were given a medical check-up, then we collected our luggage. I was very relieved when I finally saw my husband at the airport; he had come with a friend of his to collect us. We all had a cup of coffee, but it tasted horrible. To this day I dislike the taste of coffee. It wasn't until midnight, before we set off for our new home in Bolton, I was very tired and upset, feeling a sense of isolation.

In the beginning I did not like living here, I knew no one outside of the family, just my father, my husband and his friends. My life just consisted of looking after my daughter and doing all the housework. Gradually, I started to go out of the house and make new friends, then other members of our family began arriving in England and life became easier. I had a little boy in 1978. This time I had help from my mother and father to look after him. In 1980 we had to move to a bigger house because I was expecting another baby boy. After staying with my parents, my husband and I bought our own house in 1982 when I had a further baby boy.

My mum and dad always helped with the children, we were all happy. However, one day my four month old baby boy came down with a really bad fever. I was extremely worried about his condition. After a while he began to recover and I thought he was going to be fine, but after a few months had elapsed, he began to have fits so I had to take him to hospital. By this time he was one year old. To my utter shock and dismay, I was told my baby was blind. I could not believe it and became extremely depressed and very worried. I had no idea about what to do. Fortunately, my mother and father were there to help me pull through. My father supported me by doing chores such as the shopping and taking the children to the park.

Over time, I began to adjust and accept my son's condition. He started attending a special school where there were all sorts of disabled children. I could tell that even though these children were more severely handicapped, they were loved and wholly accepted by their families.

A short while after, for the first time since arriving in England, I travelled back to Pakistan to visit my in-laws, whilst the rest of my family stayed behind. However, in England my mother became very ill and she died in hospital, just as I was separated from her by thousands of miles. Her body was eventually sent to Pakistan with my brother. It was one of the most painful days of my life. I felt as though someone had ripped my heart out. I was left with a huge hole in my life, no mum anymore to listen to my problems or to console me. Up until then my mother had always been there to help me. So I turned to my father, thinking he would never let me down. He was always the rock in our lives. Now I have lost him too. He was loved and respected by all the people in our community. They always came to him for advice and help with anything they did not understand.

Whilst in England my father set up and ran the Muslim people's death committee. This organisation arranges everything to do with births, funerals and the wake. It even enables people to register newborn babies here and in Pakistan. Every person in each household over eighteen years of age pays fifteen pounds a year. This money pays for all the costs associated with a funeral, including the airfare to take the body to Pakistan, someone to accompany it, the announcement of the death in the paper to notify everyone, and the buffet. When one of our community members dies, the body is usually transported to Pakistan because we know that the graves there will never be disturbed and the deceased will rest in peace. Over here, once graves are over one hundred years old, they can be disturbed[2] by builders and developers. In Pakistan there is a greater sense of respect for the dead.

Anyone from our community in Bolton would tell you how my father helped them in some way or another. He was the pillar of the community and very generous with his time and money, as that was his nature. I know he will not be forgotten. I'd like to add that I'm very proud to be his daughter and all my family

2 English law (1857 Burial Act) stipulates that one hundred years is the maximum lease for a grave. However, the law does permit grant of ownership to be extended and some accordingly write to owners every five years offering the opportunity to 'top-up' their lease. In this manner, the grave can stay in the family for as long as they wish, though ownership will never be issued for more than one hundred years at any one time. Even where this topping up option is not offered then you (or your family) can renew the right at the end of the current lease.

have been blessed to have had such a strong, loving person as part of their lives, we are better people to have known him and hope to follow his example.

Collated by Michael Carroll

170

Cheeky Tiger

(Swee Meng Chin)

My name is Ming and I was born in the town of Batugajah[1], Malaysia, but my story takes place in 1969 in the small village of Bemban[2]. When I was five years old my whole family moved to Bemban so I could attend the school there. I was the youngest of a very big family of thirteen, with six brothers, four sisters and of course my parents. My house was made of timber with asbestos roof sheets. There were only two rooms in the house, one room for the girls and one room for the boys. We were all Buddhists and worshipped Kuan Ti who is well known for his good deeds. To the Taoists and others, Kuan Ti is the God of War, but in our faith he is not looked upon as a God, but as our Protector. He was a good and kindhearted person who lived in China at a time of great distress and chaos when the virtue of the Han Dynasty, (202 BC to 200 AD), began to decline.

There was no television in the village and we rarely listened to radio. Instead I amused myself with my group of friends by playing outside. We made toys such as wheel rollers made from two cylindrical tins and a mop stick, much like a big version of a paint roller. We made catapults from small 'V' shaped twigs with rubber bands and patches from tyres, then fired small stones at chickens and the fruit hanging from trees. Sometimes we stacked cans into pyramids, then threw stones at them from a distance. This was quite dangerous at times as each of us wanted to knock down all the cans in one go, so we chose the biggest stones we could find. We also played a stick game where a hole was dug in the ground, then a little stick was placed over it. We would get hold of a big stick, thrust it in the hole, then draw it out to flip the little stick as far as possible. Whoever flipped the little stick the

1 Meaning stone elephant.
2 Meaning a mass of people living together as a part of their own community, (an integral part of communist ideology).

furthest was the winner. In a game with Chinese picture cards, we pretended that each card represented one pow[3] and the person who matched the most cards into pairs was the winner, for they then had the most money. Another favourite card game consisted of each person dividing the pack up into two piles, then slapping them together in mid-air and letting them fall to the ground. The highest upturned numbered card represented each person's score.

All my friends were aged between eight and nine years old and I used to be the leader of our little gang. Everyday we passed through the fruit gardens, where starfruit, mango and rambutan[4] trees grew. The owner of the fruit gardens was a single old lady with a visual impairment, but she possessed very good hearing power. She was violent, abusive and swore at anyone who irritated her. Whenever we planned to steal any of the fruits, we had to be very cautious because the faintest sound would alert her senses. One day some of my friends stood on guard, whilst I climbed one of the trees to steal fruit for all of us. The old lady must have heard a noise, foreign to her environment. So she ventured towards us, trying to detect where the sound had come from. All my friends ran away leaving me stuck up the tree. I became scared as she headed towards me. Eventually, through her limited vision, she detected that I was sitting upon a branch in the tree. She picked up a piece of strong wood and threw it at me. Fortunately it missed me, but I realised I had to escape urgently and managed to scramble down the tree and run away.

Superstition played a very big part in our culture. A week later I witnessed a cyclone capturing everything that came within its reach. I rushed home and told my parents about it. They were very worried about me seeing it because in our culture we believe that if anyone sees a cyclone, something bad will

3 Slang term for Ringgit (Malaysian currency).
4 The word 'rambut' in the fruit name 'rambutan' is Malay for 'hairy', and this refers to the spiky rind or skin. It resembles the lychee (or litchee) which is in the same botanical family. The structure internally is quite similar, with a single central inedible seed and edible white flesh wrapped around it but the skin is the part that makes the rambutan so distinctive in appearance.

happen to them. Then, about a month later, I woke up one morning feeling a strange heaviness on my left cheek, it seemed to be protruding out. As soon as I touched it with my hand, I could feel it was hot. I wanted my mother immediately and began crying as I ran towards her. When I saw my cheek in front of the mirror, I gazed in amazement and was shocked. My cheek was red, inflamed and swollen. I started pressing it, to see if I could push it in, but Mum just calmed me down telling me that it must be an insect bite, reassuring me it would be gone by tomorrow. However, the next day it had grown bigger and all the family were worried. As my mother was very superstitious, she proclaimed it was an evil attack on me, believing it was due to the cyclone I had seen. The villagers were very superstitious and never viewed any ailment as just a medical condition. Any infection, rash or allergy was blamed on an ancestor's spirits or God being angry, therefore we had to undergo their curse. Dad did not believe in God or any kind of superstition and suggested taking me to see a doctor in the nearest town for some antibiotics. As we lived in a small village, we did not have a doctor, so for all ailments we used to go to the head of the village, a lady, whom everybody called Auntie. Whenever we visited her, she would prescribe herbal medicines made from roots and bark from trees. It was always Mum that cared for us, looked after us and nursed us. She was convinced that my cheek would heal this way. As Dad used to leave for work very early in the morning, worked hard all day as a carpenter and came back late at night, he was too exhausted to argue. Besides, the doctors were too far away and cost a fortune. As we were a big family we could not afford their treatment. So off I went with Mum to see Auntie.

Auntie took the dried root of a holy Buddhist tree called Putí Shú[5], crushed it, and mixed it with water. The properties of this root were supposed to calm the inflammation down and bring the blood circulation back to normal. She applied the

5 Meaning Linden Tree, from which the linden seeds are dried and used as beads for the meditation garland.

paste all over my cheek and then wrote the word 'Tiger' in Chinese upon the swelling. She told me that when I slept at night, the tiger in my dreams would pounce on the meat and eat it away, therefore deflating the swollen flesh. This concept relates to the wicked preying role that is bestowed upon the tiger in our culture, as it preys on flesh. This is why the pigs and chickens, raised for meat, were kept three to four miles away from our village in order to keep the tigers away.

The inflammation stayed for four to five days. I could not go to school during these days as I felt uneasy, could not talk properly, could not smile and could not eat. When I used to smile my lips would bunch up to one side, giving me a funny look and everyone laughed at me. Even my brothers and sisters laughed at me, and my friends. So I always hid in my room. I was told not to go out of the house whilst the paste was on my cheek. My friends came everyday to see if I would play outside. Mum told them I was not well, but the doors were usually open so they just came rushing in. They saw my cheek and became curious about it, asking what had happened, then made fun of me and giggled.

One fine morning, about a week later, I looked at my cheek in the mirror and I could see that at last it was back to normal. This meant I could go out to play once more. My mum said 'Look, I told you the tiger would eat it away'. From this moment on her belief in this superstition grew stronger.

Now that I am an adult, in my forties and married with three children, I do not believe in the superstitious traditions. If God should will anything to happen to my children or wife, such as any kind of ailment, superstitious thoughts don't even enter my mind. I arrange a doctor's appointment straight away. I believe in the medicines that have been specifically created to heal infections, illnesses, pain and various diseases. One of the reasons that the people in our village were superstitious, like my mum, was because of lack of education. However, I also believe in Chinese herbal medicine, as long as the practitioner is renowned in their field or has some kind of medical certificate.

Collated by Monica Ballani

It Couldn't Happen to You?

(Andrew Catterall)

My name is Andrew, I am forty seven years old, and happily married. Two years ago my life changed in an instant. So this is my story, a story I'm sure will shock most people because of its subject matter. I want to tell this story to educate people and make them aware of the relative issues that are rarely discussed. I would also like you to bear in mind that the issues discussed in this story apply to people and communities where you would least expect it. I know because I meet the men who find themselves in similar situations, except it is well hidden and kept under wraps.

By my mid-forties the sexual relationship between my wife and I was next to non-existent. Don't get me wrong, I love her to bits and wouldn't ever want to be with anyone else. We have been together for over twenty five years enjoying a good life and share a very close and intimate relationship. However, I was desperately frustrated, as I needed the physical intimacy that was once a part of our relationship. So what was I supposed to do without this need being met underneath the sanctity of marriage? Personally, I knew that ignoring this need would lead to all kinds of problems and resentfulness in the future.

My wife and I were having a meal at a friend's house one evening. After a couple of bottles of wine, the topic of conversation turned to whether couples with busy, stressful jobs, ever have the time or the inclination for sex. I jokingly expressed that I didn't think my wife was bothered if she ever had sex with me again. She agreed with me! However, I stressed that I did not want this aspect of my life to be over in my mid-forties. We all talked about different ways of dealing with the issue. My wife even suggested that she would not really object to me having a relationship with someone else.

Now, there was no green light to go and jump into bed with the next person I saw, but somehow there appeared a narrow window of possibility, should a suitable opportunity present itself.

Over the years I have been hit on by both men and women, but have always said, 'Thanks I'm flattered, but I'm married'. I have always been aware that I was attracted to males from an early age, but only from a distance and never in a sexual way. In fact when my hormones kicked in, at puberty, I chased all the girls and had a great time. However, about a year after the discussion at our friend's house, I had a sexual encounter for the first time outside my marriage with a man I met, whilst on holiday with my wife in Southern Spain. My wife wasn't around at the time and I didn't think that I was putting myself at any risk, but little did I know.

Back in the UK a few months later, I developed flu-like symptoms. This lasted for several days with fever, heavy night-time sweats, a rash, a hacking cough and aching bones. I was staying with relatives, where I was supposed to be doing some work, so I tried not to be too much of a nuisance, but I can honestly say I have never been as ill as that in my life before. It was Easter and all the shops and doctor's surgeries were closed. After several days, I was feeling progressively worse, so I asked my brother to take me to hospital. We arrived at the hospital at about seven thirty in the morning. A doctor examined me a few hours later and told me he couldn't find anything wrong with me, my temperature was normal and my chest was clear, everything seemed to be ok. He thought I might have a virus and advised me to take paracetomol and suggested that if I didn't feel any better after a couple of weeks, to see my own doctor. On the way out of hospital I saw my twin brother who worked there as a paramedic, he looked at me and said 'God, Andrew, you look dreadful, get yourself back to bed'. That's where I stayed for several days.

Gradually, I began to feel slightly better, but I knew that I had been seriously ill and needed to find out why. I was sure that it could only be related to my encounter in Spain and that it was more than likely to be a STI[1], but which one? I obtained a booklet from Boots on contraception and sexually transmitted infections, the opening paragraph stated:

> Anyone who is sexually active is at risk of catching and passing on sexually transmitted infections. While some infections are easily treated and cause only slight discomfort, not all of them will go away so easily. It's important to know the symptoms to look out for, as certain infections can cause serious problems later on. In some cases, they can even be fatal, so practising safer sex could not only save you from embarrassing problems, it could save your life.

Sobering words indeed. From reading the booklet it became clear that my symptoms corresponded with either a HIV[2] or a Hepatitis infection. I assumed that because my skin hadn't turned yellow, it was HIV. I felt sick; I couldn't believe I had put myself at any risk. The only thing I could think about was HIV equals AIDS. The tombstone and iceberg images of the 1980s tortured my mind. I wondered if I was being paranoid, as people tend to dwell on the worst case scenario where health is concerned.

My first visit to my doctor was to establish if I was still on his register, as I hadn't seen him for over twelve years. I was, so I asked if I could have a full medical. The receptionist suggested I had a MOT health check. I attended an appointment on 25th May, where I had a blood sample taken. Questions were asked about all aspects of my lifestyle, apart from my sexual activity, then I was weighed and measured.

1 Sexually Transmitted Infection.
2 Human Immunodeficiency Virus.

When I rang back a week later, I was told that there was a marker[3] on my liver function test and I'd need to call back and see the doctor. He told me there was a number of possible causes; maybe an infection from Spain; a virus or symptoms caused by taking paracetomol. He wasn't too concerned at this stage and suggested I had a blood test in a month's time. I asked him if any of the tests had checked for HIV. He said 'No, a HIV test can only be carried out with your permission'. However, when I asked him if I could have a HIV test, he wanted to know why. I told him I was bi-sexual. He refused the test, telling me he didn't want to do it and advised me to go to a GUM[4] clinic. I explained that if the staff saw me sat in the sexual health clinic in Bolton they would think it was my twin brother who worked there as a Paramedic, then rumours would fly. So I was provided with the contact details of clinics in Manchester and advised to ring for an appointment. This was easier said than done. Every time I rang, the line was engaged. When I did manage to get through, I was told all the appointments had been taken and to phone back at nine o'clock the following morning. This carried on for a couple of weeks, until I finally obtained an appointment at North Manchester General in early July.

I had to conceal the appointment from my family, I did not want them to jump to the same kind of conclusions as I had. When I saw the consultant, we talked about what had happened, how ill I had been and why I thought it might be a STI. I disclosed that I'd had oral sex whilst I was in Spain. He said this was a very low risk for the transmission of HIV, but added it was still possible. So he examined me, took swabs, and asked me if I wanted a HIV test. I answered yes. So a blood sample was taken. The health advisor said I might have been infected with a Hepatitis virus from contaminated food abroad. I thought to myself, I don't think so, but I hope you're right. I was asked to make an appointment a week later.

3 A marker can be an expressed region of DNA (a gene) or a segment of DNA with no known coding function. The marker can be detected and trailed.
4 Genito-Urinary Medicine: an NHS run clinic for all aspects of sexual health.

I returned on Monday 19th July. Shortly after booking in, the health advisor called me into one of the interview rooms. We sat down. She said 'It's not Hepatitis, Andrew, it's HIV'. I told her that I knew it was, but whilst I was glad of the confirmation, I was still shocked and concerned, thinking what do I do now? She explained that my previous blood sample was only tested for anti-bodies to the HIV virus, and a further sample was needed to establish the effect that the virus was having on my body. She told me it would be the most blood I'd ever have taken at one time. She wasn't wrong. I then saw the consultant, who informed me I had contracted chlamydia[5] as well. I was amazed, for I had never actually felt healthier in my life, yet all this stuff was wrong with me. I was asked to make a further appointment a week later.

I returned home and spent the afternoon confused with different types of emotions running through me. I didn't know what to do; I needed some information, but didn't want to start looking on the internet as I thought I would scare myself. However, I knew I needed to talk to someone, so I went to see a couple of gay friends. The support they gave me that day will stay with me always.

When I returned to the clinic, I learned about how the effects of HIV on the body are measured, through two main tests, checking CD4 levels[6] and viral load[7]. I was made aware that I needed testing every three months to check its progression. I found out that my levels were all right and that I would not have to go on medication immediately, only when my CD4 level decreased to around two hundred, it was currently four hundred and fifty one. I had a long conversation with the doctor about the progression of HIV. He was patient, understanding and concerned. I left the clinic feeling that at least I knew a little more and the future I faced may not be the same as those who were diagnosed in the 1980s. The drugs

5 Chlamydia is a sexually transmitted disease caused by a tiny bacterium, chlamydia trachomatis.
6 Measuring how well the immune system is coping.
7 Measuring how fast the virus is replicating.

available today, whilst having unpleasant side-effects, mean the disease, whilst not curable, is at least manageable.

I continued to attend the clinic, where my levels were monitored. My health remained good. However, I couldn't talk to anyone about having HIV for quite a while because I was confused and whilst not ashamed to have the disease, I felt unable to answer the many questions that would be asked. When it came to the check-ups, I just told my family that there was a problem with my blood and that Hepatitis was the most likely cause. In some respects it was easy to convince them this was the truth, as people don't usually question each other's medical conditions too closely.

I avoided telling my wife about having HIV for several months. We weren't having sex, so I was not putting her at risk of being infected. I was also aware of the stigma attached to HIV. Many people perceive that HIV sufferers bring it upon themselves by their risky behaviour. 'We know what you've been doing', they think, and view HIV as both confirmation and condemnation of its victim's homosexuality. I didn't want to tell my wife for several reasons. Firstly, admitting I had slept with someone would confirm the instability and imperfection of our relationship. I dreaded the issue being constantly addressed and referred to. Of course, there was the aspect of trust between us, being broken on a physical, emotional and mental level, a trust that may never be repaired. Could she accept the fact that all this was caused through my sexual encounter with a man? Could she accept or even begin to understand the reasons why?

I mentally rehearsed the way I would tell her many times and the words I would use. I had no idea how she was going to take the news. I knew that it could mean the end of our relationship. As so often happens on such occasions, when the time arrived, all the preparation went out of the window. I finally had to tell her shortly after we had booked a holiday.

Travel insurance was included with the holiday, but I knew that it would not be valid for someone with HIV. So I cancelled the insurance and re-arranged it with another company. One morning before my wife went to work, I told her about the insurance. Of course, she wanted to know why I had changed it. So I told her that it would not cover my condition. 'What condition?' she said. Then I told her I had HIV. The shock and pain immediately imprinted itself upon her face as if I had physically hit her. She wanted to know how I had caught it. When I told her, she asked me if I was still sleeping with men. I answered yes, but purely for my physiological need and I was using protection. I told her that I was well and not on any medication.

How many wives could accept their partner announcing they had been infected with HIV through an encounter with a man and not be angry, upset or disgusted? I knew I had risked everything by telling her the truth and realised how much it could hurt her. I was very conscious that I had turned her world upside down. As she set off to work, I knew my revelation would plague her mind all day long. In the evening, when she arrived home she looked ill. It wasn't possible to continue the conversation because my brother arrived, so the evening was spent trying to maintain a sense of normality. When we went to bed that night my wife turned her back to me.

I tried to reassure her that things hadn't really changed because I was still there for her. I also realised that whilst I still wanted to continue our relationship, ultimately an acceptable way forward would have to be found for both of us. Quite how this could be achieved would take some time to discover. I thought that now I should also tell my brothers about my HIV. Firstly, I told my twin brother, who not surprisingly was shocked. Not many people know anyone who has HIV, so when they come face to face with someone who has, they don't know quite how to react. Shortly after, I had an interview for a job where I was asked if I had any health problems. I wasn't sure whether to disclose my HIV status. I decided to tell the interviewer I had HIV, because I knew that in several weeks time I was due for another appointment at the hospital. He thanked me for being honest, but I asked him to keep the information confidential.

I want to tell people about my HIV status on my own terms, when I am ready and not to have other people reveal it on my behalf. Let me be the judge of who to tell and who not. Many people are still frightened by HIV and only see the disease instead of the person. I'm well aware of the discrimination people with HIV face and I am fortunate to have had very few bad experiences. Discrimination exists due to a lack of awareness, education and understanding. I have found that I have to educate people about how the virus is passed on and what the likely treatment will be. Many people think HIV will never affect them. Did you know that anyone who has ever had sex actually has a HIV status, whether it is positive, negative or untested? As the old adage goes, you only have to do it once.

I am still not taking any medication. I attend the clinic every five months or so. Am I worried about the future? No, not really, worry is a wasted emotion. I can only deal with what is happening at present. I view life positively (no pun intended). Eating well, exercising and getting enough rest slow down the progression of the disease and keep me well. If I can maintain my current health levels, I should have a long and happy life. I am also a Reiki practitioner and find that this helps me in many different ways. I hope I can prevent people from contracting HIV by talking to interested groups and individuals through my work as a volunteer in the NHS. With advancements in medical care being made all the time the outlook is hopeful, if you are living in the Western world. The same however, cannot be said of Africa. I am fortunate to be living in the UK with a decent healthcare system. Living with

HIV certainly alters your perspective on life. Like any chronic illness it sharpens your focus. Think it couldn't happen to you? It might not, but it may happen to someone you know. Take care always, the HIV epidemic is still growing, it hasn't gone away.

Collated by Michael Carroll

The Jinn Family

(Tahira Patel)

This is a true story about myself and what happened to me when I was living in India. As a child I was called 'Munni', this is a very affectionate expression given to a little girl who is very much loved by her elders. I am from a large family of about fifteen, spanning three generations. Believe it or not we all lived together in a city called Barouj in India.

When I was four years old, I had my first vivid memory of how much my parents and family really loved me. They were devoted to my well-being at all times. I became very ill with pneumonia and was taken into medical care. My condition worsened and the doctor told my family there wasn't anything else that he could do for me as they had exhausted all the medical procedures possible. There was nothing else for my parents to do, but to follow the doctor's advice and take me home. They did everything they could to make my life as comfortable as possible, attending to my every need. They did not lose faith. They never left my bedside and soon, after a lot of praying and sleepless nights, I began to feel better.

My family are very important to me. They taught me by example, how to love and respect, which is very important in eastern culture. I have fond memories of living in my father's huge house with all my brothers and sisters close by, my parents always guided us and my grandparents would tell us stories about the past.

I went to a huge all girls' school. The building was very old and situated in a row of similar buildings that cast large shadows over the small family-owned houses. Our house was massive, it was an old building with three huge floors. There were long corridors, leading into big rooms with high ceilings. We needed a big house as lots of us lived there, my grandfather, grandmother, mum, dad, three elder sisters, two younger sisters, one brother, an uncle and aunt with their son and daughter. Our home was always filled with laughter and happy family occasions. However, we soon realised we weren't the only family living there.

It all began when I was a very young girl, as far back as I can remember. One rainy and stormy night, suddenly the whole house and surrounding area had a blackout due to an electricity failure in the city. We were all in bed, when we heard a very loud bang upstairs in the attic. It was as if something very heavy had fallen over. We were all frightened on hearing this loud noise and wondered what was upstairs. So, the elders decided to investigate. Up they crept with an oil lantern flickering, projecting moving shadows on the walls, the wooden steps creaked and their hearts thumped in anticipation of what they might find. Time stood still as they crossed the threshold into the attic. The lanterns swung around only to pick out the figure of a black cat that was probably just as scared as they were. Everyone in the house and surrounding neighbourhood had heard the noise, but there was no evidence of anything that had fallen over. Over a period of time, similar incidents began to occur.

When I was about ten years old, for the first time ever, I decided to play in the attic. No one ever ventured into this room to play because it was spooky, very dark and cold with only spangled daylight appearing from the cracks in the walls and the roof. The room was very musty and filled with old clothes and furniture. I knew it wasn't really the right place for me to play, but my childish mind was curious. It seemed like a place for adventure, with a mystique and an aura. I opened the door and wandered into the room as an explorer about to embark on an epic journey. No sooner had I entered, my curiosity plunged inside me like a lead weight and my body froze with shock upon seeing a tall white spirit figure, resembling my grandfather, gliding across the darkened room.

I screamed out as loud as I could, quickly running down the stairs. In a panic, I told my family what had happened, but no one believed me. They just assumed I had let my imagination get the better of me and attempted to assure me that ghosts were only fictional creations in books and films.

Soon after that day, one morning I was getting ready to go to school; I was very anxious as I was running late and could not find the belt for my uniform. My sisters all wore the same uniform as me. I could only think that one of them must have hidden or taken it, because it was always ready for me to wear. My reasoning didn't go down too well with my sisters and an argument broke out amongst us, escalating, until we were accusing each other of all sorts of things. In the end, I had to go to school without my belt, knowing I would be punished when I arrived there. I was given a good telling off by my teacher for not having a part of the school uniform, sent to the back of the class and told to stand on a bench, criss cross my arms and hold onto each ear lobe for half an hour. When I returned home from school, my mum had found the belt upstairs in the attic. This kind of incident became a regular occurrence. My socks, items of value, such as our best china from the kitchen, and jewellery were also found upstairs in the attic.

My grandfather often wore incense on a Friday, as it is a special day for Muslims. However, the fragrance would somehow reappear around about five or six o'clock in the evening for about fifteen minutes, even though my grandfather was out. Maybe the fragrance had drifted in from next door or outside somewhere. One day whilst my grandfather was at namaz[1] in the mosque, I was upstairs in the middle level of the house playing with a die[2]. My mum was asleep in the bed next to me. My playing was interrupted by the sound of our front gate opening. We had a big iron gate in front of the garden and

1 Prayers.
2 Singular form of dice.

it was easy to tell when someone was coming in, as it would squeak when opened. I looked out from upstairs and saw my grandfather walking through the gate. He was tall with a white hat, a long white beard and was wearing a white shirvani with baggy trousers. His outfit was similar to a salwar kameez[3]. He walked along the path, past the roses and small papaya trees, then entered his own room down below at the side of the house. I went down the stairs leading towards my grandfather's room, expecting to see him there. I put my head around the door, but to my amazement I could only see my grandmother praying with her tasbih[4] in hand. Later on, I asked her where he was. She replied that he hadn't yet returned from the Mosque. I told my mum and grandmother what I'd seen, but they didn't believe me. I began to wonder if there was something wrong with me, as all these incidents never seemed to happen to anyone else.

My father is an engineer and at that time he often worked away in Saudi Arabia. On one occasion whilst he was on leave my mother, sisters and I were sitting with the front room window open. Around midnight we began to hear strange noises, as if someone was beginning to climb the stairs. My sister, who was lying down on the mat, bolted awake. We were very scared. Before our eyes, the ghost of a little girl, wearing green clothes, scampered up the wooden stairs, hurrying into the attic room. We all screamed together, but were immediately told by my mother to go to sleep, as if we could somehow magically dispel what we had just seen from our minds. However, the next day my sisters and I heard my grandfather and grandmother talking about the incident to my mother and auntie. This made us more frightened, hearing the adults finally admitting that something mysterious was going on. The night before, whilst my grandparents had been asleep downstairs on the ground floor, they too had heard the sound

3 Salwar kameez is the traditional dress worn by various peoples of South Asia. Salwar are loose trousers and the kameez is a long shirt.
4 A tasbih is a rosary probably of Persian origin, which is traditionally used by Muslims in prayer. Ninety-nine beads are divided into three sets of thirty-three, by slightly larger beads. The beads are used to recite the ninety-nine names of God or Surahs from the Quran.

of the child scampering up the stairs.

Eventually, my mother relented and told my grandfather to call an Imam[5] to our house. It was actually my uncle who found an Imam from another village. The Imam arrived and began to survey the house. As soon as he entered he could tell that there was something strange about the atmosphere. He went upstairs into the attic, then prayed and prayed, summoning his jinn[6] to check the house. After this process had finished the Imam told us all that there was definitely a presence of jinns in our house. They were a family who had come from the old schoolhouse opposite us, using our home as a walkway to go and pray in the Mosque. They often stayed in our house because they liked it so much. However, like most children, the ghost children were very mischievous and liked to play tricks such as hiding our jewellery, pretending to be our grandfather or our uncle. They liked to scare us, but the Imam told us that as the family came to our house frequently to read their prayers, they were not evil, but religious. He advised us that it was not a good idea to force them out or they would probably turn on us. However, as the whole family were scared when they realised they were sharing a house with a family of ghosts, my grandparents ordered the Imam to get rid of them. At first, he refused, but a week later, he returned to hammer huge nails on the front and back doors to ward the jinns away, he also stressed the need to pray, which we did anyway.

It wasn't long before the house became scarier. There were more noises at night, then the nails on the doors were bent backwards. We were afraid that the ghosts had turned on us. One night whilst my uncle was sleeping downstairs, he heard the sound of the display cabinet doors opening and shutting two rooms away from him, then the sound of breaking china as it all crashed to the floor. He clearly recalls going into the

5 Muslim priest.
6 Spirit.

room, not seeing anything there, but being shocked to hear a burbling sound beneath the floorboards. Apprehensively, he proceeded to follow the sound as it rolled towards his room, eventually fading underneath his bed.

One of the scariest incidents occurred whilst my father and uncle were away working in Saudi Arabia and Dubai. There was only my mother and auntie at home with us. My auntie was sleeping on the ground floor, when she was awoken by the presence of someone creeping up beside her bed. She could feel a presence approaching nearer and nearer until it towered over her. Before she could do anything, the stranger was leaning over and pressing her chest. Her whole body was paralysed, she desperately wanted to shout for someone, but could not speak or move. After a few seconds, she felt a release from this presence and was able to scream for my mother. My mother rushed down the stairs and had to calm my auntie down, for she was shaking like a leaf. Later, she went to sleep with my mum, on the middle floor. This incident really scared my auntie who became more frightened and never wanted to be alone in the house. It also affected the rest of us, so my uncle informed the Imam about the bent nails and everything else that had happened. The Imam was not surprised, as we had not taken his advice and told my uncle to take the nails out. He gave him a specific prayer from the Quran which we had to recite every day, apart from our usual prayers. He suggested that if we heard anything strange, we had to try and ignore it. We followed the Imam's instructions and gradually things started to improve. The incidents became less threatening and although they were still scary, the jinns became an accepted part of our lives.

Many years later in 1997, after I was married and had a young daughter, I returned to India to visit my family. To my amazement, incidents were still occurring, the ghosts were still as mischievous as ever. Whilst I was sleeping there, they threw water on my face. Another incident happened to my brother. On his way home from work, as he passed the old school buildings, he could hear noises and voices calling him. He dared not look back and carried on walking. This occurred on two or three separate occasions, until my brother would no longer walk home on his own, my father had to go and collect him.

I have had a happy childhood and have fond memories of my family. I still have a close relationship with all my brothers and sisters. Even though our house possessed the presence of ghosts, I don't let it cloud my memory of the happy times I spent there. The jinns chose a family like ours because of the warmth and friendly atmosphere in our home. Sadly, my grandfather passed away, but before he died he gave half of the house to my uncle and the other half to my father. Later, my father built another house on the other side of the city Bijlinaghar. Up until recently my uncle was still living in the old house and for the past two years had not experienced many incidents with the jinns. He prayed regularly as the Imam had advised. However, my uncle then wanted to sell the house, but no one wanted to buy it because of the huge dark spooky corridors. Maybe they thought it was haunted. Now, with a tinge of sadness, I can disclose that the house has been sold, but I'm not too sure how the new owners are getting on with their guests.

Collated by Michael Carroll

Mustafa

(Afsaneh Karbla Zadeh)

Afsaneh was born in Tehran in 1970 and later lived in Shomal, which lies to the north of Iran. She was married when she was twenty-two years old and now she has a little daughter and a son. Her family has been living in the UK since 6th January 2000. Last month she invited me to her son, Aria's birthday party. She was very happy and didn't have any worries. Everybody was enjoying the party. I chatted to Afsaneh about her family and asked her if she had any brothers and sisters. She regretted that she had no sisters, but told me about her two brothers whom she loves very much, especially the youngest one, Mustafa. She told me that Mustafa was twenty years old and was currently undertaking his military service. With a sparkle of pride in her eyes, Afsaneh explained that Mustafa was engaged and how she was looking forward very much to his marriage, when he had finished his military service.

Afsaneh reflected fondly on her relationship with Mustafa. They used to live in a big three bedroomed house which had a big sitting room and a big garden. When she was a child, she used to play an imaginary game, common amongst the children in Iran at the time. Mustafa would pretend to be a grocer, with all the imaginary fruit and vegetables laid out along his stall. Afsaneh would then pretend to be a customer coming to choose what fruit and vegetables to buy. The scenario very much mirrored the market stalls in the city centre of Shomal. Both of them had hours of fun developing these scenarios then changing roles. Although they used to enjoy playing together very much they would often argue and fight about the most trivial things. As they grew a little older, Afsaneh became more responsible and would clean the house only to see Mustafa messing it up again and again. She grew tired of cleaning up after him, which caused her to swear, curse and even fight him. Once she slapped him across the cheek, but Mustafa light heartedly said that she could slap him on the other cheek as well, if it made her happy. Whenever she wanted to go to the cinema with her friends though, she would never go without the very big-hearted Mustafa, who took care of her and protected her. Her friends also enjoyed his company. Afsaneh described how she still keeps in touch with her parents, brothers and other relatives in Iran by phone every week, but of course, how she speaks mostly with her youngest brother Mustafa.

Shortly after Aria's birthday party, Afsaneh received a phone call from her aunt, at home one evening. However, her auntie just asked to speak to Afsaneh's husband, Farhad. Afsaneh sensed from her auntie's voice that something was wrong, so she asked if everything was all right in Iran. Despite her auntie saying that everything was fine, Afsaneh was suspicious that she was hiding something and asked her why she wanted to speak to her husband. She pleaded with her aunt to tell her what had happened. Her aunt told her not to worry, that everything was fine and she merely wanted to speak to Farhad because she had heard he wasn't well. Afsaneh relented, but Farhad wasn't at home anyway, so her aunt asked her to pass on a message to him, that she would call tomorrow. After the phone call, Afsaneh was still worried and thought about it so much that she could not sleep that night, despite her husband's assurance that there was nothing to worry about.

At five o'clock, early next morning, the phone rang, making Afsaneh's heart sink. Farhad answered the phone and after a minute, went downstairs to continue the conversation, thinking Afsaneh was still asleep. When he had gone downstairs, Afsaneh got out of bed, put the bedroom phone to her ear and listened to the conversation. It was the voice of her aunt asking Farhad to contact all of Afsaneh's friends and invite them to offer their condolences because her younger brother, Mustafa, had died. As soon as she heard this Afsaneh put the phone down, feeling very dizzy as though she was whirling in a dream. She could not believe what she had heard and immediately called her father in Iran. Ali, her older brother, answered the phone. In tears, Afsaneh desperately wanted to know what had happened to Mustafa. 'I know something has happened to him, please tell me the truth' she cried. Ali told her not to worry and that nothing had happened. This only caused Afsaneh's trembling voice to plead with Ali to let her speak to Mustafa. Ali replied that this was not possible, as Mustafa had been posted to another city, as part of his military service. 'Please, please, please tell me the truth!' cried Afsaneh. Then there was a minute's silence as her brother Ali cried, he could not speak anymore and put the phone down. About an hour later Ali called Afsaneh back, admitting the death of their younger brother was true. He acknowledged the love that Afsaneh and Mustafa had for each other, but told his sister there was nothing they could do. He stressed that the family would need a great deal of patience and time to cope with their loss.

Later, Afsaneh found out that whilst Mustafa had been serving as a soldier, one day he believed his gun to be unloaded, but as he handled it and clicked the trigger, the weapon blasted him, killing him instantly on the spot.

The minute Afsaneh's friends found out about her brother's death, they felt so sorry for her. Afsaneh still cannot believe her young brother Mustafa is dead. She thinks that if she returned to Iran, he would still be there waiting for her. In her mind he is alive, every time she goes to bed all her memories of him come flooding back, particularly the times when they played together as children.

Hurtful tears streamed down her cheeks as Afsaneh told me about Mustafa's death. She had only spoken to him just two weeks ago and he had told her how his wishes were about to come true as soon as he was married. Afsaneh had told him she was going to send him a very special present. Unfortunately, nobody can foresee the future and just by the simple click of a trigger, a life can end tragically. Life is too short and unpredictable.

Collated by Nasim Rezaei

The Language of Home Movies

(Elizabeth Coburn)

There were eight of us in our house, Mum and Dad, my two older brothers, two younger brothers and younger sister. There can't have been many children who had an upbringing like mine with two deaf parents. It's amazing how sound, or the lack of it, can affect your environment. For example, Dad had a fish tank with Perch and Roach in it. He fed them Kitty Kat cat food, which caused an uproar in school when my younger brother chose to do a presentation on his home life. Sometimes the filter broke on the fish tank. The rubber seals wore away on the pump causing a continuous annoying buzzing sound that could be heard all over the house, even at night when we were trying to get to sleep. When we asked Dad to change the seal, he refused saying that he could not hear the sound so it did not bother him. The problem was never alleviated until his next planned trip to town. We also had to contend with one of the great unsolved mysteries of the universe. How did Dad know when we were jumping about on our beds upstairs? He used to take his leather belt off and bang it on every one of the wooden steps as he came up to our rooms. By the time he reached the upstairs landing we were in bed. He then stood in the doorway and told us off for jumping up and down on the beds. We used to say to each other 'How does he know? He can't hear us'. It wasn't until a few years later that the mystery was solved. One evening as I sat downstairs, I could hear my younger brother bouncing up and down on the beds upstairs, but I could also see the light flickering on the ceiling above me and realised how Dad knew. Well at least we could jump up and down on the beds until our hearts were content during the daylight hours.

It amazes me when people talk of having this or that culture. In our household it was like having our own separate culture. Could this be celebrated as part of my national heritage? I doubt it. As you can appreciate, communication in our house was quite different from the norm. Sometimes if we wanted Mum and Dad's attention we stamped our feet on the wooden varnished floor, so they could feel the vibrations. The lights in our house also played a big part in communication. If we were upstairs and Mum or Dad wanted one of us, they flicked the landing light switch on and off from downstairs. Someone came to install a special doorbell from the Welfare for the Deaf. When pressed, it switched the front room light on and off. In theory it was a good idea, until the kids on our street got to find out about it. They would sneak up, press the doorbell and run away.

Mum and Dad learned sign language long before they met each other at the local deaf club. Being from Yorkshire, Dad's sign language alphabet was slightly different to Mum's Lancashire alphabet, just like the spoken dialects are different from each other. Their deaf friends from our estate sometimes came round to gossip. As kids we got bored when they came because they had long conversations and we could not understand their language of the hands. Cruelly, we then began to imitate the sounds they murmured and started to laugh, causing them to ask us why we were laughing and give us some attention.

Because of my deaf parents, we were teased a lot and bullied by the other children on the estate who used to say 'The dumby kids are here'. Sometimes they hit us and taunted 'You can't go home and tell your mum and dad'. I had a lack of confidence at school that affected my ability to express myself so when incidents happened I could not communicate them to Mum and Dad. I kept a lot of things to myself. Though my name is Elizabeth, Mum and Dad pronounced it 'Alibeth'. If Mum wanted to know where the sugar was, she said 'Where Kugar' accompanied by her sign language. She said 'milek' instead of milk. Dad was easier to understand. They both uttered the main words of a sentence, excluding small words like 'is', 'a' and 'was'. I was Mum and Dad's voice for the outside world because anyone from outside of our family did not understand what they were saying. As children we learned their verbal language accentuated by bits of their sign language.

We never actually had a radio, or a wireless as they used to be called, because of course, they were useless to Mum and Dad. So I missed out on all the radio programmes as a very young child. It was only when my older brother bought a radio when I was eleven or twelve that I got to hear the music on stations such as Radio Luxemburg. I realise that we hadn't sat around the wireless as other families did at the time. Instead, all our family sat around a silent film projector. As far back as I can remember, when I was a little girl in the fifties, Dad always had a silent movie projector in the main room downstairs, a huge ugly monster set up on angle iron, with a big brass body, standing on its own heavy frame covered up with black cloth when not in use. When the black curtains were drawn over the windows, on the inside there appeared a white screen that Dad had somehow painted upon them with distemper[1]. Usually, every Sunday night there would be a film show, a big family occasion that everyone looked forward to. We had our baths first then the show would begin. Some of us sat on the floor because there was not enough seating. The reels, nearly as big as old dustbin lids, the same size as they had in the cinema, began to whirl making a clicking sound, but drowned out by the projector's motor, like a washing machine on a slow spin dry. As there were no carpets in our house, we could feel the vibrations through the bare varnished floorboards. Sometimes it was a film that we'd seen before, sometimes a new one. Some of the films were silent movies in sepia or black and white, where a frame of dialogue followed a few frames of visual action. Some of the films were talking movies; however, the projector was not equipped for sound and, of course, made

1 An old form of paint made from whiting and glue.

no difference to Mum and Dad's silent world. Half-way through the film, whilst waiting for Dad to change the reel over for the second half, we'd jump in front of the projector to be hit by a big blast of light and perform hand shadows on the screen, imitating rabbits, dog and birds. We became so engrossed in the films; you can imagine our disappointment when the film strip snapped. A congregational groan emanated from all of us when the images suddenly became a blank white canvas. Dad got the green ribbed octagon shaped bottle marked with the words 'poison' and proceeded to repair the film by cutting the film strip, then paint it with the fluid, smelling stronger than nail varnish remover.

On a Saturday afternoon the house was like the local cinema for the kids on the street. Dad charged them a penny each towards the electric. He wrote out the names of the films and slotted them into a frame to advertise them, 'Showing today: Jesse James; Showing next week: Crimes Highway'. We were thrilled by the antics of Mickey Mouse, Donald Duck and Colonel Blood. I remember a trailer for Walt Disney announcing 'Coming Soon Walt Disney in Colour'. It began in black and white, then I became fascinated at the images that followed. Water lily buds in black and white slowly opened up, blossoming into colour with pink petals and green leaves. Frogs jumped off the lily pads whilst dragonflies flew around them. I imagined the absent music underscoring the beautiful coloured scenery.

The next door neighbours were a nowty pair. Because there were six kids always shouting at Mum and Dad or stamping on the floor to get their attention, once, the neighbours contacted the Superintendent from the Deaf Club, complaining about the noise. The Superintendent came down to our house, lined us kids up and told us we were all too noisy. She said it was the responsibility of the elder ones to keep the younger ones quiet. We could not believe the neighbours had complained because we could often hear them bickering amongst themselves next door. It was scary listening to their shouting matches as a child. It was very different with my parents. They had their arguments, but of course they used their hands flapping about in sign language. At least their arguments were quiet. When we asked them what they were arguing about, they pointed at their noses, meaning 'Mind your own business!' The grumpy next door neighbours were one of the first on our street to get a television when they first appeared in the shops. However, they were not very happy and complained because Dad's projector was interfering with the picture on their screen. They came round knocking at the front door, shouting right in front of Mum and Dad. They believed that if they shouted loud enough Mum and Dad would be able to hear them. Then they just stormed off. Dad relied on us to communicate what had been said. His attitude was that he could not hear the noise of his projector so it didn't matter. He thought they had a cheek in the first place as their kids used to come in and watch the films. One week though, I noticed Dad was looking a bit worried. He sat on his chair, pipe in mouth, deep in thought. I could tell something was playing upon his mind. A few days later I was off school as I was not feeling very well. I remember Dad showing me a postcard from the GPO[2] he had received the week before. He told me they were coming to visit our house in the afternoon, to investigate the projector's interference with next door's television. I realised what had been concerning him. I think he was worried about his much loved projector being taken away or that he would not be able to use it again. So that afternoon after showing me the card, he went out to the shops and came back with a little device; I think it was a suppressor. He winked at me and then said 'Watch this... I've won'. He connected the small brown rectangular device to the wiring from the projector then left it until the officials from the GPO arrived in the afternoon. Two of them turned up and told him to run the projector whilst one of them went next door to turn

2 General Post Office.

on their television. Ten minutes later the official came back from next door and said to Dad you're OK, then left. Dad was ecstatic because he had got one up on the grumpy next door neighbours and made them look foolish after their complaints. No evidence of any interference could be found. 'I've won, I've won!' Dad exclaimed.

I think Dad purposely put off getting a television as he saw it as a major threat to the equilibrium of the household. We were one of the last families in the street to get one. Before this, us kids would find ways of going to other people's houses to watch television. A woman across the road said to me when I was about ten 'Go and get a paper for me and you can come and watch my television for half an hour'. I could not wait as I had never seen television before, so I dashed off and bought the newspaper for her, but was nearly run over by a wagon due to my excitement. I was mesmerised by her television showing Children's Hour at five o'clock. I could hear people talking, it actually had sound! Fortunately there was no heavy whirring motor like Dad's projector.

When television finally arrived in our household, Dad became annoyed with it because he could now not understand what was going on. Mum and Dad would not let us watch programmes like London Night at the Palladium because it contained singing and music without any action, yet they would watch a film for its visual content and pester us when they could not understand something. 'It's not fair we can't hear it', Dad would say. 'What's he saying? What's he saying?' This annoyed the rest of us as it shattered our engagement with the film. Eventually, as our televisions became bigger throughout the years, Mum began to watch more and more TV, especially when colour became popular. However, Dad was in the shed practically every night making his model wooden trams. The introduction of television in our house led to Dad getting a small scale projector which was relegated to one of the rooms upstairs. When alone in the house Dad watched

Laurel and Hardy and Charlie Chaplin films, usually whilst we were out shopping on a Saturday afternoon with Mum.

After Dad died, nearly twenty years ago, Mum took a liking to the foreign films shown on BBC2 because they included English subtitles. Then Ceefax and Teletext were introduced which meant, eventually, Mum could watch all the programmes with subtitles, like having her own version of the silent movies she watched with Dad. I remember visiting Mum one day as she was watching Dallas. She said 'What have you called for?' Then she sat back down to watch the programme with subtitles on Ceefax and completely ignored me. She must have watched the series three or four times once subtitles became available.

Now, it is good to know there is still a demand for the black and white films that we used to watch as children. As adults we can sit and watch them on DVD accompanied by the sound that used to be absent. This makes me appreciate even more the sense of sound, but I also recognise the sense of equality Dad's silent film projector brought to our house.

Collated by Michael Carroll

Adventures of a Very Curious Girl

(Pasmia)

This story is about a very curious girl called Pasmia, from the small village of Mattu in Pakistan. She always used to get into mischief whilst playing with all her cousins. Pasmia was only a two-year-old baby when her sister Zenab took her for a visit to Auntie Sabira's house, which was in the same village, to play with her cousins, Rehana, Semi, Nagina, Robina and Shabou. Auntie Sabira's house was huge, like a mansion. Attached to the house at ground level was a veranda with pillars and arches looking out onto the garden. The garden was filled with fragrances from all the fruit trees; the guava, pomegranate, orange, lemon and especially the mango. It was like paradise on earth. Whenever they visited they always collected some fruit from the garden so they could take it home afterwards.

On the day of the visit, the sun was blazing hot, accompanied by a very light breeze. Pasmia was playing happily with her cousins in the veranda with some toys and pebbles near the mango and orange trees, when her uncle's sparkling bike caught her eye. The bike was shining brightly, glistening in the sun as it leaned against a pillar just under the entrance of the veranda. Pasmia was immediately lured by the new toy and trotted off to investigate. She stood in front of the bike, mesmerised by its glinting texture and began to stroke its surface. It wasn't long before her cousin, Rehana, joined her in a mutual appreciation. They both delighted in exploring the bike and the opportunities it presented to their imaginations. They became fascinated by the different shapes making up the object. Then Pasmia discovered the parts that could move. She slid her hand along a springy chain leading to a wheel with teeth. She asked her cousin what it was, but in a split second, Rehana turned the pedal, rotating the cog, which caught and crunched Pasmia's finger. Pasmia let out a piercing scream, her finger throbbed so much, she'd never experienced such pain. She yelled and cried for her mum. Realising that she had done something terrible, Rehana began to panic and she too began crying and shouting for help. Pasmia's sister, Zenab, and Auntie Sabira, who had been chatting and enjoying a glass of sherbet, came rushing out of the house to see what the noise was about. Zenab realised something awful had happened. She knelt down on the ground next to Pasmia and tried to free her trapped finger from the bike. It was a slow process, with Pasmia sobbing and suffering. Zenab was near to tears herself, as all she could see was blood oozing from Pasmia's finger onto her clothes and the ground. At last, she managed to free Pasmia's finger. It was flopping limply and cut to the bone, but Zenab gritted her teeth as she placed her baby sister's hand in hers and took her straight to the doctor's surgery about five minutes away in the neighbouring village.

It was a very traumatic experience, not only for Pasmia, but for Zenab too, as she was held personally responsible for her sister's well-being and felt that she had let her down. The doctor cleaned up Pasmia's finger with antiseptic, and wrapped it up with a bandage. He visited Pasmia regularly after the accident to clean and check the wound, but this did not compensate for him not setting the bone right, as he was not a surgeon. So until this day Pasmia's finger is still pulled and scrunched up. There was no hospital near the village, it was too far away. In those days, people had to make do or find the money to hire an available car to take them there.

A couple of years later when Pasmia was about six, she was playing with Billa, Billy, Shanou and some other cousins just outside her house across the road, where there were acres and acres of land as far as the eye could see. Here the neighbours grew galia melons, tiger melons, vegetables and rice depending on the weather and season. Pasmia and her friends sat upon the branches of trees as they had heard the jingle of bells in the distance, almost like wind chimes. They knew that this signalled a procession of tradesmen journeying through the village to sell their wares. A man appeared in the distance, clearing the path in front of the procession and walking ahead to announce their arrival. Pasmia and her friends were excited, but also a little scared as they gazed at the camels, donkeys and goats, carrying huge bundles of cotton and cloths along the road. The bells, hanging around the animals' necks, were clanging, and the camels' gungroos[1] jingled around their feet.

When all the camels, goats and donkeys had passed by, a horrible smell lingered from the manure, but some of the villagers collected it, to dry and use it as fuel for their handmade chullas[2]. Pasmia was hanging on the branch of a tree swinging to and fro, when Billy saw a thick gooey substance oozing out of the trunk. Billa suggested to the others that they should try and taste the stuff, so they all dipped a finger in the sticky texture and were surprised to find that it tasted like a sweet syrup. Whilst Pasmia's hand rested against the trunk of the tree, a shooting pain charged through her finger. She screamed with shock and was horrified to find a squirmy black insect attached to her finger. Whilst she was crying, her cousins Billy and Shanou began shouting at each other, not knowing what to do. Pasmia started shaking her hand about to try and get rid of the insect, but the tiny black creature would not come off. This caused Pasmia to cry even louder. She even slapped her hand against the tree in an attempt to get rid of it but the insect remained intact. At this stage, fortunately, Pasmia's Auntie Suraj came running from across the road to rescue her, yanking the insect off her finger. Taking charge of the situation, Auntie Suraj wrapped Pasmia's hand in her grandad's shirt, which she was about to hang out to dry. She took Pasmia home, then ordered one of her cousins to take her to the doctor. However, in the doctor's surgery, it gradually dawned on Pasmia that it was the same doctor attending to the same hand and the same finger that she had

1 Anklets with small bells attached.
2 Small handmade red clay ovens.

previously trapped in the bicycle chain. Again the doctor cleaned the finger up and put a bandage on it. He commented on how Pasmia always seemed to be getting into mischief.

A few days later, Pasmia's cousin Billy came over on an errand to ask for some vegetables to cook dhal, as her family were short of food. Billy's mother had told her not to be long and to hurry back home, but Pasmia was so bored and just wanted someone to play with, so she persuaded Billy to play with her for a while. However, it wasn't long before Billy became hungry, so the obliging Pasmia offered to share her lunch outside, underneath the shade of a tree. It was a beautiful sunny day as they sat eating lunch on the mangi, a bed made from vines, resembling a hammock. All was well between the two friends, but as soon as Billy had finished eating, she got up to go home. This angered Pasmia so much that she demanded Billy give back her lunch. Billy was baffled. This was impossible, for she'd already eaten the food. However, it did not deter Pasmia from demanding that Billy should extract the food from her stomach. All Billy could do was cry as she could not meet her cousin's demands, nor make her see any sense. Pasmia's older cousin, who was passing by, carrying some pickles, heard all the commotion and stopped to laugh upon hearing such an absurd conversation. She called Pasmia's mother and told her what her daughter was demanding. Her mother emerged to break up the bickering and gave Pasmia a good telling off, then sent Billy home.

Billy was really upset because she had forgotten to ask for the vegetables she had gone for. She got into trouble for being greedy, selfish and arriving home empty-handed. However, Pasmia got away with being so horrible because she was still recuperating from her insect bite and managed to obtain lots of sympathy. Although Pasmia's finger had suffered from the skirmishes and scrapes she'd got herself into, at least she could still wrap the rest of her family around it.

Collated by Nusrat Rafique

206

Ghungo

(Monica Ballani and Kanyalal Bhagchandani)

Back in India I lived in a three storey building in the town of Thane, Maharashtra. It was a cooperative block of flats, much like in the UK, where everyone is expected to contribute to the repairs and maintenance. I lived with Mum, Dad, my Grandma and my younger brother. At the back of the apartments was a slum area of brick huts with asbestos sheets as roofs. There was always a foul filthy smell because the huts were only serviced by public toilets, which were often full, in which case the residents there just used any convenient space they could find. It was such a relief to stand on the front of my balcony instead and breathe in the fresh aroma of warm bread and biscuits from the bakeries, wafting above the chaotic main road.

My story actually begins back in 1966, six years before I was born, when my dad, Kanyalal Bhagchandani was a young and single twenty-five year old bachelor. Dad is from a lower middle class family and used to own a little shop in Dadar, selling bleaching powder, bleaches, disinfectants and soaps. The shop was on the corner of a row surrounding the busy central market, where the other traders sat on the ground selling their wares. It was the busiest place in Mumbai during peak hours in the morning and evening. Vehicles drove in and out amongst the masses of people, to off-load products and groceries. There was a great hustle and bustle about the market amidst the aroma of freshly made spicy food, tea, heaps of turmeric, coriander, garlic, ripe mangos, custard apples, and paw paws to name but a few. The honking of horns from the traffic and the shouts of 'Ten rupees a kilo potato' from traders trying to undercut each other, mingled in the air.

For about a year, a beggar had been sleeping on the floor next to Dad's shop. At night, he safeguarded his little pocket of money by placing it in his bag of clothes, which he used as a pillow whilst he slept. After the beggar awoke each morning, he approached the hotels around the corner from Dad's shop for leftovers about to be thrown away. One afternoon at four o'clock, as usual, the tea boy appeared with the kettle from the tea stall and poured out Dad's tea. Looking forward to his daily chat with one of the shopkeepers about the day's business, Dad tipped half of his tea into the saucer and wandered along the front hoping to offer the other half in the cup to a companion. Much to his disappointment, everyone was either too busy to drink with him or had just finished their own tea. So, feeling bereft of company, Dad wandered back to his shop. Just as he was about to enter, the beggar caught his eye, sitting on the ground counting the change he had collected. Dad bent down and nudged him, asking him if he would like some tea. The beggar did not say anything, he just raised his head and without a reply grabbed the tea from Dad and began to drink it. Dad assumed he was either shy or short of manners. He observed the beggar's dirty, half-sleeved shirt, trousers and chappals[1], wondering when they had last been washed, for they reeked of a stale, sweaty smell. He was very skinny with a beard even though he was only about fifteen years old. His skin was a dry scaly unnourished black with scruffy stiff rough hair, as he never washed. There were open wounds around his feet. He had a gaunt look about his face with his eyes set back in their sockets and he had broken brown, discoloured nails. He breathed a ghastly stench of breath. Despite all this, at least Dad knew that if ever he was short of someone to share his cup of tea with, he could turn to the beggar. After a short while, Dad had to leave him to attend to some customers.

Later on, the beggar timidly brought the empty cup back to the shop, holding it out to Dad uttering the words 'Aa pa pa'. Dad

1 Slippers.

asked 'What is it?' wondering what language he could be speaking. He asked his name, but the beggar just kept repeating 'Aa pa pa... aa pa pa' signalling to his mouth and ears. 'Oh!' Dad thought, 'Aa pa pa, that's his name', so he began to address him as Aa pa pa. However, it eventually dawned on Dad that the reason the beggar was pointing to his mouth and ears was because he was deaf and dumb. From that day onwards, Dad shared his cup of tea with the beggar, as the other shopkeepers could afford theirs.

Over the next few days, the other shopkeepers became curious about the relationship developing between Dad and the beggar. One by one, they drifted over seeking more information about him. Dad explained about the beggar always being there beside his shop, that he slept there each night and that he was deaf and dumb. Ghungo, meaning dumb, then became the name by which the beggar was known. The shopkeepers told Dad that whenever it was past lunchtime, to send Ghungo across to them for any leftovers or a share of their food. Following this, every shopkeeper gave Ghungo food from their tiffin[2]; biscuits, rusk, samosas, wada pav[3], chapattis, curried vegetables, Indian snacks such as Bombay mix, chai[4], water, and even some loose change.

Sometimes in the off peak hours when business was dead after lunchtime, the shopkeepers became bored. It was during these hours that Ghungo became their favourite pastime. As Ghungo counted his little bag of change, one of the shopkeepers snatched it, causing him to scream 'Aa pa pa! aa pa pa!' chasing the shopkeeper up the street whilst the others laughed. Then the bag was thrown from one shopkeeper to the next, only serving to escalate Ghungo's fury as he helplessly attempted to reclaim his most prized possession, thinking it was going to be stolen. The whole street was full of laughter and screams as everyone enjoyed the entertainment, apart

2 Round pyramid shaped metal lunch box.
3 Spicy potato ball inside a bread roll with chutney.
4 Tea.

from Ghungo of course. However, he was rewarded for his role at the end of the game, as every shopkeeper filled his bag with change. Calming down with a big grin on his face, Ghungo walked back to his place at the side of the shop to count the bulging bag of money.

Some weeks later, Dad was expecting his delivery man to come and collect an order placed by a customer. He waited and waited, but the man did not turn up. Dad had given the phone number for the hotel reception next door to all of his customers, as he did not have a phone. When the calls began to come in from the irate customer expecting his order, Dad had an awful time trying to explain the situation; he could only say that the delivery man had not turned up. To avoid losing the order Dad had an idea. He calmed the customer down and assured him that his delivery would arrive soon. He locked his shop, got the order ready and signalled Ghungo to come towards him and pick up two cloth carrier bags full of bleaching fluids and cleaning powder. Dad also carried two bags in his hands and they set off to deliver the goods. Feeling very pleased after the delivery, as Ghungo was such a valuable help, Dad took him to a restaurant as a reward and bought him lunch and a packet of bidis[5]; a matchbox and gave him a ten rupee note. However, this confused Ghungo who just stood there holding the ten-rupee note, not knowing what to do with it. He handed it back to Dad indicating he did not want it. Dad gestured 'Why?' asking if it was too little, but received no response from him. Then, in a moment of inspiration, Dad went to get the note changed into ten rupees worth of coins. Receiving the big bagful of loose change Ghungo was overwhelmed. He could not believe his eyes that all of the money was his. How silly of Dad for not realising Ghungo had never received a bank note before. From this moment on, whenever there was such an emergency, Dad knew he could rely on Ghungo. He even began to trust Ghungo to mind the

5 Ready-made dried tobacco rolled up in a
dried leaf, tied with a tiny thread.

shop, if he had to leave for a short break. It was not long before Ghungo was helping Dad with the packing, filling, weighing, labelling and sealing the packets of bleaching powder. However, Dad was very careful to communicate to Ghungo the importance of wearing a face mask during the packing, as the chemicals were very strong.

A year later in the monsoon season there was very heavy rain; the roads became flooded and were more like rivers. Standing outside in this rain is equal to buckets of water being continuously thrown over you. During this time of year, Ghungo slept under a covered area, on an empty counter, used to display goods in the daytime, but even the counter had been washed away. Concern about where Ghungo was going to sleep enveloped the shopkeepers, as he peered through the opening at the front of the shops with his sad eyes, clinging on to his belongings like a drowning cat appealing to be rescued. No one did anything, as they were more concerned about themselves and how they were going to get home. Dad, however, took pity on him as intermittent thoughts ran through his head. Where would Ghungo sleep? What if he died of pneumonia? What if the trains stopped running and Dad was unable to return to work the next day? So, Dad closed his shop quickly and gestured at Ghungo to come along with him. A big smile beamed across Ghungo's face. Dad took him to the train station just a short walk away. However, wading through a river of water up to their knees, with a prolonged waterfall cascading across them, in strong howling winds, made the journey akin to an epic expedition. With the tip of an umbrella, Dad felt for manholes and potholes under the muddy murky water imparting the odour of sewage into the rain swept air. This was the best use for umbrellas as people's lives had been claimed by underwater death traps.

They arrived at the station to find the trains were still running, so Dad bought Ghungo a ticket. After a treacherous journey, they reached home. They were both drenched through from head to toe, but no sooner had they entered the apartment, my uncle, auntie and grandma demanded to know who the foul, servile creature was. My short-tempered auntie was angry because he was ruining the floor after barging inside the house. 'Why is he coming into our house? Water dripping everywhere on the stone tiles... What's he doing in here?' Dad explained that Ghungo had nowhere to sleep and that he was deaf and dumb. He told them not to worry as he would take Ghungo back to Dadar tomorrow. Ghungo was scared that he might get kicked out after my auntie's rant, meaning he would not be able to find his way around the unfamiliar surroundings of Thane. Auntie insisted that he should at least sleep outside the apartment in the corridor like a servant. She didn't want the dirty beggar inside with the family, as she also had two daughters and one son living there. Having also weathered Auntie's storm, Dad gave Ghungo one of his towels and a clean set of his clothes, a cup of tea and some food. He was given a bed sheet to sleep outside the apartment in the corridor. Ghungo was relieved to have a place to stay and from this moment on began to trust Dad as a friend.

When the morning arrived Ghungo was awoken in a state of shock and anger to find himself being kicked by the milkman who thought he was an intruder off the streets. Ghungo screamed 'Aa pa pa! Aa pa pa!', banging on the door, pleading for help. Much to her dismay, Grandma got up out of bed and rushed to open the door to see what was going on. She calmed Ghungo down by giving him signs of assurance, sitting him down. She took the milk and awoke Dad. As Auntie and Uncle were still asleep, Dad asked Grandma if Ghungo could use the toilet and bathroom. Dad wanted to give him a proper scrub, shampoo his hair, shave his beard, cut his nails and give him a bath. Grandma agreed. Having slipped into the bath, Ghungo enjoyed the luxurious smell of soap as it dispelled the engrained dirt from his body. He was dried afterwards and dusted all over with talcum powder. Dad gave him a new toothbrush and told him to brush his teeth, but he did not know how, so Dad had to do it for him. He gave him a clean set of underwear, vest, shirt and trousers. Clean-shaven and with a new set of clothes, Ghungo was amazed to see how he looked in the mirror. He could not believe the big change that had taken place and wore a big happy smile upon his face. Ghungo was given something to eat then he and Dad set off to work.

The conditions were still horrendous. When they arrived at the shop and opened the door, a torrent of water, knee high, gushed out onto the muddy and squidgy street. Ghungo was very helpful placing all the containers of fluids and powders onto the highest shelves and sweeping the water out of the shop. All of the traders had lost money because there were no customers and the flooding had ruined their goods. As there was no improvement in the weather, Dad took Ghungo back home in the evening. He made Ghungo sit outside the apartment whilst he went with Grandma for a little chat, explaining about the atrocious weather conditions in Dadar. Grandma was very sympathetic and kindly agreed that Ghungo could stay until the conditions improved. As it was Grandma's house this was a big assurance to Dad, he could afford to ignore the harsh attitude towards Ghungo from Auntie and Uncle.

As the days passed by, the family became accustomed to Ghungo's presence and Grandma decided to have a chat with Auntie about letting Ghungo stay as a member of the family. However, Auntie disagreed because keeping Ghungo would mean extra work for her, on top of having to look after her own children. Grandma tried to convince her that Ghungo would be no trouble at all. He would just come home every night with Dad, have his food, go to bed, get up and use the bathroom and toilet facilities in the morning, before going back to work with Dad to Dadar. Therefore, he would not be in her way. Auntie was still not happy and Grandma was disappointed with her response. However, Auntie was very cunning and had a plan up her sleeve. She suggested that Ghungo should help her with the household chores, such as sweeping and mopping the tiled floors, washing up the dishes, washing the clothes and doing the shopping. This way she and Uncle would save money by getting rid of the maid they paid to do this work. So eventually, Ghungo was able to sleep inside the apartment instead of outside in the corridor. He had his own corner where he kept a rolled up mattress. He was provided with his own set of cutlery, bowl, glass and a plate, his own bag of clothes and toiletries. Dad gave him ten rupees daily as pocket money for helping at the shop and sometimes helping at home. At work, Dad bought Ghungo's meals and cups of tea. They ate together, smoked together, drank tea together, travelled together and worked together. Dad and Ghungo became inseparable as they both enjoyed each other's company so much.

Because Dad had a monthly train ticket, he would board the train without buying Ghungo a daily ticket, otherwise it would mean having to queue up for two hours at a time, as is usually the case in India. One day the inevitable happened. Ghungo was caught without a ticket by the ticket collector. Dad had to pay his fine, but explained he could not get Ghungo a monthly ticket because he had no identity. Also, because of his personal circumstances, there was no information that could be written for him on a monthly pass. So the ticket collector helped Dad. The name Ghungo was actually written on the pass, his current address, with a note 'Adopted from the street' and his thumbprint was used as a signature. Dad then bought him a travel pass every month.

Slowly, Dad and Ghungo started to build up a series of gestures in order to communicate. Dad taught him to write a few basic words such as his age, his name and a signature for his railway pass instead of using his thumbprint. He even managed to teach him to write numbers, from one to ten. Ghungo learned a special sign to signify each person in the family. The sign of a sign of a bindi[6] on the forehead symbolised Auntie. The sign of a moustache under the nose meant Uncle. A gesture of a headscarf on a head depicted Grandma. The sign of a nose ring symbolised Mum and a hand on his heart meant Dad 'Whom I love the most – my friend'. Aw! So sweet!

During the next four years the relationship between Ghungo and Dad grew stronger and stronger, Dad was really attached to him. He never treated Ghungo as a servant, but as a younger brother. In 1971 when Dad turned thirty years of age, he married Mum, which meant an extra member coming into the family. She did not know anything about Ghungo and it never even crossed Dad's mind to ask Ghungo to leave the house in order to accommodate Mum, such was the bond between them. Within a few weeks of Dad getting married, one day some of his relatives unexpectedly paid a visit. Dad was not at home, so Mum had to attend to them, but unfortunately, she did not have enough food in the house, so she wrote down a list of snacks for Ghungo to go and buy from the bazaar, attempting to communicate this to him through her hand gestures. She even wrote down for the traders: six samosas, one packet of Bombay mix and paapri[7], and gave Ghungo a ten-rupee note. So, off Ghungo went to the bazaar. Time passed by and Mum became anxious about her guests, she was ashamed that all she had to offer them was tea and biscuits. She wondered where Ghungo had got to. So much time elapsed that the guests left before Ghungo returned. Eventually Ghungo turned up, but there was no sign of any shopping. Accompanied by what gestures Mum could muster up, she asked angrily 'Where have you been? What took you so long? Where is the shopping?' With a gesture to his mouth and stomach, Ghungo signed 'This list, I ate it all away'. Mum just stood there gob smacked. When she asked about the loose change, Ghungo took some bidis from his inside pocket. Mum

6 Hindus wear a tilak (a red dot by women and an elongated dot by men) on their foreheads, between the two eyes. This point is known by various names such as Ajna chakra, Spiritual eye and Third eye. It was said to be the major nerve in the human body, in ancient times.
7 A savoury crisp made of chickpea flour.

became furious. She proceeded to blame Dad for bringing such a good for nothing into the house who just ate, ate and ate. She waited for Dad to return home and told him what had happened. Dad just laughed and explained that he had once made the same mistake of not communicating the gestures properly, leading to Ghungo eating a whole load of sandwiches intended for his business colleagues. So, Dad calmed her down and after that day he taught her how to express all the right gestures for Ghungo.

In 1972 a year after Mum and Dad were married, I was born. My brother, Shailesh, was born two years later in 1974. Shortly after this, my auntie and uncle moved out of the house with their children and Mum no longer had anyone to help her with the household chores. Mum mopped, washed clothes, dusted, cleaned, ironed and cooked for the house. When Shailesh was only one year old, due to the hot weather he crawled about naked in the house. One lunchtime, as Ghungo sat on the floor eating his food, Shailesh toddled towards Ghungo to show him his new rattle, waving it in front of his face. However, Ghungo was too engrossed in his meal. My baby brother soon caught his attention when he released a squirt of wee all over Ghungo and his food. 'Aa pa pa!' Aa pa pa!' Ghungo shot up, aggressively throwing his plate of food to the floor. He carried on screaming as his beloved food was ruined. His screaming scared Shailesh and he burst into tears thinking Ghungo might hurt him. Rice, dhal, chapattis covered the floor in the puddles created by Shailesh. Ghungo rushed towards Mum in the other room, dragging her in to see the mess. He was only concerned about his food. As Shailesh paddled in the mess, Mum came in and picked him up. She gestured to Ghungo in order to find out what had happened. Ghungo just kept tapping Shailesh's arm indicating that it was his fault. Mum did not know what had happened for sure, so she kept asking how the mess had occurred. She checked the water pipe to see if it was leaking, she wondered if Shailesh or Ghungo had knocked a glass over, but Ghungo pointed to

Shailesh's lower regions. Then Mum realised what had happened and burst out laughing along with Grandma as she handed Shailesh over to her. Then she began to clean up the mess whilst chuckling to herself, but the incident was also an eye opening indication of Ghungo's aggressive behaviour.

Ghungo had a huge appetite and Dad never refused him food. It was during one of Ghungo's gorging of food moments that Mum noticed an awful smell. She was horrified to discover that Ghungo had soiled his pants, yet he was still quite content to sit at the table and carry on eating and eating. She became angry, but nevertheless washed his soiled pants. This started to become a regular occurrence and after an appointment with the doctor, Ghungo was diagnosed with a stomach disorder, he could not control his bowels. Because of this illness, Ghungo no longer went to work with Dad. Instead, he stayed in the house all day just eating and sleeping. Mum found herself having to wash his pants everyday. She could not stand doing this disgusting task on top of all the other chores and broke down crying, cursing her misfortune and fate, she could not take any more. Once, Ghungo was sat in the eating area, right next to the cooker near the little shrine on the wall. Mum could smell that Ghungo had soiled his pants even though he was just sitting there eating. He did not seem aware of this at all. Mum shouted 'How can you just sit there with that in your pants and eat at the same time?' As she carried on shouting, Ghungo could only understand she was angry with him. She snatched the plate from his hand and told him to go and wash himself. Thinking he was not going to get his beloved food back, Ghungo raised a fist in anger. Mum grabbed hold of his shirt collar and pushed him towards the bathroom, telling him she was not going to tolerate his nonsense anymore. Later that day she complained to Dad, about Ghungo. Mum also explained he did not act as a mature person and now was even displaying signs of threatening behaviour and anger. She argued that Ghungo was over thirty years old now, that I was ten years old and growing up, so they could not afford to keep him in the house any longer, as he could be a risk to my brother and I. In particular, she was so sick of having to clean Ghungo's mess. She told Dad that Ghungo would have to go.

Reluctantly Dad began to think of ideas of how he could send Ghungo away. He came up with the plan of buying Ghungo a local rail ticket to the end of the Victoria Terminus, one hour away from Dadar. So, the day came when, with a heavy heart, Dad bought Ghungo the ticket. Walking onto the train with him, he made sure Ghungo sat in his seat and gave him some bidis, a matchbox and some money for his journey. With a deep sense of betrayal, Dad gestured 'You go, I'll come after, I've got things to do'. He left the train with a tear in his eye, making sure Ghungo did not see how sad he was. Dad arrived home that day with an extreme sense of loss and told everyone that Ghungo had now gone away for good. Dad could not eat nor sleep that night because of his guilt and sadness. He missed Ghungo so much. The next day Dad went to Dadar as usual. Whilst in his shop he lamented the loss of Ghungo all morning. Outside his shop around lunchtime, he surveyed the scenes of people buying and selling their wares as he reflected upon life. A figure in the distance caught the corner of his eye, it looked vaguely familiar, as it drew closer it looked like Ghungo, it was Ghungo! Dad could not believe his eyes; he was so shocked yet so happy. They both hugged and celebrated Ghungo's return, and then Dad went to buy him some lunch. Though he was so happy at the return of his close friend, Dad now faced the dilemma of taking Ghungo back home, no doubt to the shock and horror of Mum. Later that day upon arriving home, Dad somehow managed to convince Mum to let Ghungo stay for the time being. Neither he, nor anyone else could explain how Ghungo had managed to find his way back to Dadar. However, Dad was forced to concede that he would still have to try and get rid of him permanently.

A few weeks later Dad tried putting Ghungo on another train, but again much to everyone's disbelief, Ghungo found his way back. Dad was at a loss of what to do next. He confided with a business friend about Ghungo's problem at home. His friend was about to leave by train on a business trip to Pune, so he advised Dad to put Ghungo on the same train. He assured Dad that Ghungo would reach Pune and would not come back. So, Dad bought Ghungo two packs of bidis, a matchbox, gave him one hundred rupees in cash, a ticket to Pune and some food and water in a bag. As before, Dad fared Ghungo goodbye with tears in his eyes, watching the train setting off for Pune. Surely this time Ghungo would not be coming back.

One day, two days, then three days passed and there was no sign of Ghungo. There was an empty void in the house and in Dad's heart. It was the saddest moment of his life. He missed Ghungo every day and every night; during meal times and during smoking times when Ghungo used to sit on a box next to Dad in the shop, giving him such good company. When Dad had his afternoon tea break, he stared at the vacant space beside the shop, where he first shared his cup of tea with Ghungo fifteen years ago. Fifteen years, a long time to share a special relationship with a friend. We do not know what happened to Ghungo after he was sent to Pune, but Dad still has tears his eyes whenever we speak about him. I phoned Dad yesterday in India asking for more details about Ghungo's story. He said it has been twenty-three years now and he still misses him. They had a wonderful time together. God bless Ghungo wherever he is. Amen.

Collated by Monica Ballani

Hospital Blackmail

(Anonymous)

Elsie was born in Bolton on 20th May 1938, the week when King George VI and Queen Elizabeth paid a visit to Bolton, just before the war. A friend said to her uncle 'Have you heard the Queen's coming?' Her uncle replied, 'The Queen has arrived' meaning Elsie. Elsie was an only child and grew up in a loving family.

In 1949 when Elsie was ten years old she had to go into hospital to have a mastoid ear operation because the bone behind her ear was diseased. During the morning of Elsie's appointment, she traipsed around the house lovingly saying goodbye to all the rooms and objects in the house, including the grandfather clock and all of her toys. Elsie had never been away from home before. Unfortunately, her mum had to work that day, so it was down to her dad to take her to the old Bolton Royal Infirmary just off Chorley New Road, where David Lloyd's Leisure Club now stands today.

It was a cool breezy day, there was not a cloud in sight. Elsie's father collected her from school later that morning and they both walked to the hospital. The journey was quicker than expected as they walked through the back streets. Both of them were quiet as they walked along, each contemplating from their own perspective how Elsie's stay at the hospital would transpire. As they neared the end of their journey, Elsie felt the dampness of her father's palm as he gripped her hand tightly. On entering the hospital, Elsie became very scared, but at the same time, she tried to put on a brave face for her father who was trying to cheer her up. They waited nervously until it was time for Elsie to see the consultant. He explained that she would be staying in the hospital, but he could not predict for how long.

It was soon time to say goodbye to her father. They both wore brave faces, trying not to cry and Elsie tried her best not to show how nervous she was. They both gave each other a big bear hug before her father departed to leave his little girl.

Elsie was taken to the children's Chadwick Ward. She felt strange as she entered the long ward with a column of beds on both sides and lots of children's eyes peering at her. The beds were big old fashioned iron beds, surrounded by dirty brown coloured walls, not very bright and cheery at all like the children's wards of today. The ward smelled of disinfectant and ether, a gas used for anaesthetic. The nurse's desk station was positioned like a teacher's desk at the top of the class.

Above Elsie's bed there was a brass plaque, which read 'This bed has been donated by Bolton School Girls Division'. Though she did not know it at the time, the plaque would turn out to be a premonition of things to come for Elsie. At seven o'clock that night a couple of nurses shaved off Elsie's hair just above the ear, as her operation was due the next day, Saturday. The shaving of her much revered locks of hair was a traumatic experience for her, as it would be to any girl of her age. At least there were quite a few books in the ward to help comfort her, as Elsie loved to read.

The next morning, off Elsie went for her operation. An incision over the mastoid bone had to be made in order to remove the infected bony material under a general anaesthetic. Elsie cannot remember much about her operation, as in those days anyone undergoing an operation of this type was usually unconscious for at least twenty-four hours. Elsie did not regain consciousness until Sunday, all she remembers is how she felt after the operation. Because of the ether gas, she felt dreadful and was physically sick. When asleep she constantly shouted 'Oh my ear!' Despite this, the operation had gone well, but Elsie had to remain in hospital until she had fully recovered.

In the children's ward there were no visiting hours, making it a distressing time for Elsie and her parents. Elsie's dad had to phone the hospital from a public payphone to ask how she was coping. Little effort was made to make the children feel comfortable. The nurses were very strict and not at all friendly. They were figures of authority and all the children were in awe of them. Today parents can visit their children in the wards and even stay overnight to comfort them.

The most exciting time on the ward was the anticipation of all the children as they awaited parcels from home. All of their eyes would light up when the parcels were brought in on a big stretcher. Elsie used to get excited and wandered around impatiently, waiting for the stretcher to arrive. The parcels consisted of letters, sweets, stamps, papers, and anything to cheer the children up and keep them occupied. From time to time, Elsie received a shoebox of goodies from her family and letters from her school friends. One day Elsie was very happy when she received sheet music in a parcel from her mum, motivating her to walk over to a neighbouring children's ward to play the piano. She played the happy childlike tunes her mum had sent to her in the post until her heart was content. Her piano playing was too loud for the quiet environment of the hospital; sometimes she would play the piano at six thirty in the morning, driving the nurses mad.

Whenever the children received any food in their parcels, they were supposed to pass them over to the nurses. One day, when Elsie opened her shoe box, much to her delight she found a bar of chocolate inside and couldn't resist keeping it to herself, to nibble under the covers. However, the girl in the next bed knew about Elsie's secret and decided to blackmail her. She demanded that if Elsie did not give her a stamp, she would tell the nurses about the chocolate. Because of the strict regime in the hospital, Elsie was afraid, so she complied with the girl's wishes. However, this only served to whet the girl's appetite even more to extract further gifts from Elsie throughout the rest of her stay. The mean girl continued to blackmail Elsie over the chocolate. As Elsie felt intimidated and frightened she handed over any gifts that the girl asked for. It was the first time in Elsie's life that someone had a hold over her and she didn't like it one bit. After a while Elsie had had enough, she decided she was not going to give in to the blackmailing anymore. One day Elsie refused to hand over a gift that the girl had demanded. However, her bully was determined to have her own way. All it took was for her to shout the word 'Nurse!' and Elsie was frightened once again into submission. Reluctantly, Elsie handed over her present.

Elsie had had enough of this girl. She also felt bored in the hospital and she was missing her family so much. Despite there being a strict regime in the hospital, Elsie's curiosity often took her wandering off into other wards. Aware that she was able to get away with this, Elsie decided to try and escape from the hospital. She planned to see if she could make it to her grandma's house. Elsie actually managed to walk through the whole hospital undetected and stepped outside the grounds onto Chorley New Road. It would have been easy for her to find her way to her grandmother's house, not too far away on Chorley Old Road, but her conscience got the better of her and she decided to turn around and go back to her ward.

After nearly three weeks, a doctor came around to speak to Elsie and her blackmailer, as they had both had the same operation at approximately the same time. Elsie was overjoyed, as she was told that she would soon be going home, before her mean friend. At last, Elsie thought she would be rid of the bully and the boredom that plagued her, but to Elsie's amazement, her cruel companion was actually sent home first by the nurses. Elsie wondered if there was any justice in the world. Despite being disappointed and irritated, she was at least glad and extremely relieved to see the back of her, so there was still some sense of freedom.

When the day did finally arrive for Elsie to go home on 1ˢᵗ April 1949, her dad came to collect her. She was very excited when she saw him walking down the corridor. They were both overjoyed to be reunited after such a long time. Elsie was also looking forward so much to sleeping in her own bed for a change. Later that day, Elsie found out she had been offered a place at Bolton School Girls Division, a well known grammar school with an excellent reputation and tradition. It was a very welcome surprise and news of her place was printed in the local paper.

Today, Elsie says that her three weeks in hospital were the longest three weeks of her life. She recounts the premonition of the brass plaque, above her bed as having a double meaning. Not only did she end up studying at the same school, but later in her life she became involved in the same type of fundraising.

Collated by Selma Kadva

Feelings that can Last a Lifetime

(Raisa Ivanovna)

My name is Raisa Ivanovna; I am seventy six years old. I used to live in Bolton, but now live in an ordinary, very English looking house situated in the Leeds suburbs. Although the exterior of the house looks English, the interior and the back garden are pretty much a little piece of Russia. My imported Russian furniture is arranged around the house in an orderly fashion. Russian relics of cutlery line the shelves on the walls in the living room. I have transformed the back garden of the house into a small Russian vegetable garden, where I grow my tomatoes and cucumbers.

One March morning, in the year of 1976, I was just about to go into the garden and water the vegetables, when the phone started to ring. So I took my gardening gloves off and trundled off into the living room to answer it. 'Hello?' I said as usual. A German sounding voice replied: 'Hello? Raisa Ivanovna? Raisa, is that you? ...' I know this voice I thought, it sounds familiar, I'm sure I've heard it somewhere before. I could not put my finger on who it belonged to. Again the voice said: 'Hello? Hello? Raisa, are you there? Raisa? Is that you?' So naturally I replied: 'Uh ... yes, it is me ... Who is this?' He responded: 'Raisa, I'm so glad I found you! It's me, Martin! Martin Redfern! Raisa, are you there?'

I had fainted, dropping the phone. All the events connected to that voice had flashed before me in an instant. When I was sixteen, in the year of 1942, during the Second World War, I was taken captive from my birthplace, the village of Borowljany near Minsk in the Ukraine, bundled into a big suitcase and sent to work in Germany for free, as a slave. I think I was chosen because at the time I was a very beautiful girl. My kidnappers, in the Ukraine on a visit, had been ordered to kidnap someone for their master's household. I remember them to be two very broad and mean looking men. They approached me from behind, turned me round to examine my face and physique, then drugged me with a cloth soaked in chloroform and bundled me into a massive trunk. I wandered in and out of consciousness and registered very little. I remember vaguely that the trunk was quite spacious. When I regained consciousness for short periods of time, I could hear the steady beat of the Russian train tracks. I could smell a faint fragrance of tobacco, lavender soap and vodka.

After a long journey, we arrived at the train station, where I was released from the trunk. I had no way of telling how long the journey had lasted, but I felt like I had slept for a few days, though that could have been the effect of the chloroform. I was placed in the back of a plain but beautiful horse drawn carriage and taken to the house of my future owners. On my arrival I was taken aback by the grandeur of the place. We rode up a winding driveway through a beautiful park-like flower garden adorned with every different kind of flower and tree imaginable. It was a large forbidding farmhouse in the German countryside, near the city of Leipzig. It was obvious that the house was the property of someone very important who could afford this kind of luxury. At the back of the house there were animal enclosures, vegetable patches, fruit trees and a vineyard. The big spacious family house had huge windows, a red tiled roof and impeccably brilliant white walls. It could have been a fantastic place to live, but for my status as a slave. Later I found out that it was the home of a very important German government official. There were some rumours and wild guesses circulating amongst the slaves as to who this person was, but nobody could actually know for certain, as he seldom visited the place.

The Lady of the house, my owner, usually lived in the house on her own, whilst her husband was away on business or at war. She was extremely beautiful, with rosy cheeks, a cute button nose and marvellous brown eyes and hair, not one strand of it was out of place. Her physical form and shape was most feminine and perfect. She wore all the elegant dresses of the time. However, her bad character and disregard for the slaves far outweighed her beauty. She was the cruellest and nastiest person I have encountered in my life, a scary authoritarian figure. She did not say much to us personally and treated us with contempt.

There were sixteen slaves on the farm, I was the only woman. We survived on only one meal a day and even that was very meagre. We all had to get up very early in the morning, at the crack of dawn, usually five o'clock, and start work on the farm, sowing seeds, pulling weeds, looking after the animals, cleaning up after them and feeding them. All of this may not sound like hard work, but the fields were absolutely enormous, containing large numbers of pigs, cows, sheep, goats, and a multitude of different birds. There was a huge amount of work, even for sixteen slaves. Despite it being a very efficient farm household, the Lady of the house always walked the grounds voicing her dismay about anything she didn't like to her paid employees in charge of the farm. They in turn shouted at the slaves and punished those that didn't obey the orders exactly as specified. According to her Ladyship, all the problems on the farm were the fault of the slaves. We knew when she was talking about us even though we could not understand German. Her tone of voice was clearly vicious and expressed scant regard for us. My life was so very miserable; I was treated like an animal during my captivity. I was never spared the hard physical work because I was a woman. I had to do any job I was told to do from chopping wood to cleaning the enclosures of pigs, which was one of the hardest tasks. I had no freedom, wasn't allowed outside of the farm's walls. I had no spare time, the only thing I was allowed to do was sleep and work. In one instance, I hadn't eaten in two days, as I was working on the far side of the fields and so was late for my meals. During the night of the second day, I was so hungry, I sneaked out of the slave's quarters to get some food from the larder, but I was caught by a German worker. Despite trying to explain I hadn't eaten for two days he savagely beat me with his walking cane so hard, he knocked my two front teeth out. Each whooshing blow signalled a clear intent to leave visible signs of the beating as an example to the other slaves. I was dragged to the slaves' quarters and dumped on the floor for all of them to see. They had to help clean me up as I was in too much agony and pain to do it myself. The next day, I had to return to work as usual. Losing my two front teeth meant I also lost my beauty. No one could replace teeth, not in the Second World War.

Being a bright young girl and a natural linguist, after a while, I managed to learn how to pick up the German language quite well. This was noticed by my owner. She called me to her room and began to tell me about her ten year old son. From this moment, as well as the other tasks, I was put in charge of looking after him. His name was Martin, Martin Redfern. My main responsibilities were to check his homework, look after him and cater for him. However, our relationship was far from a master and slave relationship, it became more of a little brother and big sister relationship. He was not doing as well as he should have been with his school work and he needed help with his homework. I helped him as best I could by providing analogies and breaking down certain methods he had to learn into easy steps. After a while he began to do so much better in his classes and we were both very pleased. When he needed a break from his tuition we were able to go outside and play together in the gardens. He had certain anxieties as any young boy would have and he shared them with me. In turn I consoled him and reassured him there was nothing to worry about. He was not very close to his mother and so had no one to take on the role of his confidante. I would tell him of my troubles and he reassured me by putting in a good word for me with his mother, making sure I was spared some of the harder work. Martin looked up to me. I loved him like a sister loves her little brother because he was the only friend I had. Apart from my relationship with Martin, like any other slave I led the most miserable life imaginable. After three years, in 1945, when the Second World War ended, I was freed and ran away to England.

I missed Martin greatly, and thought I'd never see him again. However, this voice, this strange, but at the same time very familiar voice on the phone sounded like a grown-up Martin. I could not believe it was him and that I had actually fainted, missing the opportunity to speak to him. Later on that day, when I had regained my consciousness and composure, he phoned again. He and I talked and talked endlessly about how much we had missed each other over the last thirty one years. Martin told me how hard he had tried to find me. I didn't try to look for him because I thought he wouldn't like me anymore. I assumed that what we had over thirty years ago; all those warm feelings would have worn away as he grew older, but he told me quite the opposite and contradicted my worst fears. Martin assured me that even after thirty years he still felt the same flame of brotherly love towards me.

After phoning me back everyday for the next couple of weeks, Martin suggested that we meet in Paris. I was very happy with this proposal; I was over the moon in fact and phoned the travel agent straight away to book a ticket. When I got on that plane to Paris, even the butterflies in my stomach had butterflies! We were to meet on the fourteenth of April on a bench along one of the banks of the Channel of St. Martin, at eleven in the morning. I can still remember it, as though it was yesterday. He told me he'd be wearing a bright red top. Now, there were lots and lots of people wearing red tops that day and I must admit, for a while I was scared. I thought I would not recognise Martin in the crowd, but I did recognise him, I don't know how, I just knew it was him. I stood up, went up to him and embraced him in a tight bear hug. We stayed glued to each other for a long time and broke out in tears of joy. Seeing Martin after all those years brought back all the good feelings that we had towards each other. It also brought a combination of joy through meeting him again, but sadness because I didn't keep in touch with him after the war. I felt sorry it took thirty one years for us to be reunited again. However, all that was in the past, at least we were together now, better late than never. Martin and I spent the next three weeks together touring France.

After arriving back home, no sooner had a month passed, we decided to meet in Paris again, this time with our families. I took my English husband and my two sons. Martin took his Russian wife and his daughter. Since then, our families have even enjoyed holidays together. We have travelled to Russia, Germany and around England. Now, Martin and I still love each other very much; phone each other every month and our families still go on holiday together every year.

Collated by Elena Taban

The Holiday

(Anonymous)

Ali was born in 1972 in the city of Shiraz, Iran, where he later attended school. He had an older sister and a younger sister, his father was a mechanic and his mother was a housewife. He loved his childhood life in Shiraz. One of his most favourite pastimes was playing football with his friends. Usually when boys grow up into their teens they just want to play and have fun, behave irresponsibly, yet still want to be treated as adults. However, throughout his childhood, Ali always had time for other people. He was very happy with his family. Whenever his mum wanted help with the cleaning Ali would only be too pleased to assist. He would also go on errands whenever his mother needed something from the shops.

At fourteen years old, as Ali had proved he could act responsibly and his older sister was now eighteen years old, his parents decided that they both could look after themselves and their younger sister who was ten years of age. Ali's parents had wanted to go away on holiday for a quite a while, just so they could both have some time together, away from the children for a change. They decided to travel towards the north of Iran, to the seaside. Further towards the north of Iran the climate is milder and there is similar countryside to Britain. There is a lot more greenery than in the dry south of Iran and only the richer people live in the north, as houses are more expensive there. Ali's parents were not worried at all about leaving their children for a couple of weeks. It is fairly common in Iran for parents to give children such responsibilities. So the day finally arrived when his parents set off on their holiday, trusting Ali and his older sister to look after their youngest daughter.

Their parents had never left them this long before so Ali and his sisters enjoyed a new sense of freedom, but also a sense of responsibility. It was an opportunity for Ali's older sister to practise the cooking skills that she had learned from her mother. Most of the food that they needed had already been bought, but Ali did any additional shopping they needed and took responsibility for the menial chores around the house. Everything went extremely well, apart from Ali's younger sister missing her parents as soon as they had left. So Ali also had the task of keeping her occupied by playing games with her. Eventually they all began to realise just how much they depended on their parents and began to look forward to their arrival home. As the day of their arrival approached, Ali and his sisters made an extra special effort to make sure that everything in the house was clean, tidy and prepared to provide a warm welcome home for their mother and father, to express just how much they had missed them. Everything was ready in time. All that Ali and his sisters could do now was wait in anticipation of their parents' arrival.

At last, later on that afternoon, the phone rang, so Ali immediately grabbed it to speak to his father. Ali wasn't greeted by his father's voice, as he had anticipated; instead, a stranger's voice dissolved all of Ali's enthusiasm and expectancy, sending a cold shiver up his spine. She said she was a nurse and in an apologetic murmur, informed him that his parents had been involved in a car crash on their way home, that his father had died and his mother was about to undergo surgery for serious head injuries. The words from the nurse were unreal, but continually floated around Ali's mind as if waiting to be accepted. Suddenly the accustomed structure of the world was distorted, nothing appeared safe or secure anymore. The care and love the children had invested and manifested in every part of the house to welcome their parents home, lingered as an unrequited embrace.

Words cannot convey the sense of loss suffered by the children and the strength and hope they all needed to pray for the survival of their mother. Barely had they even began to contemplate coming to terms with the loss of their father, their mother too, passed away. The only way that Ali could physically feel being a part of this world anymore was to involve himself in some of the tasks regarding the preparations for the funeral.

During the traditional mourning period of fourteen days, relatives and friends descended upon the house. There were many tears shed from Ali, his sisters, aunts and uncles. The men and women mourned in separate rooms, praying, paying their condolences, respect and remembrance. Ali ensured there was enough food to cook meals for the guests during the whole two weeks.

After the mourning period was over, an even bigger sense of responsibility began to grip Ali, which helped him in his grieving process. He walked with his sisters to the cemetery to talk to their parents' grave every week. His uncle and auntie volunteered to support and look after all of them. However, Ali decided that he could not continue his study and left school early, in order to look for a job, so that he could support his sisters alone.

Ali had to work away from home, but he did accept the occasional help from his uncle. It was a very hard time for Ali as he had been used to growing up in a comfortable family environment. This secure environment had enabled him to contemplate many dreams and wishes to fulfil when he grew older, but now they had been shattered. Ali applied for any job available and eventually found a cleaning job in a restaurant. He worked very hard at the restaurant for very little money which made him become increasingly depressed. He grew friendly with one of the other workers at the restaurant, who was also desperate for money. He seriously suggested to Ali that they should draw up a plan to rob a jeweller's shop, as there are many jewellers' shops in Iran. Fortunately, Ali was sensible enough not to take his friend's advice as he is now in prison for committing this crime. A second stealing offence in Iran would result in a thief's hand being cut off.

Eventually, Ali was able to take on other jobs and ended up working all hours of the day. He became extremely exhausted and when he finished work, all he could do was climb into bed. He never received the opportunity to enjoy himself or even think of taking a break or a holiday. His primary concern was his sisters' welfare. Ali began to mature as he worked over the next few years and was a pillar of strength for his sisters. His older sister became married when she was twenty-two years old and his younger sister soon followed.

Ali is thankful to God the Almighty who helped him to overcome all the difficulties and hardship he faced during those agonising years. His sisters are very grateful to him for all his hard work and support. Two years ago, Ali had to leave his country for political reasons and came to live in England.

Collated by Nasim Rezaei

Little Sparrow

(Nyla Anwar)

Iftikhar was born on 2nd February in 1962 in Shahadapur, a small town in Sindh, Pakistan. Iftikhar started school at five years old, attending primary school from 1967 to 1972, then High School from 1972 to 1977. He successfully studied for a degree in art in 1985 and a Masters in Political Science in 1987 then worked as a school teacher from 1984 until 1992.

Iftikhar remembers very well the small town of Shahadapur where he lived as a boy. Around his house neem trees grew, also known as 'wonder trees' for many centuries, renowned for their health properties. On a blistering hot day, the temperature under a neem tree can be ten degrees lower than the surrounding area. Iftikhar remembers fondly the sweet smell of the flowers, especially just after it had rained. He remembers the taste of his favourite dish, a traditional sweet made from flour and dry mango, which he enjoyed very much. The most exciting event that occurred in his town was the occasional procession of camels passing through at sunset. The camels wore small bells around their necks and legs, playing sweet melodies filtering through the air, accompanying their movement. Iftikhar would often stand with his friends to watch and listen as the camels strolled by, carrying cotton from the villages to a ginning[1] factory.

Iftikhar's town of Shahadapur suffered from poverty and was politically unstable. It was among the large desert hills which meant there were hardly any places for playing games like cricket and football. It was very hot there, around fifty degrees Celsius. Whilst Iftikhar loved these games, he was frustrated at the lack of opportunities to play them. This made him bored, restless and very unhappy. His town certainly did not

---

1 Ginning is a process to separate the cotton seeds from the raw cotton which was handpicked from the cotton fields.

have any money to provide any leisure activities. There was a very untidy, neglected, piece of wasteland where there used to be an old cottage. It was here that Iftikhar used to go and play, practising his football and cricket skills. He really appreciated this place and loved playing there as a form of escapism from his strict and angry father.

Iftikhar was also interested in nature, particularly birds. He longed to catch a sparrow and often dreamed about this, as in his rural culture, especially amongst the villagers, it was a privileged few who were fortunate enough to catch and keep a bird. Possessing such a bird was a matter of pride and distinction, but Iftikhar also wished for one to be his own personal companion, as he was a very lonely young boy. He knew this would be a very special experience for him and often observed the birds as they flew to and from the surrounding trees.

One day Iftikhar went alone to the wasteland to practise his footballing skills. As he walked to the old cottage, the sun was blazing hot and the wind was blowing gently. As he passed the wild untamed flower bushes, which reached high up into the sky, he was sure that he had heard a little squeak. He stopped in his tracks and parted the long, spiky bushes, full of thorns, to see what it was. There, to his utter amazement, was a sparrow, but it seemed to be in some kind of distress. As he knelt down, he noticed the sparrow was bleeding. It looked like its wing was injured and maybe broken. Iftikhar realised that a large thorn was stuck into the bird's wing. He assumed that the sparrow must have fallen from the trees and onto the spiky thorns of the wild flower bushes. Iftikhar gently picked out the thorn and discarded it, then picked up the bird and headed off towards home. His hand was shaking as he tried to hold the sparrow carefully. At the same time, a sense of pride and joy filled his heart as he carried it along his journey.

As soon as he had arrived home, he rubbed some mustard

seed oil onto some rags and bandaged the bird's wing. He then covered its wing with a clean cloth, provided by his mother. His dream of catching a sparrow had suddenly come true, though not in the way he had envisaged.

After a few days the little sparrow had begun to get better and was moving about a lot more freely, even flapping its wings. Iftikhar had become attached to his little friend and wanted to keep him. He thought about putting the sparrow into an old broken cage and hanging the cage from a tree next to his house. So, with the cage in one hand, he put his foot up onto the window ledge of the room nearest to the tree. He stretched, leaning over towards the tree, grabbing one of its branches. As he lifted one leg towards the trunk of the tree, he tried to maintain his balance by holding onto a wire, which was hanging loose from the wall of his house. Just at that moment a tremendous bolting shock buzzed through his hand and flung him away towards the tree, where he managed to hold onto a couple of branches, swinging backwards and forwards. He was in great pain, feeling the full force of the electricity. He let out a piercing scream. He began to cry and his body was shaking like a leaf. Everybody came running out of the house. Iftikhar's mum tried to pull him by one of his legs, but she received an electric shock too and let go immediately. Neighbours and friends soon gathered round and the electricity supply was shut off. One man brought a stick and prodded Iftikhar who then fell to the ground. He was physically weak, in a mental state of shock and could not stand on his own two feet. He had placed his hand on a bare piece of wire, which was not properly fitted. The electricity supply had been newly introduced into the small town at a domestic level. However, there were no properly trained electricians who were knowledgeable enough about fitting electrical wiring or fully aware about the dangers of electricity.

Iftikhar soon found himself tucked up in bed. His neighbours made him some warm milk with a spoon of turmeric to help restore his energy. Everyone around his bedside was frightened and some of the old women began to curse the electrical supply, saying that it was a bad omen and that lanterns were much safer. Then Iftikhar's grandmother began to shout at him, exclaiming that the accident had been caused because Iftikhar had captured the sparrow. She decreed that the only thing left to do was to free the bird, otherwise there may be other disasters lurking ahead. This thought frightened her, but she was also like a bird, a very wise old owl. Nature had intended the bird to be free to fly and not caged up. His grandmother believed in the old saying 'You reap what you sow'. She had always preached this to Iftikhar, but it was only now that he was beginning to understand the true meaning of her words. Despite his best intentions to nurse the bird back to health, he had annoyed it by wanting to hold onto to it and keep it in the cage, therefore taking away its freedom. Iftikhar began to wonder too, if he was being punished for his actions.

After Iftikhar had recovered from his misfortune he was still very reluctant to release the sparrow because he was so fond of his little friend. He wrestled with his thoughts about setting the sparrow free, for this would mean the loss of a companion that he could not replace. However, soon Iftikhar began to come to his senses and actually felt a sense of pride that he had helped and cared for the bird. It was precisely because of his care and attention that the bird was now well and ready to fly away on its own. So Iftikhar opened the door of the cage and without a moment's hesitation, the little sparrow fluttered its wings and flew off towards the trees. As Iftikhar watched his friend fly away, he also felt a sense of freedom, for he discovered a part of himself that he did not know existed.

Collated by Tahira Patel, Nusrat Rafique and Benaz Amen

The Salon

(Faruk Amen)

I love my car. It is a Vauxhall Astra 1.7 Turbo Diesel and very economical. I can drive it for at least one month on thirty five pounds worth of fuel. I remember when I used to see this beautiful black shiny machine parked every day near the barbers where I got my first job in this country. I fell in love with its curved shapely body so much that I found out who the owner was and bought the car off him. Now it is my pride and joy.

On the morning of 18th December 2004, I awoke with a headache, because the previous night I had had a nightmare about my beloved car being stolen. I climbed out of bed, went to the bathroom and washed my face with cold water, then went downstairs and turned on some nice, calming, classical music. After my breakfast I was ready to go to work. As I opened the door, a cold blast of air rushed onto my face. Outside, a veil of white frost had descended and crystallised everything in sight. When I saw that my car was still there, a smile came to my face, even though it was now white. I breathed a sigh of relief, as my nightmare had not come true.

Despite the freezing cold, my baby started first time as usual and I set off to work towards the centre of Bolton. On my way I saw a fellow Kurdish friend waiting for a bus. I managed to pull over immediately and called him to hop into the car. I had met him some months ago at Rice and Three, whilst he was working there and I was having my lunch. Along the journey to work, we engaged in the topical conversation of car parking. I was so fed up because I had to pay three pounds and fifty pence every day to park my car and yet I'd still spent about three hundred pounds in parking fines due to traffic wardens being over zealous. My friend asked me where I usually parked my car. I told him that I parked it just behind the hair salon where I work. He asked why I parked there, when I could park my car for nothing behind his work place, just across the road from the hair salon. I was overjoyed at this news, free car parking in Bolton! Needless to say, I took up his offer!

I had worked at barber shops in Iraq and Turkey, but in these countries the haircuts were just a case of a short back and sides for the men. I remember using a thin metal holder with a kind of wick at the end. This would be dipped in alcohol or petrol, set alight, then used to burn the fine hairs off the men's faces, near the eyes and around the ears. However, when I tried introducing it in this country, it scared people off. Over here the unisex hairdressers are a very different experience. The women are very demanding, their focus is entirely on the artistic merits of the hair style. When I first began working in the unisex hair salon I did not really understand what they wanted, in fact, once a woman was so dissatisfied, she walked out and refused to pay.

After dropping my friend off and parking the car in my new parking space, I walked across the road to the salon. This particular day, the salon became extremely busy because it was a Saturday. I did not even get an opportunity to eat any dinner as there were always customer appointments. We had to work fast, as we could not afford to keep the customers waiting long. We counted ourselves fortunate if we were able to get a break and go to the toilet for a rest, but even that was out of the question on this day. As English is not my first language, it was difficult to keep the customers entertained whilst drying their hair or waiting for a dye to take effect. I found myself asking the same questions about their work and their holidays. 'Have you been anywhere this year? Did you enjoy it? How much money did you spend?' I even took on the role of waiter serving them tea and coffee. Then the peroxide began to get too much for me, I hate the smell, I kept opening the door to let it out and tried to avoid having to do dyes or perms. However, this was contrasted by the delightful fruity fragrance of the shapers, perfumed waxes used for styling short hair. For the guys I also applied a special aftershave from Turkey that makes you feel very mellow and calm. One lady rang for an appointment, making a special request for her hair to be cut by the Italian guy. We all laughed as we knew she meant me, the Kurdish guy. Hmmm, quite a difference between cultures! Following this, I could not believe the man with the bushy hairdo who walked into the salon. I had cut his hair very short, only a week ago. 'Wow!' I said, 'I cannot believe how fast your hair grows!' He replied 'No, it wasn't mine, it was my twin brother's hair you cut last week!'

I was extremely tired at the end of a long day, after I had finally finished cutting and styling everyone's hair. So, when the manager asked if I was going to the pub for a drink, I had to refuse. Before going home, I thought I'd just nip to the toilet. However, when I came out of the toilet I was surprised to find myself in total pitch black darkness. I managed to find my way to the front door, but it was locked. I could not believe it. I was so tired and angry. Under my breath, I swore at the manager for not checking to see if I was still in the salon. Fortunately, I had his mobile phone number, so I called him straight away, but all he could do was laugh and laugh. He thought I had already left the salon. I told him to hurry up and not to be late because I just wanted to go home. As he was in a pub nearby, it wasn't long before he arrived. Despite my anger, I was finally relieved to get out of that prison, especially as I had been slaving there all day. Straight away I went to the car park, looking forward to going home and sleeping. I was stunned when I arrived there because I could not see my Astra. I felt so strange, as I appeared to be reliving my nightmare. I was very upset and wondered what else could go wrong. I decided there was nothing else to do, but to report my stolen car to the police. So I walked to the police station feeling very sorry for myself, wondering how much more time would elapse before I could go home. I could not help thinking that even if the police found my car, it would probably be damaged or burnt out somewhere.

The police station was quiet, there was just a middle-aged woman sat there waiting. I was fuelled with panic and anger. However, when it came to my turn at the counter, as soon as I opened my mouth, my snarled lips suddenly turned to a smile, a smile of sheer delight, then I laughed and laughed. The woman and the police officer stared at me in disbelief. The officer asked if I was OK and what was going on. I just thought 'Oh my God!' Relief and joy spread through my body. It had just clicked in my mind that I had automatically gone to my usual car parking place and not to where I had actually parked my car, behind the restaurant. I explained to the police officer that I thought my car had been stolen, but I had forgotten where I had parked it. He laughed and just advised me to go and find it. I actually ran over there as fast as I could and there it was, my pride and joy in the restaurant car park. By coincidence my friend also came out of Rice and Three at the same time, as he had just finished work. He asked me why I was laughing. I asked him if my car was really there. 'Of course it is!' he replied. 'Are you OK?' I said 'No, not really, I will take you home and tell you my story!'

Collated by Michael Carroll

Firestone

(Jenneh Masaquoi)

My story happened in a small town called Firestone in Liberia. I was eighteen years old living with my parents, my older sister who was twenty-two years old and my younger brother who was fifteen years old. Our house was a three bedroom terraced house much like the terraced houses in England. The town was nice and quiet with lots of rubber plants growing here and there. Firestone is well known for its rubber plantation, where the rubber for Firestone tyres comes from. However, the workers there are poorly paid and the tyres are actually made in America.

We were well aware of the war that was going on in the northern part of Liberia, it had begun in the state of Nimba. Over a number of years the Madingos from Guinea had settled in the state of Nimba. The Mandingos appeared as a rich race and looked down on the Nimbians, even beating their children. They would say 'I'll beat you now and pay for you later', meaning they would pay off the police with bribes. Word also spread that they were putting caustic soda into tobacco they were selling to the Nimbians, therefore killing a number of them off. A very influential figure in the government called Charles Taylor, who was allocated funds to buy items such as cars for the ministry, mysteriously disappeared from the country for four years and returned on 24th December 1989 as the head of a guerilla force of one hundred to five hundred men called the National Patriotic Front of Liberia (NPFL). The NPFL settled in Gbarnga, some hundred miles northeast of Monrovia. Taylor said he had returned to topple the government. He joined with the Nimbians and began a war with the Mandingos. There were constant reports on the radio that the two sides were going to put their guns down. However, the war still progressed in the North of Liberia.

I was happy in the close knit community of Firestone, the neighbours were really friendly. Most weekends our family would eat together, visit relatives, friends, go on a trip out for a picnic or go to the beach which was quite a long way away. My father was a mechanic at a garage and the chair or the head of the local community, which meant that effectively he had links to the government, much like a councillor in England. He helped sort out people's problems and was involved in development projects. At the end of my day at college studying business, I used to go the local park five minutes away with friends to play tennis or basketball. Our family was quite religious, every Sunday we went to church and I sang in the church choir. I enjoyed watching movies at home and going to see musicals at the local theatre.

As usual, early on the morning of 1st July 1990, I got up out of bed, took my bath, and then prepared the cornmeal for the whole family's breakfast. My brother set off to school early with a packed lunch. He always went to school early so he could go to the library and work on his assignments.

Po...pp! Wow, I thought, that was some blowout coming from the street; it must have been a big fat tyre. Then lower more rapid noises followed like fire crackers. As we wondered what it could be, a muffled megaphone voice reverberated from outside. 'Everybody stay inside and lock your doors! We have entered this town. We will ask you to open them later. Lie down on the floor, do not stand up in your house!' A sense of shock froze us in our daily routine. Then a sense of reality about the situation began to seep in. The town was under siege. The rapid fire continued. I screamed. I was so confused and disorientated. I did not know where to go in my own house. Come into the living room Dad said, but I feared the shots ricocheting here, there and everywhere. I ran up to my bedroom, then to the bathroom, the toilet, everywhere in a panic trying to get away from the shots, with my sister following me. I ran back to my bedroom and hid under my bed.

I cried hysterically with fear, I could hear my sister and Mum crying. Dad shouted at everyone to stop as we were making the situation worse. Under my bed I kept praying 'Please God, have mercy on us! Protect me and my family!' Amidst the intermittent rattle of machine gun fire, I could hear the next door neighbours crying in their house. The air carried with it the smell of dust and gunpowder. A bomb, nearby, shook the whole house with its blast. Mum was so distraught about my brother, wondering where he was. My sister frantically phoned friends and relatives to find out, but no one had seen him. Mum was told to try and calm down and maybe he would find his way home as soon as the shooting ceased.

It was a good three hours before the shooting stopped. The megaphone announced: 'We want everybody to open your doors. If you don't we will open them and kill everybody in the house!' Dad called us all into the living room. He didn't want to open the door fearing what might happen, but Mum was terrified they would carry out their threat if we didn't. She argued if they have any questions to ask, we should answer them, if we cannot answer, we will just say we do not know. She had noticed that other people on the street had opened their doors and urged us to do the same. Dad relented, telling her to open the door... we followed behind her in trepidation. The opening door laid us bare, our privacy escaped before us in the face of the invaders. We followed Mum through the door, onto the street, standing in front of our house. There, black balaclavered men, stood with big guns and knives lining the whole street. Five naked men with their hands tied behind them were being held in a group. A staunch air of authority filled the street compelling our attention:

> Who is working for the government...?
> Who is a soldier...? Whose father is a minister...?
> Who can speak Madingo...? Who can speak Kirm...?[1]

---

1 Language associated with the government.

A few of the militants approached us. They asked where my father was working. 'At a garage', he replied. They asked him for his ID card and asked how many children he had. They stated that they were in control now and if anyone had links to the government, they would kill them. The father of the family next door was asked what job he did. He told them he was not employed. They checked his legs to see if there were any marks left by wearing army boots. He was fortunate they did not notice any so they just left him. I knew he was a soldier. However, over the next three days, people in the town began to point their fingers at each other, telling the new authorities that a soldier lives there..., this person is a minister..., that person has links to the government.

After three days they came back to our house. There was a knocking on the door very early that morning. A voice yelled 'Open the door! If you don't open the door we will break it down!' I heard the door smash open, I hid beneath my covers. Boots clambered into the house ... 'Where is your husband?' one of them cried downstairs. Mum and Dad, in the bedroom next to mine, did not answer. I could hear the sliding of drawers and the banging of cupboard doors beneath me, as they looked for clues. A jolt shot through me as a balaclavared man appeared in my room unleashing a big harsh shiny knife. Wielding it at me, he asked 'Where is your father? I told him I didn't know where he was this morning. The soldier darted out of my room. I sat on the edge of my bed listening to what was going on. I could tell that a group of them had herded into Dad's bedroom, I heard a slap, they demanded to know if Dad had links to the government. I dashed into his bedroom. My father was laid there in his underwear with his hands tied. Five soldiers beat him on the floor with their rifles, thud, thud, thud. I felt my sense of existence desert me, being so helpless, I could not do anything. Through our streaming tears Mum and I pleaded with them to untie him. 'Are you a soldier?' they demanded. 'No!' Dad cried. 'Have you any links with the government? These are the kind of people we are getting rid of.

There is no use denying it, people have informed us about you'. Dad told them he was the chairman of the community. They ordered him to get up so they could take him to see their Commander. The butts of their rifles whooshed through the air, cushioned by Dad's bloodied red back as they forced him out of the house. Helpless feeble faces peered through the windows of the houses as Mum and I followed behind thirty soldiers marching Dad to their base.

After ten minutes, we arrived at a big house. I realised that it had previously belonged to friends of the family whom the soldiers had kicked out. We stood in front of the Commander who was sitting with other soldiers on the veranda of the first floor. He saw the commotion and asked what was going on. Without giving Dad an opportunity, a soldier explained about his links to the government. The Commander merely said 'Take him away, these are the kind of people we do not want here. Take him away and kill him!' 'No...! Don't kill him, don't kill him, please don't kill him' my mother and I screamed in a frenzy. The Commander told us to shut up and leave as we would also be beaten. Oblivious to this, as Dad's life was at stake, we continued our turbulent tirade. Four soldiers rushed at us with guns, knives, and a whip lashed my arm and back. We began to run and scurry to avoid the thrashing weapons. Before we knew it, we had arrived back home. Despite the beating we had taken, we could only think of Dad and what was going to happen to him. We were all fraught with anxiety. The next day we went back to the base early in the morning to see if we could see him.

The soldiers standing outside the base told us that it was not time for us to see him. I knew in my heart, after what they had said yesterday, they'd killed him. Mum though, tried to hold onto the thought that maybe he was in a prison cell.

Over the next three days, time passed agonisingly slowly, as we awaited news about Dad. I could not eat or drink, I was physically sick with worry. Mum could not control herself, she cried all day long, not knowing if her husband or her son were alive. To make matters worse some neighbours came around and told us that when these people say they are going to kill someone, they do it. Of course this badly affected Mum and set her off in hysterics again.

The next day there was very heavy gunfire in the streets between the government soldiers and the rebels. There was no longer any difference in danger between staying in the house or running onto the streets trying to escape the civil war. People were now running in fear of their lives. My Mum, sister and I decided it was best to join them, staying could mean being raped or killed anyway. So we ran onto the streets, with no food or belongings. We ran into the machine gunfire spraying from the roof tops, the mortar bombs demolishing the occasional building. We ran into the sea of bloodshed, no film could ever depict, where women and children fell before us, but only became hurdles for us to leap. Their mothers could not stop to pick them up. So alive, on the brink of death, like savage hungry dogs snapping at the meat of survival, no time for the children being felled like chicken in the baptism of fire, roaring from the surrounding houses. Yet women gave birth on the roadside surrounded by circles of other women shielding the disgrace of giving birth in public with their lappers[2]. Even cultural tradition was trying its best to survive, but the rampaging bullets were not taking any notice. We trampled the arms and legs of the slaughtered, crying with their last breaths. We bustled and barged our way through the bloody massacre of the human abattoir, where hell would have been a welcomed heaven.

We were fortunate to survive the carnage, but God only knows how. We arrived at a deserted village with about two hundred others. Here the pain and suffering began to descend upon

2 Aprons.

those grieving for a lost child, haunted by their guilt to leave them dying on the street and those with bullets in their legs to be carved out with a knife. Over a course of two weeks we stayed there. Mum's feet swelled up and she became sick. My sister and I had to go onto other people's farms asking for cassavas or potatoes to feed her. Some asked first that we work for them. Despite this and potions obtained from a herbalist, Mum became too weak and died. She was given a bath, bathed in oils and then her hair was lacquered. My sister and I did not have time to grieve for her properly in the middle of desolation surrounded by war and with nothing except the instinct to survive. There was no coffin, no priest to give her a proper service, I just prayed over her body before it was lowered into a makeshift grave. I prayed her soul would rest in peace. Her burial would have been so different in normal circumstances. She would have had a beautiful dress, a beautiful coffin and buried in a vor[3], in a proper plot where we could have drawn up her embalmed body when we visited her and see her face, at least for a few years. We would have mourned her for two weeks in a wake. We would have sung in praise of her, but we had not the physical strength here, amidst the sufferers, suffering in war torn Liberia.

Collated by Michael Carroll

3 Shrine.

Thomas

(Thomas)

Thomas was born in 1982 in the Princess Anne Maternity Unit at the Royal Bolton Hospital. He lived with his parents in Deane, Bolton, until he was fifteen years old. He attended St. Ethelberts School, which he enjoyed very much, then went to Mount St. Josephs School, which, unfortunately, he did not like at all. In fact, Thomas hated the school so much that one day in 1995 he told the school that his family was moving away from Bolton. He even forged a letter to support his story, which the school surprisingly believed and wholly accepted. So Thomas actually only went to school until he was thirteen years old. Amazingly, Thomas got away with his truancy as his parents worked long hours all week and his nine brothers and sisters had already left school.

During the months of his truancy, Thomas still wore his uniform when he left and returned home to make it appear as if he had been to school. However, Thomas was actually working on a milk float and spending the money he earned on pot, beer and motorbikes. One day, Thomas and two other truant friends hopped onto a bus to Manchester with the intention of just hanging around the bus station. Little did they know about the reception that would greet them when they arrived. As soon as they got off the bus, they were immediately spotted by a gang of youths armed with all sorts of weapons and wearing spiked knuckles on their hands. To avoid any trouble, Thomas and his friends decided to walk up onto the high street. As they rounded the corner, an almighty blast of power hit Thomas, like a giant demolition ball swinging and hitting the whole of his body fast, taking him to another part of the street. The sound of the impact was eclipsed by the powerful force.

All that was left were the remnants of destruction. Glass was strewn everywhere, clothes were floating about like feathers in the air. It was as if Thomas was in the middle of a film as he witnessed blood trickling down people's faces like tears, people walking around disorientated in a daze, crying in despair, screaming, trying to make sense of what had just happened.

The boys stood up trying to run in sheer shock and disbelief with their legs shaking beneath them, not knowing where to go amongst the taste and smell of metal lingering in the dusty air, stinging people's eyes. Buildings had crumpled as if they had been bulldozed.

Thomas and his friends grabbed each other spontaneously in an instinct of survival. Their bodies were soaking with sweat. The salt from their sweat intermingled with the dusty air particles and irritated their eyes as they ran. There was no logic, no awareness, no time to stop and think in order to try and comprehend the situation, no thoughts about catching a bus home, just a blind desperate run from the bewildered chaos. Thomas' subliminal consciousness filtered through a fear of being caught by the police for being present in this battlefield and, worse still, being found out by his parents for never going to school.

During their desperate attempts to find their way home on foot from Manchester to Bolton, the friends felt sick through hunger, leaden with the residue of sulphur in their mouths and nostrils. Thomas felt as if he had been living and breathing in a room full of burning matches.

As the pangs of hunger became more apparent, Thomas stole an apple whilst they passed a stall outside a fruit shop. It was the tastiest apple he had ever eaten, oozing with sweet juice.

This is the first time Thomas has spoken about the terrible tragedy of the bloody Manchester bombing[1] that hit the world

1 The 1996 Manchester bombing was a terrorist attack in Manchester,
by the Provisional Irish Republican Army (IRA).

emotionally like a tidal wave.

Thomas arrived home in such a state and of course his parents found out about his truancy. At first his mother hugged him, glad that he was alive and Thomas cried with so much pent up emotion from his ordeal. His parents were shocked that they had been lied to for such a long time and that Thomas had never mentioned anything about his dislike of Mount St. Josephs School. They had always assumed he was safe and sound there, whilst in reality he had been hanging about in bus stations or on street corners.

Thomas was grounded for months with many other punishments, but he also needed time to reflect upon the bombing as the slightest sound made him jump.

Later on, Thomas became very mixed up about his life's course of events, so much so, he ran away from home, living in tents or other people's homes here and there. Once he had left, he was too proud to return home. Thomas broke the law on various occasions, which resulted in him being sent to prison in 2000 and 2001. Drugs were easy to purchase in prison, which didn't help matters.

Thomas moved to Darcy Lever after being released from prison and lived with his parents. He worked here and there for a while until he had a big row with them. They threw him out of the house, which Thomas admits he deserved.

With no home to go to, the only option he had was to live rough, mainly in the country parks of Bolton. He slept in Queen's Park, Leverhulme Park and even Crompton Lodges. This didn't really bother Thomas, as he liked the crisp lush green smell of the grass in the morning and the feeling of freedom. Even the crawling, tickling insects didn't bother him.

One day a child from our environmental group, the Wacky

Cleaners in Darcy Lever, came into the community centre to tell us about a homeless man. He had been discovered sleeping on a bench in Leverhulme Park earlier that week. As this was in our neighbourhood, we decided to investigate the matter and went to meet him. He looked tired and cold, his clothes were ripped and he was very hungry. It was sad and very humbling to see a person in such a state, so we looked after him as best we could and made enquiries about getting him somewhere to live. Within a week we managed to find a flat for him. He was initially provided with some rent money and household items by the Wacky Cleaners in exchange for some decorating he did for us. Now this man has a full time job and helps out at our centre. His name is Thomas of course!

The Manchester bombing affected Thomas greatly. It was a very traumatic experience for him. He also sensed that his parents did not trust him anymore, once they had found out about his truancy. He feels that if he had been at school and not in Manchester where the bombing occurred, his life would have taken a completely different path. Thomas was just one hundred yards away from the actual explosion and he will never ever forget it, even though it still seems unreal.

To any reader of this story, Thomas would like to say 'West life', a street term meaning peace on the streets. He also hopes that if you are ever offered any help or support, don't be too proud to accept it.

Collated by Teresa Bolton

The Thief and the Show Stopper
(Kennedy Mupomba)

Having enjoyed a two day stay at a lodge in Kariba, I decided to pass through my aunt's place on my way back to Harare where I worked as a public prosecutor. Thus, driving into the township that morning everyone was taking it easy. As the old saying goes 'There is no hurry in Africa' and arriving at a local shopping centre, I found some local folk drinking beer outside a bottle store illegally. Despite the high risk of being arrested for public drinking, it is a popular spot countrywide to meet friends, drink and catch up with all the local and international news. It is also a popular spot for detectives to get rich information, but this morning all were jocund with the latest topical story doing the rounds, which I shall now attempt to recall.

Whilst the ordinary folk of the Nyamhunga Township in Kariba had drifted asleep amidst the pitch darkness and the biting mosquitoes from the Zambezi Valley of Zimbabwe, Tinos was up and abound mulling over how to eke out a living. The Mugabwe regime of Zimbabwe had ousted the farmers from their land who had previously generated an important source of income for the country through the export of their crops. Mugabwe had also stopped the repayments of the country's loan to the IMF[1]. These factors, not to mention the tortures and beatings that were going on, had a disastrous effect on the country's image and economy. This township, which was built on a hillside overlooking the beautiful lake Kariba, had in the past, relied on tourism, but the tourists were now only coming in trickles. There were now no speed boats or sunset cruises along the lake, as there was a shortage of fuel. Here, where temperatures rise up to a scorching dry heat of thirty seven degrees Celsius and where the only means of survival was now

---

1 International Monetary Fund.

to fish in a climate where the fish population was dwindling due to over fishing, Tinos sought to raid a fishing company's premises that night to steal diesel from one of the trucks in order to make himself some money. He had spotted an old truck the other day and because it was used early each morning to ferry fish from the boats, he anticipated that it would probably be filled up with diesel before daylight. This would be an easy steal and quick money, according to Tinos' calculations of the likely reward if he sold the fuel on the black market.

Situated a thirty minute walk away from the township through a snaking dirty road was his intended raid. As groans from his stomach signalled a void from the last whole meal eaten the day before, Tinos put any reservations about his task behind him, remembering the old adage 'Nothing ventured, nothing gained'. Without further ado the lean gaunt ebony figure of Tinos, in his shorts and bleached ragged t-shirt, set off on his quest, arming himself with a twenty litre plastic container, pliers and hose pipe piece. Sneaking along in the darkness, the image of wild animals, especially lions, who for some strange reason loved to relax on the road at night, played upon his mind. He called upon his ancestral spirits to protect him. As he skulked onto the dusty road, the no man's land between the township and the company premises, Tinos feared the protective spirits may be abroad. The croaking of frogs from the lake etched into the sinister night and swarms of mosquitoes queued to draw blood from his body. Tinos wondered about the other predators the dark night might be harbouring to set loose and maul him. He trembled at the prospect of meeting the dreaded hyenas feared for their cowardly gnashing pack attacks with jaws to crush any type of bone and shrills of evil laughter. Worse still maybe he would meet the wicked witches riding and commandeering the hyenas on a night's errand, searching for their delicacy of human flesh. Sweating with fear as if about to be burned as a sacrificial offering, Tinos cooled with relief to see the much welcomed dim lights of the premises in the distance.

Security at the premises was lax with two elderly security guards, facts which Tinos had earlier canvassed. Sneaking around the back of the premises, off the road, amongst the bushes, Tinos set about cutting the wire of the two-metre barbed wire fence with his pliers. Tiptoeing, through the hole, he edged towards the targeted truck parked on the arid ground whilst watching and listening for the security guards. He willed the diesel into the container as fast as it could go, for time appeared to have ground to a halt in the urgency of the criminal deed. If the security guards saw him now he'd be caught red-handed. Finally, the deed was complete and hoisting the heavy container to his right shoulder he began creeping out of the premises. However, the silence of the night was broken by the shout of a security guard, who began to give chase. Tinos clambered through his entry point in the fence. With the twinkling stars too far away to illuminate his way and choosing to put his fate into the wilderness rather than the police, Tinos plunged into the thick forest laden with his loot, attempting a short cut in a roughly estimated homeward direction. In the savage wilderness there are no rules, it is survival of the fittest, where danger lurks in slithering snakes, rampaging rhinoceros, lethal leopards, lordly lions and barging buffalo. Tinos blundered into the bushes with one hand holding onto his loot slung over his shoulder in the blindness of night. His other hand charged before him brushing and breaking cumbersome branches. Crashing into trees, tripping over shrubs, thorns ripping his flesh, Tinos clasped his holy grail of diesel. In the distance he could hear the guards breaking bush in hot pursuit. Suddenly a thicket entangled him. Hacking in a ferocious fit of panic he fought it off, but valuable time had dissolved into the darkness. Agonisingly the security guards drew nearer shouting at him to stop as they would fire. However, Tinos became the leopard, accustomed to the dark night he could now distinguish between openings and objects sifting and gliding through the night forest like a buzz saw. He weaved through the bushes with eyes roving backwards and forwards. His feet danced the borrowdale[2] rhythm of the landscape. Jetting on the fuel of fear, his momentum thrust into overdrive, scorching the undergrowth, he dodged tree trunks, he soared through leaves which murmured in appreciation, he leapt over mounds of vegetation, he scuttled through groves, he flew like an arrow and Bang!

In a dazed stupor, his eyes hazily registered a large solid object darker than the night thundering away, trembling the ground in its wake and heralding a trumpeting cry. Tinos had charged into a massive wild elephant. Shocked at such a realisation and given that not many live to tell of an encounter with such a beast, instead of adrenalin flowing through his body to spur him on he just lay prostrate on the ground, wailing for help and calling for his mother. It was in this state the guards' torches found him and triumphantly 'nicked' him in the process recovering the loot surprisingly still intact. So pleased were they that they bore him straight to the police station oblivious of the human excrement flowing from what remained of his shorts.

Well, some of the stories you hear at a bottle store are normally a version spiced up sometimes by those who are too broke to afford a pint of beer. Thus, such a storyteller would occasionally get a free pint from the well-to-do who are sport for such tales. I did not believe the story and left for my aunt's. However, after arriving there not only did I find out that the story was true, but that the protagonist of the story was my cousin, so I left immediately to visit him in the police cell.

Now a police cell is neither lodge nor home, a fact that can be deduced from the overwhelming stench travelling its way to the charge office, so bad as to blast away a newcomer from

2 Zimbabwean dance similar to the rhumba.

such a place. In the corner of the cell was the cell toilet, a twenty litre container where green flies were busy feasting on human excrement. With no provision for a bath the heavy stench saturated the inmates arrested from Friday, waiting until the court was to sit on the Monday. Looking haggard and hungry, Tinos had to lean against the wall for support as other relatives thronged the police station to see him, for indeed various versions of the story had already circulated the township. One version depicted that the thief had lost various limbs in the ordeal and another that the thief had been crushed beyond recognition except for his identifiable clothing. Affording a thin smile Tinos hugged me. Attempting to ignore the reek and dishevelled appearance I embraced him too. He perked up as soon as he saw me, seeing the potential in me to pull a few strings for him to alter the course of justice. However, I could not do this. I offered him some sadza³, which Tinos wolfed down in between telling his story. After his harrowing narration, all the relatives left amidst relief that at least he was alive, but also worried about his sentence for the courts these days were talking of deterrent custodial sentences for fuel thieves. Despite the money that I gave him in case he incurred a fine, the local magistrate stated that Tinos could do with the money anyway and sent him to prison for a month.

Collated by Michael Carroll

---

3 A kind of dense bread.

Mixed Faith

(Tariq Abaker)

Once described as the breadbasket of the Arab world, Sudan is a country of high, though largely unrealised, economic potential, which is presently crippled by civil war, a foreign debt of around fifteen billion US dollars, and climatic effects which have brought both drought and flooding. It is a multicultural and multi-religious country. Islam is the main religion with Christianity as the next major faith. Arabic is the official language, but there are more than two hundred tribes owning more than five hundred dialects. This colourful culture gives Sudan its unique identity between all Arab and African countries. There are quite a few mosques and some churches, relative to the population of Muslims and Christians. The only way you can tell who is Muslim and who is Christian is when it actually comes to prayer times and religious festivals. Both Muslim and Christian males usually wear a jalabia[1] and all the females tend to wear a toub[2]. Despite the diversity of Sudan, there is a very strong relationship between the different cultures.

The city of Madani is about one hundred and fifty kilometres south of the capital city, Khartoum. Madani became known as the city of culture, stemming from the 1970s and 1980s, when it provided about sixty percent of Sudan's singers, poets and musicians. Everyone in the city shares their lives together and helps each other. Five years ago in 2001, floods devastated Madani and destroyed all the houses and huts, yet everyone bonded together and helped each other to build new homes. Whenever there is a death in the community, usually a big marquee is erected where people of all faiths can come and comfort each other throughout the mourning period. A lamb is slaughtered to feed everybody and the people can chat over tea

---

1 Long white robe.
2 Sudanese women often wear a traditional toub, a long garment that is similar to an Indian sari and covers most of the body. Like a sari, a toub (which is also worn in Mauritania and Somalia), is quite beautiful and can be very expensive. The women, however, do not cover their faces, as in conservative Muslim countries such as Saudi Arabia.

and coffee. These activities reflect how the community in Madani live in harmony. However, whilst the cultures are very tolerant of each other, this community is quite conservative and everyone aspires to certain values. For example, it is unthinkable for a couple to have a child out of wedlock.

There was a simple Sudanese man called Soliman. His family originated from the Nuba tribe, an African tribe originally from West Sudan. In parts of West Sudan the Nuba tribe is still very rural. They wear the bare necessities of clothing and traditionally hunt for their food. However, Soliman was born and brought up with the traditions and customs of a Muslim family in the city of Madani. Originating from the Nuba tribe, his skin was darker than the people of Arabian tribes in Madani and he spoke his own regional African dialect, apart from the main language of Arabic. Though Soliman was a Muslim, he was not fervently religious.

Initially, Soliman worked as a farmer. Whilst working on his land he came to know a neighbouring Muslim farmer, who would often invite Soliman back to his house. There, he met the farmer's sister, Mariam, and he was struck by her big brown eyes and her caring nature. After becoming acquainted with one another, Soliman and Mariam's families began to visit each others' homes regularly as Soliman started to develop a close relationship with Mariam. It wasn't long before Soliman and Mariam eventually fell in love. However, one day a dispute arose between Soliman and Mariam's brother. Their farms were separated by a channel of water about one and a half metres wide with narrow channels of water branching out into each of the farms, enabling water irrigation[3]. Soliman's neighbour contested that his farm was not getting its fair share of water. He thought that Soliman's farm was draining most of it, therefore affecting the growth of his own crops. This matter caused deep resentment between them both and had

---

3 Irrigation is when people add water to plants and crops, to help them grow when there is insufficient rainfall. Irrigation water can be pumped from rivers, lakes or wells or allowed to flow to the fields by the force of gravity along pipes or open canals.

to be referred to the Sheikh[4] to decide how it could be resolved. The Sheikh took into account the size of each farm and the amount of water each farm needed to grow crops. He ruled that there was no manipulation on Soliman's part and that both farms were receiving their equal share of water, therefore no adjustments to the water irrigation were necessary. Though Soliman's neighbour had to accept the Sheikh's judgement, deep down he disagreed, and so harboured a grudge against Soliman.

Soliman became known to be very helpful and well known for his community work. He always made himself available to help people and would drop whatever he was doing at a moment's notice. He lent a hand to build and repair neighbours' houses and to gather crops for neighbouring farmers during harvest time. Due to his caring nature, he was approached by a Christian charity to work for them, so he readily obliged. His main duties included distributing food and clothes to the needy and looking out for the poor who were reluctant to approach the charity. There are lots of poor people in Madani who do not have any land to farm and so have no crops, no goats or other animals to provide them with food. Yet these people are proud, too embarrassed to ask for help and too ashamed to beg. Due to his active involvement with the charity, in time, Soliman converted to Christianity. Initially, this was a great shock to his parents who could not accept his conversion, but Soliman stood firm in his belief. Seeing how strong their son's conviction was, Soliman's parents eventually relented and accepted his decision.

Despite Soliman's conversion to Christianity, he and Mariam decided to get married, but the fact that he was Christian and she was Muslim became a big obstacle. There was no doubt that her family would object to the marriage. However, Soliman's family was happy to know that he was in love with

4 A village leader, though not like an Arab Sheikh, who has been elected or has inherited the position. He is well respected and acts as a local judge, his decision is final. The system, which is similar to a civil court, dates back to British colonisation of Sudan.

a Muslim girl and hoped that this could influence him to revert back to Islam.

Soliman suggested to Mariam that they should leave Madani and head to the capital, Khartoum, where relatives of his could provide some protection, until he found work there. However, Mariam refused because she believed that her family could still react violently against Soliman. The only choice for them was to stand firm and face her family, no matter what the consequences would be.

Soliman's parents agreed to visit Mariam's family to ask their consent for the marriage, as is the traditional practice in Sudan. Mariam's eldest brother was the first one to refuse and insisted the marriage would never take place as long as he lived. Apart from Soliman now being a Christian, Mariam's brother still felt resentment towards him over their previous land dispute. Mariam's parents were both reluctant to give their consent, but also cautious about refusing the proposal because they knew how determined and strong willed their daughter was. They were also worried that she might harm herself or even commit suicide, then they would never forgive themselves. So, they did not reject the proposal, but they did not accept it either. Instead they told Soliman's parents that they needed some time to think it over.

Soliman became very anxious as he awaited a decision from Mariam's parents. Three months passed and there was no reply from them. So, Soliman decided he could no longer wait and asked his parents to visit Mariam's family once again to obtain their consent. On the second visit, Mariam's parents felt obliged to accept, but on one condition, that Soliman reverted back to Islam. Soliman refused this condition, for he felt he had found himself through Christianity and it was now a deep part of him that he could not compromise. Christianity was his chosen path from which he could not veer, even for the sake of his love for Mariam. Mariam's brother also declared that he would refuse to accept his sister's marriage to Soliman even if he did revert back to Islam.

The problem had become very complicated, but Soliman and Mariam had thought of a plan to solve their dilemma. Mariam was to approach her mother with the news that she was pregnant. Hopefully, then, Mariam's parents would be forced into arranging a quick marriage, thinking they were preventing Mariam from having a child out of wedlock, therefore avoiding dishonour and the destruction of the family's reputation. It was a big lie for Mariam to tell and ordinarily she would not conceive of doing such a thing. She lacked the courage, but her love for Soliman provided her with enough strength to carry out the plan. Mariam knew that her mother would prefer her to die rather than see her have a child outside marriage. However, to tell her father or brother about her supposed pregnancy would be too risky. So, Mariam told the story to her mother, who of course was very shocked, but realised she had to act quickly to save the family's honour.

Mariam's mother had to wait for the right time to tell the news to her husband; very late at night, whilst he was calm and quiet. Even though he was very angry, he insisted that their daughter must marry Soliman as soon as possible. Both Mariam's parents agreed to keep this secret from their son, for their daughter and Soliman's safety.

In May of 1970, two weeks after Mariam told her mum about her fake pregnancy, the marriage took place, without her brother's consent and without him knowing the reason why his parents had arranged the speedy wedding. When he found out, he reacted badly to the news. He disowned his sister and moved out from the city. Three weeks after the couple returned from their honeymoon, they told Mariam's parents the truth about their story. Her parents were very angry, but nothing could now be done as Soliman was already part of their family.

After nine months and three weeks the couple had their first child, Salah. Salah spent a lot of time with his grandparents and relatives in Madani. The first child in a family always has a special place in the hearts of the grandparents and being the first born, Salah was doted upon. His grandfather was a very influential figure and took him to the Mosque and prayed with him. His mother Mariam remained a Muslim. Because of these influences, Salah also became a Muslim too.

In time, Soliman and his family moved to a small city called Rabak, where he was offered a job as a manager in a new branch of the Christian charity. Here, Mariam gave birth to Raja, Imad and Randa. As there was more of a Christian influence and the family were living away from their grandparents and other relatives, Raja, Imad and Randa grew up as Christians. The family soon got to know their neighbours and became strongly involved in their new community. They celebrated the Muslim festival of Eid by visiting Muslim families and celebrated Christmas as well, with visits by Muslim friends to their home. These are festivals which all Sudanese celebrate together. Soliman and Mariam believe that there is nothing more natural than love between two human beings and that neither culture nor religion should be an obstacle. They only wish that a marriage of diverse faiths could be reflected in a broader context, on an international scale, then there would be greater peace in the world.

Collated by Michael Carroll